CLAY COUNTRY
SPEEDWAY

CLAY COUNTRY
SPEEDWAY

Robert Bamford & Dave Stallworthy

TEMPUS

First published 2002

PUBLISHED IN THE UNITED KINGDOM BY:
Tempus Publishing Ltd
The Mill, Brimscombe Port
Stroud, Gloucestershire GL5 2QG

PUBLISHED IN THE UNITED STATES OF AMERICA BY:
Tempus Publishing Inc.
2 Cumberland Street
Charleston, SC 29401

British Library Cataloguing in Publication Data.
A catalogue record for this book is available from the British Library.

ISBN 0 7524 2727 X

Typesetting and origination by Tempus Publishing.
Printed in Great Britain by Midway Colour Print, Wiltshire

CONTENTS

INTRODUCTION

Cornwall has seen some peaks and troughs in speedway racing over the past few years. Here, I will pick up on just a few of the special moments, which thrilled spectators from far and wide. For me, the re-birth of speedway at the Clay Country Moto Parc on 3 June, 1997, was truly amazing. A carnival atmosphere was generated by over 2,500 people, who watched the St Austell Gulls take on local rivals the Western Warriors in an Amateur League fixture. It might have been a defeat for the fledgling club, but no-one gave a damn as they had witnessed Brian Annear launch a new chapter of speedway history, for after a speedway void of 34 years, the quarry venue had blasted off.

Obviously, Steve Bishop made a significant contribution in the first two seasons for the Gulls, but inclusive of bonus points, Truro's Wayne Barrett out-scored 'Bish' in 1997, and continued to provide sterling service over the four years of their activity, prior to helping Trelawny in 2001. One can only wonder what might have happened had Brian started the new club a few years earlier, for it could have meant a second shot at the big time for Wayne, who had begun his career at Weymouth in 1984, before riding with some success at Poole in 1986 and 1987.

Personally, I was pleased for my friend Paul 'Grizzly' Adams, the *Western Morning News* reporter, who fulfilled an important ambition to ride a speedway bike. Not only did he do it, but he also bagged £1,000 for the Cornwall Air Ambulance charity in the process.

On a sad note, I would have loved another friend, Chris Julian to have seen just one match. Sadly, he never did, as he was taken from this world in a flying accident, the very day before the press and practice call at the Moto Parc in the summer of 1997.

The 1998 campaign saw Adrian Newman, Chris Harris and Seemond Stephens launch their careers on the shale. Harris has certainly come on since and looks to be one of England's brightest prospects, whilst Stephens still proves to be one of the quickest gaters in the business. The season's high was bringing the Knock-Out Cup back from Mildenhall in October. The first-ever piece of silverware was quickly followed by the Conference League Championship to complete a great double for the Gulls.

For me, the popularity of Cornish speedway flagged a little because the management failed to grasp the fact that the public was ready for the club to go up a notch into the Premier League.

The 1999 highlight was the Knock-Out Cup afternoon, when the Gulls pipped Newport. It was speedway heaven to watch Seemond Stephens cross the line ahead of Chris Neath and Andrew Appleton, in what was his final race for St Austell. I can still picture little Lloyd Barrett's face as he proudly clutched his dad Wayne's leg – it really was a magic moment.

Rider of the year, for me, in 2000, was Newquay hotelier Will James, who was lured back into speedway after many years in retirement. Will proved to be a gutsy performer on an old upright Weslake. Sadly though, the last Gulls side found that silverware was to elude them.

The 2001 season saw the birth of the new Trelawny Tigers, and although the opening match was memorable, it lacked the fever pitch of 1997. Action packed meetings sustained the loyal fans; however, I really couldn't separate the top Premier League lads. Many impressed me, including Charlie Gjedde, Armando Castagna, Les Collins, Sean Wilson, Leigh Lanham, Carl Stonehewer, Paul Thorp, Neil Collins and Robbie Kessler to name but a few.

In conclusion, I can only hope the consortium now running Cornish speedway can build on their success. Despite being in a near wooden spoon league position in 2001, Trelawny is alive! Star turn for the club is pint-sized local hero Chris Harris, while other favourites are Czech Republic ace Pavel Ondrasik, his compatriot Richard Wolff and Argentinean racer Emiliano Sanchez. The 2002 side has a good balance of local riders and imported points plunderers and, hopefully, this will be the key to their success. To them, good luck for the future and thanks for the memories to all Gulls and Tigers since that marvelous night in 1997.

Finally, I'm pleased that Robert Bamford and Dave Stallworthy have gone to such lengths to record the history of such a unique and wonderful speedway venue. The book was originally only going to cover events at the Moto Parc and indeed it does to a fine detail, but for the sake of telling the full and often-humorous story, Robert has also added in a synopsis of every away match undertaken by the Gulls and the Tigers. I am happy to commend this publication to all speedway enthusiasts: please enjoy an excellent account of all that happened over the fabulous five-year period between 1997 and 2001.

Jeremy Jackson
Cornish motorcycle enthusiast, speedway writer and historian
June 2002

ACKNOWLEDGEMENTS

The authors would like to thank a whole host of people, who over the short history of the Clay Country Moto Parc helped to make the whole experience enjoyable, and who latterly, have helped in various ways with the production of this wonderful story. These include *www.mike-patrick.com* for the stunning cover photograph, plus John Yeo, Les Aubrey, Neil Ferguson, Bernard White, Dave Payne, Ted Humphrey, Alan Basham, Phil Hilton, Alan Baker and David Collins for the additional images used throughout these pages. Special thanks go to Brian Annear and his family for making everything possible at the marvellous Moto Parc, and latterly for being so kind as to let us borrow all the officially marked referee's programmes from the Gulls era. Grateful thanks are also due to Jeremy Jackson, Tony Lethbridge, Glynn Shailes, Albert Poulton, John Jarvis, Paul Adams, Eric Barnes, Ken Westaway, Carol Pitman, Fred Paul, Godfrey Spargo, Peter Dearing, Ray Purvis, Shirley Stephens, the *Cornish Guardian*, the *Western Morning News* and all the marvellous supporters of the Gulls and the Tigers.

STATISTICAL KEY

CLAY COUNTRY MOTO PARC RESULTS AND HEAT DETAILS

In order to save any confusion, the following abbreviations are used throughout the heat details contained within this book:

M = 2 minute exclusion
T = Tapes exclusion
R = Retired or engine failure
F = Fell
X = Excluded

The statistics for each year appear at the end of each chapter.

1

1997

The roots of speedway in the Duchy lay in the pioneer years of the early 1930s, when grass speedway was held on the outskirts of St Austell at Rocky Park. This gave Cornish supporters their first opportunity to see some of the top speedway stars of the time, including the likes of Bill Kitchen, Jack Parker and Billy 'Cyclone' Lamont. Other familiar names that appeared before the war were Bert Jones, an Australian who also rode for Southampton Speedway, plus local riders Bob Collins, Tommy Kessell and Ivan Kessell.

Following the success of Rocky Park, pukka speedway first came to St Austell on 14 June 1949, promoted by Chirpy Richards and John Luke, under the banner of Cornish Stadium Ltd., at Par Moor. The opening meeting saw a Peter Robinson Select defeat a Cyril Quick Select 46-37, in front of an audience of 12,000. Challenge matches continued to be run, initially using 'Pixies' as a moniker, but on 12 July, this was changed to 'Badgers', before the name 'Gulls' was first used a week later. The Gulls subsequently joined the Third Division of the National League in 1950. Bizarrely, on 4 August 1951, a sheepdog trials event was promoted at the track, with the programme being identical to the ones used for speedway, even down to including photographs of riders in action!

With new promoter John Selleck at the helm, St Austell joined the Southern League in 1952. Sadly though, just one further season of action followed before the track was taken over by car racing events. The final season of regular team racing was marred, however, when 26-year-old Australian Ted Stevens died following a crash on 14 April 1953. What turned out to be the last meeting for five years was held on 13 October that year, when the Gulls lost 39-46 to Norwich in a challenge match.

Promoter Trevor Redmond brought speedway back to the venue in 1958, opening on 30 July with a Best Pairs event that saw Jack Geran and Gerry Hussey triumph. Including the Gulls participation in the regional Western League in 1960 and 1961, open licence events continued until Neath (another of Redmond's tracks) used the stadium to complete their fixtures in 1962. The first of these meetings occurred on 10 July, when Edinburgh were beaten 42-36 by the Welsh Dragons. The Neath team subsequently completed their run of four league matches at the venue on 5 September, with a 44-34 success over Newcastle.

There were plenty of the great riders who wore the famous Gulls race-jacket with distinction during the Cornish Stadium era, namely Norman Street, Harold Bull, Ray Ellis, Bob Duckworth, Maurice McDermott, Allan Quinn, Maurice Hutchens, Ticker James, Ken James, Max Rech, Mick Mitchell, George Newton, Jack Gates, Ken Monk, Alf Webster, Chris Julian, Ray Cresp, Glyn Chandler, George Major, Chris Blewett and

Trevor Redmond

Trevor Redmond himself. All were aces of the track, who provided plenty of thrills and spills from a truly marvellous era of speedway.

Trevor Redmond continued to run the show in 1963, with the return of the Gulls in Provincial League action, but that was to prove the final season of team action for St Austell until Brian Annear resurrected the side at the Clay Country Moto Parc in 1997. The last meeting at the Cornish Stadium took place on 1 October, 1963, when Cornwall defeated Devon 33-21 in a challenge match. Stock car racing was later staged at the stadium, but the last such event in 1987 was followed by the site being sold for redevelopment.

The aforementioned Brian Annear used to help out on race nights at Par Moor in the 1950s and 1960s, along with his father, who was a member of the track staff. Brian had been involved with bikes all his life, including running a spares van at various motocross circuits over a ten-year period. He had also been heavily involved with the stock car racing at the Cornish Stadium, as well as the running of the first-ever indoor speedway meeting at Trago Stadium, Bodmin on 31 December 1980, when young riders participated, mounted on motocross machines.

Co-author Dave Stallworthy first met Brian in 1990, when researching stories for inclusion in a book written with Tony Lethbridge entitled *The Story of Grass-track & Speedway in Cornwall*. Later on, when interviewing Brian for this publication, he revealed that he had seen an advertisement in a local newspaper in 1996, indicating that the ECCI (English China Clays International) had an area available for use as a motocross track. Sometime afterwards, the ECCI invited possible club members to a meeting at John Keay House, along with youth associations and the police. A successful

The orginal motocross circuit, 1996.

The original motocross circuit, 1996.

outcome saw the formation of a new club, and Brian set to work with Tony Stephens to cut out a track. It was then decided that adults could also use the circuit upon the payment of a membership fee. However, as things turned out, the track didn't get as much use as had been hoped for, so Brian asked the owners about the possibility of introducing speedway. Thankfully, ECCI were keen on the idea and so began a huge amount of work, which culminated in Brian fulfilling a wonderful dream that many thought would never reach fruition.

Together with grass-track ace and former Plymouth junior, Mike Bowden, the entrepreneurial Brian Annear took another look at the site and decided what needed to be done. Within a month, a huge rock was blasted out of the way by the ever-helpful ECCI company. Brian was full of praise for all the help he received from the quarry owners, revealing that ECCI had often donated heavy plant that could have cost up to £700 an hour to hire. Alan Robertson, who had constructed his own track up at Linlithgow, West Lothian, offered plenty of good advice in the initial stages, including the suggestion that they keep the circuit on the small side. So, the most important work began. Brendan Joyce initially designed the track, although the Annear family later slightly altered the shape by working around the radius with a knotted rope. This was how the famous wide, sweeping bends came into being, and what wonderful racing they were to create. Tyres from the motocross track were used to help with the safety fence and the track was eventually constructed in October 1996. This was a remarkable achievement as work was only carried out on Sundays.

Unbeknownst to anyone, former Gulls chief Trevor Redmond had been down to look at the new track, leaving a New Zealand sticker as a calling card, with Brian quick to realize who his famous visitor had been. It transpired that Trevor wanted £1,000 to use the Gulls name, but Brian laughed this off as a joke and no money ever changed hands of course.

Prior to the completion of the work on the track, Reading Speedway announcer Dave Stallworthy had been watching a meeting at Exeter in September that year, when Brian Annear tapped him on the shoulder and proudly announced 'I'm going to open up St Austell Speedway.' Dave later admitted that his heart ruled his head at the time, but his reply was 'Well if you need an announcer, keep me in mind.' Dave had long since fallen in love with Cornwall and taken many holidays in the St Austell area, often dreaming of what it would be like to resurrect the Gulls, so it somewhat ironic when Brian approached him. Dave heard no more about the new venture until just before the season opened in 1997, when Gulls press officer David Collins penned an article in Speedway Star, stating that he would indeed be the announcer at the renamed Clay Country Moto Parc. Dave initially told his wife Hazel that he would only do the job for a few weeks, but he was to end up serving the track throughout five remarkable years!

Many people came forward to help, once they heard that speedway was returning to Cornwall and it is only right to run through the list of other officials for that first season. Nigel Prynne, a former Cornish Grass-track Champion was in charge of track preparation, while the experienced Brian James, very much a part of the set-up at Exeter Speedway, was the Clerk of the Course. Brian's assistant was a veteran grass-track organizer by the name of Dennis Huddy, with the pits marshalls being Honey Sanford and Robert Glanville. Former all-round motorcyclist Phil Williams, was one of the machine examiners, with Tony Stephens ably helping with the duties. Andy

The new track takes shape.

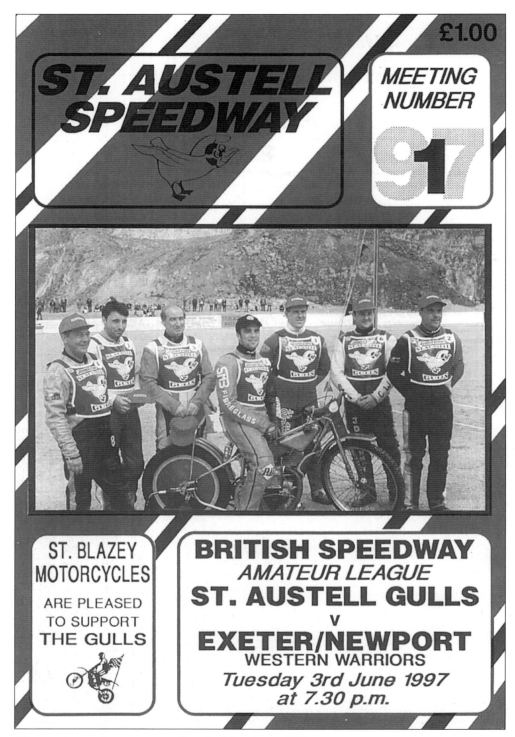

The opening meeting programme from the Moto Parc, 1997.

Mitchell, formerly from the north of England, took on the main role of starting marshall, and Cliff Sanford, who hailed from the Exeter area, backed him up. Of course, both Cliff and Honey Sanford had a long-standing speedway connection, being father and daughter of the late Tony Sanford, who unfortunately lost his life in a track crash at Exeter in 1981.

Prior to opening at their new venue, the new Gulls had made their bow at Exeter on 26 May, when they went down to a narrow 38-40 defeat. Wayne Barrett produced a sparkling display, netting 14 points, while new team-mates Chris Bennett (6+2), Darren Matthews (6+1) and Jason Prynne (6) chipped in with good contributions. The performance of Barrett was particularly remarkable as it looked as if he'd been lost to the sport after last appearing for Poole way back in 1987!

So, the great day dawned on 3 June 1997, when the reformed Gulls entertained the Western Warriors in a British Amateur League match. The Warriors, incidentally, were a composite side, who split their home fixtures between Exeter and Newport. Their team manager Colin Hill marched his team out on to the track and while they lined up neatly in a row, the new Gulls, many of whom were used to riding on the grass-tracks, merely ambled across the track. Announcer Dave Stallworthy still had time to kill as the start was delayed until 8pm in order to let the large crowd in, so he began to interview various riders. All of a sudden, from the pits, mounted on a vintage motorcycle with 'No.1' emblazoned on the front, came promoter Brian Annear, sporting a pair of shorts and a red shirt! Speedway Star reporter Tony Hoare and photographer Mike Patrick were there to record Brian's antics, which culminated in him receiving his licence from SCB manager David Hughes.

The Moto Parc and its wonderful setting.

The fans who attended simply couldn't believe the sight as they came down the hill and entered the disused pit, with the area looking like something from outer space. A landscape of cliffs surrounded the track, while a large glistening pool stood beside the third and fourth bends. It was totally unlike any other track in speedway and this was reflected in the meeting programme, which contained a warning notice headed !!IMPORTANT!!, which went on to list eight things the public should or shouldn't do: 1.Keep off the cliffs; 2.Keep away from the pool; 3.Do not trespass onto adjoining land; 4.Do not exceed 10mph to and from the track; 5.Give way to ECCI vehicles (they always have the right of way); 6.Do not cross fences around the buildings and plant yard on the right as you leave – they are protected by solar beam alarms and video cameras; 7.Respect the local people in the nearby roads; 8.Park only in the car parks provided.

Referee Mick Barnes had been known to get a little excitable at times and David Hughes obviously wanted to make sure there was plenty going on throughout the evening. He apparently suggested that Gulls team manager Steve Annear (son of Brian) ought to create a fuss and wave his arms in the air about any refereeing decision in order to create a bit of atmosphere. As a result of Steve's outbursts during the meeting, Mick Barnes got quite rattled at one point, although he did see the funny side of it afterwards.

The scene was set in the very first race, when Gary Lobb took the lead, only to be caught and passed by Wayne Barrett, proving that Clay Country Moto Parc was going to be a very special racetrack indeed. Since then, there have been literally hundreds of overtaking manoeuvres, both in the Amateur and Conference League days of the Gulls, and of course, in Trelawny Tigers first season of Premier League activity in 2001.

A large proportion of the big crowd (estimated at 2,500-3,000) were new to speedway and initially they were very quiet, but they were just

Roger Lobb and Jason Prynne.

Brian James and Mick Barnes.

waiting to erupt and when they eventually did, it was absolutely incredible. The spectators gradually warmed to the sport, helped in no small way by Brian Annear's clever idea to buy a batch of air horns and sell them at a subsidised price. The volume went up notch by notch and eventually, could be heard all around the track.

The two teams for the historic match, which ended in a 41-34 victory for the visitors are recorded for posterity as follows: St Austell – Wayne Barrett, Chris Bennett, Darren Matthews, Mark Phillips, Jason Prynne, Mike Bowden and Simon Phillips; Western Warriors – Gary Lobb, Richard Ford, Roger Lobb, Nick Couch, Paul Oughton and Andy Carfield. It was wonderful as the whole St Austell team actually came from Cornwall, even Mike Bowden, who was from the Saltash side of Plymouth. Interestingly, no less than three of the visitors would also later go on and appear for the Gulls, namely cousins Gary and Roger Lobb, plus Richard Ford.

On the night, Barrett gave an impressive performance for the Gulls, scoring 13 points, while Prynne, who had only previously ridden on grass, chipped in with a well-taken paid 9 point return. Barrett, in fact, went into the record books as the first race winner, when he set the track record time of 61.62 seconds, although this was subsequently twice bettered by Roger Lobb in heats two and four, with the record standing at 58.43 seconds by the end of the night. The super fast Lobb headed the Warriors' score-chart, weighing in with a terrific 15 point maximum, while cousin Gary and Paul Oughton lent solid support, each netting 9 points.

There was one race in particular that featured almost everything, and that was heat 8. At the first time of asking, Darren Matthews, Richard Ford and Mark Phillips all ended up in a heap on the track, with referee Mick Barnes excluding Phillips. The re-run was quite unbelievable and saw Gary Lobb suffer an engine failure on the final lap, with the Warrior pushing his machine home, accompanied by local rider Greg Daniels. Inadvertently, Daniels touched the back of Lobb's machine, which meant he had to be excluded for receiving outside assistance. Meanwhile, both Darren Matthews and Richard Ford had crossed the finish line, only for Matthews to then be excluded after an objection had been raised about an illegal silencer on his machine. So, after all that, the race resulted in a 3-0 advantage for the visitors, with 'Fordy' being the only finisher!

Many things were unique about the Clay Country Moto Parc, not least the fact that the meeting officials were perched in a caravan, which was facing end-on, towards the track. It was akin to being at a grass-track meeting, where the spectators are almost within touching distance. Announcer Dave Stallworthy enthused that it was ultra-exciting, having the crowd literally on top of the officials' caravan, even to the point where they were sometimes looking directly in! Beryl Sinclair was due to be timekeeper and incident recorder for the meeting, but Roger Nettlefold of Reading, Swindon and Oxford fame, took care of the duties, in order to give the less experienced officials an idea of what to do. For subsequent meetings, however, Beryl diligently dealt with the recording of incidents, while Terry Hooke completed the timekeeping duties.

Afterwards, David Hughes simply raved about the place and there was champagne to celebrate Brian Annear's great triumph in bringing the sport back to the Duchy after an absence of 34 years. The fact that the Gulls had lost didn't matter a jot, because it was all about the occasion. For announcer Dave Stallworthy, it was one of his highlights of his career, the memories of which would last forever. Afterwards, he was in no rush to leave, preferring to just soak up the atmosphere, but eventually, on the drive back, it took him until had reached Exeter for the adrenalin to start dying down. Accompanying Dave, were long-time speedway friend Eric Barnes and timekeeper extraordinaire Roger Nettlefold, who had left his transport at Eric's house in Upper Seagry, near Chippenham, Wiltshire. Dave got to his Yate home at 2am, and Eric promptly set off to drive Roger back to Upper Seagry. However, Eric was suffering with a tooth abscess and was in great pain, so much so that he missed his junction on the motorway and had to go to Wotton Bassett before turning around and coming back. By the time Roger had collected his mode of transport and journeyed home to Abingdon, it was 4.15am and he had to be up for work at 6 o'clock! To this day, Roger Nettlefold has never been seen in Cornwall since!

The press covered the meeting well, with Paul 'Grizzly' Adams writing in the *Western Morning News* of 4 June, 'History will show that the Warriors defeated the reborn Gulls, but the result of the Amateur League match was surely secondary to the occasion.' On 5 June, David Collins wrote in the *Cornish Guardian* 'Speedway roared back to Cornwall on Tuesday, when the Western Warriors completed the double over the St Austell Gulls, winning 41-34 in a thrilling match at the new Moto Parc, Nanpean.' *Speedway Star* included a brilliant four-page spread on the opening of the track in their issue dated 14 June, featuring many of Mike Patrick's brilliant photographs, which captured the wonderful feel of the occasion.

The euphoria of the opening meeting was brought down to earth with a bump the following week, when, with visitors Peterborough waiting in the pits, the rain came down by the bucket load and the meeting was postponed. This was the first time that announcer Dave Stallworthy began to question his own sanity at undertaking a 360 mile round trip each week! As previously mentioned though, it would be a further five years,

Chris Bennett.

Steve Bishop leads the way against the M4 Raven Sprockets.

before he finally decided that he could no longer carry on. During that time, of course, the enthusiastic man with the microphone became a firm favourite in Cornwall, not least for his off-the-wall style of presentation, but also for his varied taste in music, which stretched from Daniel O'Donnell to Abba!

Prior to the scheduled match against Peterborough, the Gulls had travelled up to Belle Vue on 6 June, when they were roundly beaten 29-48. Wayne Barrett fought a lone battle, scorching to a magnificent 18 point maximum against the Colts, who boasted three men in double-figures: Phil Knowles (11+2), Glenn Furniss (11) and Scott Donovan (11). Unfortunately, Jason Prynne broke a collarbone in a heat 10 fall, but the Gulls acted quickly to plug the gap, signing former top grass-tracker and Exeter Speedway rider, Steve Bishop on loan. 'Bish' was to go on and become the top rider at the Clay Country Moto Parc, becoming almost like a pop star, with young girls chasing after him for photographs and autographs. Steve's popularity was quite amazing and he became such a cult figure that he even turned on the Christmas lights in St Austell!

The next match at the Moto Parc was on 17 June, when the Shuttle Cubs (a combined Wolverhampton and Long Eaton team) were the opponents. Steve Bishop made his debut in this match, mounted on a machine that Jason Prynne and his sponsors had managed to come up with. The Gulls were looking for a morale-boosting victory and they certainly got it, by 53 points to 25. That man 'Bish' fairly romped to a 15 point maximum and by the end of the night, he had established a new track record time of 58.09 seconds in heat 2. This was the match when the St Austell supporters witnessed

Steve Bishop's famous race winning routine, when he circumnavigated the 230-metre circuit standing on the saddle with one leg in the air! Wayne Barrett had set a new track record time of 58.22 seconds in the opening heat, prior to this being eclipsed by 'Bish' in the very next race. Wayne, along with Darren Matthews provided the Gulls new top man with solid backing, each plundering paid ten point returns. With 12 points, Paul Lee gave a great display for the visitors, and he would later go on and ride for Hull, Sheffield and Swindon at Premier League level, as well as spending a season in the Elite League with Coventry.

One of the announcements that evening concerned Mark Phillips, who had just acquired sponsorship from Graham Grose, the local funeral director. Mark of course, would later acquire the nickname of 'The Undertaker' as a result of this! At the time though, due to his spectacular style of riding, his entrance to the track was usually marked by the playing of 'Wild Thing', and at times, he was introduced as 'Mad Mark' in order to get the crowd going. Meanwhile, the ever-smiling Chris Bennett was proving to be quite a character and a crash sequence involving him was actually used to start all the meeting highlights filmed by Re-Run Videos. Chris, a Cornish grass-tracker, was the son of Claude Bennett, who himself was a former grass racer of note. Talking of the top quality meeting videos, they were on sale at the Re-Run Videos stand, priced very reasonably at £10 each.

In the track shop, an extensive range of goodies were available, including T-shirts, baseball caps, sun visor strips, plus aerial photographs of the track. Air horns were also on sale at £5, along with autograph books, with the young fans subsequently crowding around the pits to get the riders to endorse them. Meanwhile, Wayne Barrett's wife Kaye was on the lookout for team sponsorship at £1 per point.

On June 22, the Gulls raced at Buxton, and although rain washed out the final heat, the result stood as a 40-32 win for the homesters. Jamie Young topped the scoring for the Hitmen with 11 points, whilst Steve Bishop scorched to a 14 point tally for the battling St Austell boys.

Back at home on 24 June, the Gulls were up against Belle Vue Colts and they managed to chalk up a 47-31 victory in what was a typically entertaining encounter. In spite of an engine failure, Steve Bishop still recorded a paid 12 points, while Wayne Barrett went one better, recording paid 13. For the visitors, Simon Cartwright, who later rode for Hull, Sheffield, Stoke, Glasgow and Berwick, plundered a paid 10 points, with Jamie Isherwood scoring 9. Going back to 'Bish' though, he again lowered the track record to 58.00 seconds in heat 2, but after the gremlins had rendered his bike out of action, he had to use an elderly track spare machine that was known as 'Team Pigeon'. Steve was so pleased to win a race on this bike, he asked if he could use it for the Gulls next away match at Wolverhampton! The machine that 'Bish' blew actually belonged to Jason Prynne and upon hearing this, a representative of Batteries and Brakes Ltd. generously offered to finance the repair bill.

Prior to the match, the Colts had arrived early in the afternoon and had gone to Brian Annear's garage in order to prepare their equipment. While there, they were supplied with traditional Cornish pasties by Hendra Bakeries, and they were also treated to Cornish cream and jam scones made by Amos Putt. Needless to say, Belle Vue team manager Terry Vernon and his charges were completely bowled over by the hospitality of the Cornish people. Talking of Belle Vue, local photographer Bernard White, who was supplying the local press with superb shots of the racing from the home of the Gulls, used to attend meetings at the famous old Hyde Road venue several years previously!

In the programme for the Belle Vue match, promoter Brian Annear revealed that as a gesture he had given pit owners ECCI £1,000 to donate to a charity of their choice. In turn, the owners of the open-cast quarry decided to pass the money on to the Friends of Churchtown Lanlivery Field Centre, and the cheque was subsequently presented on Thursday 17 July. The money had been raised from the previous two home meetings, and this was despite incurring a huge loss, due to the cost of advertising and programmes etc., from the rained off match against Peterborough. Brian also explained that he had been advertising extensively in newspaper and holiday booklets throughout Cornwall, and had even used the *Daily Mirror*.

So, to that match at Wolverhampton, which brought the Gulls face to face with the Shuttle Cubs once again. Aside from Steve Bishop (13 points) and Wayne Barrett (9), the rest of the St Austell side had difficulty in getting around the Monmore Green circuit, and it was no surprise that the homesters avenged their defeat in Cornwall with a 50-28 success. The aforementioned Paul Lee again showed his class with a superb 12 point maximum, while Rob Clarence netted 11, and Nathan McDonald scored 10.

A Swindon and Reading composite side called the M4 Raven Sprockets were next at the clay raceway, and in what was a closely fought match, the Gulls secured a 44-34 win. Darren Matthews was asked to stand down from the side, having encountered numerous mechanical problems, and this allowed the fit-again Jason Prynne to return in the no.4 berth. The position of the race control certainly created some unique problems, one of which occurred in the middle of a race, when, with the referee fully focused on the action, a young lad without a worry in the world, stood in front of the caravan and obliterated the view while he scoffed a tray of sausage and chips!

Anyway, back to the meeting, and Steve Bishop was at his brilliant best, racking up a fabulous 15 point maximum, with Wayne Barrett again providing splendid backing as he piled up a paid 13 points. Bobby Eldridge scored paid 14 for the visitors, while Gary Phelps, who would later link with the Gulls, recorded a fine 12 point tally. Martin Williams was another member of the M4 Raven Sprockets team and he would also later don the famous Gulls race-jacket. David Collins certainly enthused over the match in the *Cornish Guardian*, stating 'This had been tremendous speedway all evening, with passing and repassing on what surely has become speedway's most exciting track.'

In the programme, Brian Annear thanked a chap by the name of Godfrey Spargo from London, who provided the old Weslake that was used as the track spare. Godfrey of course, would later become heavily involved at the Cornish venue, as part of promotional team that introduced Premier League racing in 2001.

Local firms were beginning to get behind the riders and apart from the previously named companies, Nippy Bits were helping out both Chris Bennett and Simon Phillips, while New Way Carpets were providing Chris with additional assistance.

The St Austell boys faced two away matches before they next graced the Clay Country Moto Parc. The first stop was Berwick on 5 July. The Gulls were without Steve Bishop,

Mark Phillips.

so Darren Matthews returned to the fray, but unfortunately they slumped to a 24-54 defeat. Only Wayne Barrett offered any real resistance to the onslaught from the Border Raiders, scoring 11 points from six starts. Peter Johnson was in tremendous form for the homesters, however, sweeping to a paid 15 point maximum, while both Anthony Barlow and David McAllan were paid for 10 points.

It was much better news the day after though, as the Gulls brilliantly raced to a 43-35 success at the Heathersfield Stadium home of Lathallan. Again, without the services of Steve Bishop, the Gulls looked to be up against it from the start, as Simon Phillips was a non-starter, having badly lacerated a leg at Berwick. The six-man side rallied, however, and although Wayne Barrett was the star man with 14 points, the other team members all made telling contributions, thus: - Jason Prynne 9; Darren Matthews 7+2; Mark Phillips 6+1; Chris Bennett 4+2; Mike Bowden 3+1. At no.1 for the home side, Paul Taylor put together a superb performance, and it was only in the final race that he was denied a full 18 point maximum, when Wayne Barrett held on to defeat the Edinburgh born rider.

Back home on 8 July, Buxton provided the opposition, and very good they were too, inflicting a 37-41 defeat on the Gulls. Steve Bishop was back in harness and had little difficulty in knocking up a 15 point maximum, but it was the Hitmen that possessed the strength in depth, with three riders being paid for double-figure tallies thus: Stephen Read 10+1; Jon Armstrong 10+1; Paul Macklin 9+2. The meeting featured one spectacular effort from Mark Phillips that ended in disaster. The Gulls were 4 points adrift after heat 10, and with 'Bish' leading the way, Mark stormed past Jamie Young, but in trying to pass Neil Painter, he took off and landed awkwardly on the track. He was unconscious for several minutes and was taken to hospital for a check up. Mark appeared to be dazed, but as one of the nurses shone a torch into his eye, the Cornishman with the wicked sense of a humour shouted 'Boo', sending all the medical staff jumping with shock!

An interesting point about the St Austell race-jacket was that unlike the old style, a comic gull was featured. Following on from this, the programme from 1997 featured a regular cartoon strip and the programme for the match against Buxton was no exception, depicting three riders and a gull flying overhead, accompanied by the caption 'When Brian started they were pterodactyls, not gulls!'

A week passed before the next track action on 15 July, when the Anglian Angels (a combined Ipswich and King's Lynn side) arrived at the Longstone pit for a league encounter. The gutsy Mark Phillips was straight back in the side after his knock the previous week, while coming in as track reserve was Dean Garton, a former Cornish grass-track rider of note. Dean had previous speedway experience with the Isle of Wight, beginning in 1996, but had also won the South Western Speedtrack Championship - a grass-track event staged on the shale at Exeter's sweeping County Ground circuit back in 1991. Quite a bit had been expected of Dean, but as he only appeared in the nominated heat, he didn't really get a chance to fully demonstrate his undoubted ability.

The Gulls had no difficulty in racking up a convincing 55-21 victory against the Angels, who actually had to borrow Mike Bowden and Cornish youngster Martin

Brian Annear with Dave Stallworthy.

Matthews to complete their side. Skipper Jason Prynne produced the best performance of his short speedway career thus far, romping to a full 15 point maximum, while Wayne Barrett also weighed in with a 12 point full-house. Steve Bishop recorded 9 points, but would have certainly joined the maximum men, but for an engine failure in heat 5. 'Bish' did have the distinction of further lowering the track record though, clocking 57.44 seconds in heat 2. Meanwhile, for the beleaguered visitors, the potential packed 15 year old Matt Read topped the scoring with 8 points. The highlight of the night was undoubtedly a tremendous opening race, which saw young Matt Read pass Wayne Barrett, while Mike Bowden initially held third position from Chris Bennett. Going into the third lap, Wayne swooped ahead of Read, while at the same time, Chris roared around Bowden to give the Gulls a 4-2 advantage in what was another example of the super racing the circuit had fast become renowned for.

Before the racing had started, promoter Brian Annear had addressed the crowd from the start line and asked whether the Cornish fans would like to see Premier League racing? This followed an approach from the Skegness management to see if they might use the Clay Country Moto Parc to fulfil their fixtures, having left their Marsh Lane venue in Lincolnshire. Doubts that the supporters might want to see anything other than the Amateur League fayre they had become accustomed to, were quickly dispelled with air horns a-blasting when Brian asked if those present wished things to remain as they were. Following that response from the crowd, Brian cheerily presented a cheque for £500 to the Fowey River Lions, a local charity that he was supporting. Incidentally,

1997 Gulls, from left to right: Wayne Barrett, Dean Garton, Steve Bishop, Chris Bennett, Mark Phillips, Jason Prynne and Darren Matthews.

among the crowd were a group of elderly residents from Athelstan House in Bodmin and one gentleman was 93 years old!

Local author Jeremy Jackson had a column in the programme, entitled 'Gulls Supporters' Notes', in which he mentioned that Steve Bishop had recently finished fifth in a German grass-track meeting. Jeremy was also trying to find sponsors for young mascot Chris Harris, while reminding local businesses that they could sponsor a rider for as little as £1 per week, under the scheme organized by Kaye Barrett.

Five days after the Anglian Angels match, St Austell journeyed to Peterborough, but, in spite of a determined effort, they went down to a 34-44 reverse. Wayne Barrett was top man with 11 points, while Steve Bishop chipped in with an 8 point total on the pacy 355 metre Alwalton circuit. The young Thundercats side, managed by Peter Oakes, was absolutely packed with talent and this was fully emphasized by their top three performers, namely David Howe, who rattled up a 12 point maximum, while Oliver Allen scored 11 and Simon Stead garnered 10. The meeting actually formed part of a double-header, which also saw the main Peterborough side take a 57-33 victory over the world famous Belle Vue Aces in an Elite League fixture.

Back in Cornwall on 22 July, the Gulls blasted their way to a 58-20 success over Berwick, with 'Bish' simply flying to a 12 point maximum. After a fine paid 7 point return at Peterborough, Dean Garton came up with a brilliant paid 11 score against the Border Raiders, including a couple of very impressive race wins. Jason Prynne gave another captain's performance with a paid maximum, while the ever-reliable Wayne Barrett also scored heavily with paid 11 points. The battling Mark Phillips, who had been likened to the 1960s favourite at Par Moor and Exeter, Chris Blewett, recorded paid 12 points from five starts on what was a real bonanza night for the Gulls. For the visitors, who were an awfully long way from home, Peter Johnson gleaned one race win in his 6 point tally, while David McAllan was their only other heat winner, with a paid 6 points to show for his endeavours.

After the main match, there was a second half event sponsored by Damerells, which saw Steve Bishop win his heat, before beating Jason Prynne in the final to take the £200 prize. All the action was taken in by a number of guests on the night, including Bob Radford, a well-known writer from the *Speedway Star* and former announcer of note at Swindon, Reading and Newport. Also in attendance was Exeter Speedway's genial scribe Tony Lethbridge, who was soaking up all the action along with his wife Chris. It was around this time that the Gulls challenged Exeter to an end of season charity match and Dave Stallworthy used his humorous style of microphone banter to encourage Tony to accept the challenge, with the losing side having to donate £1,000 to charity. Poor Tony was somewhat put on the spot, but eventually responded by saying he would have to discuss it with Falcons promoter Colin Hill! This was only one example of the rapport that went on between Messrs Stallworthy and Lethbridge during the Gulls era, and it actually became quite a feature of meetings at one time, with the supporters wondering quite what comedy routine they would be subjected to next!

There was another amusing story about this meeting, which involved a Berwick supporter who had travelled down and got lost amongst all the hills. The gentleman concerned had stopped to ask one of the employees of the china clay company for directions to the track. Goodness only knows which route this chap ended up taking, for he actually ended up coming down the hill at the back of the pits and as far as anyone connected with the track knows, he remains the only person to ever take this route!

On Tuesday 29 July, it was the turn of West Lothian based Lathallan to visit Cornwall, and their long journey proved fruitless as the Gulls had little difficulty in knocking up a 53-25 victory. Steve Bishop again led the way, scorching to a 15 point maximum, while Jason Prynne lent solid support with a paid 14 point tally. Mark Phillips missed this meeting as he was actually in the Czech Republic, attending a speedway training school. With 12 points, Blair Scott stood out for the Scottish side, but he fought a lone battle and they were well beaten. Blair's performance included two wins, both of which were greeted by the sound of bagpipes as Dave Stallworthy got up to some of his antics with the cassette player! Before the racing had got underway, a mobile crane planted a large H-frame lighting tower in the middle of the centre green. Obviously, this was put in place in readiness for when the evenings started to draw in towards the end of the season.

On an evening of lousy weather, a full feast of speedway was provided, for as well as the Amateur League fixture against Lathallan, the 1,800 folk in attendance were also treated to a demonstration of vintage speedway. Three heats were staged, which really rekindled memories of the pre-war days at Rocky Park. Jim Gregory, a former rider with Wembley, Rayleigh, Wimbledon and Oxford, rode well to accumulate 8 points on board a 1931 Rudge machine. Alan Patis, a man with rally driving experience, as well as grass-track and cycle speedway, scored 5 points mounted on a 1929 Douglas. Riding a 1930 Rudge, the enthusiastic Tom Richardson notched up 3 points, meanwhile completing the line-up and scoring 2 points was Adrian Kessell. This was a real throw back to when

Adrian Kessell and Brian James.

speedway first began at Par Moor of course, as Adrian was one of the original Gulls. As well as riding a Rudge machine, Adrian also brought out the famous 1926 Zenith that his father Tommy had used when winning the 350cc Cornish Championship at Rocky Park in 1933. It was quite appropriate that Vintage Speedway Magazine editor Peter Lipscomb should make his first trip down for this meeting, and he was most impressed with entertainment served up.

Earlier weather forecasts had proved accurate, with mist and drizzle descending on the Moto Parc, making the size of the crowd truly remarkable. Referee Barry Richardson was worthy of great praise for keeping the meeting going as at one point, he had to view the action from the centre green, while Terry Hooke manned the controls in the caravan. This was to cause great amusement amongst the spectators, for when the referee wanted to put the riders on 2 minutes, he had to say the words 'Bleep, bleep' into Dave Stallworthy's microphone!

On 5 August, Mildenhall were scheduled to make the journey down for Amateur League business, but the meeting was cancelled to save them travelling, as the whole area had been covered in a thick blanket of fog for three successive days.

It was away action next for the Gulls, with a trip to Oxford on 8 August. The match formed the second half of a double-header, which had earlier seen Oxford gain a 54-36 victory over Exeter in a Premier League encounter. The Amateur League match that followed was balanced on a knife-edge throughout, with St Austell finally winning 39-38, thanks to a last heat 4-2 from Steve Bishop and Wayne Barrett over Simon Wolstenholme.

Jim Gregory with Jeremy Jackson.

This completed a faultless 15 point maximum for 'Bish', while Wayne totalled 10 points. Meanwhile, for the Oxford side, Wolstenholme notched 13 points, whilst Philip Ambrose scored 11.

The return match with Oxford was next up at the Clay Country Moto Parc four days later, but thanks to heavy rain, the meeting only reached heat nine, before being abandoned. Fortunately, the Gulls held an unassailable 43-11 lead at the time and the result stood. At the time of the stoppage, both Jason Prynne and Steve Bishop had gleaned 9 points apiece from their three starts, while Wayne Barrett (8+1) and Dean Garton (6+3) also remained unbeaten by an opponent. Before the conditions had deteriorated, the amazing 'Bish' had again burned up the track to establish a new track record of 56.38 seconds in heat two.

A week of inactivity was followed by more fast and furious action at the clay raceway, when the Ryde Wizards provided the opposition. Skippering the side from the Isle of Wight was Greg Daniels, who was a somewhat unpopular figure at the Clay Country Moto Parc, as he had originally agreed to sign for the Gulls and had actually sported a St Austell race-jacket on the press day. However, before turning a wheel for the Gulls, he had opted to join the Wizards.

In another link with the past, the Ryde side were managed by George Major, who had been a star performer at Par Moor in the early 1960s. There was no joy for the visitors in the match, however, with St Austell running out fairly comfortable winners by 45 points to 33. That man 'Bish' again did the business, scoring a paid maximum (14+1), while Wayne Barrett (14) and Jason Prynne (10) completed a powerful three-pronged attack for the Gulls. Bobby Eldridge headed the Ryde scoring with 8 points, while Kevin Phillips notched a paid 8, and the previously mentioned Daniels gleaned 7. This match saw Dean Garton's stint in the side come to an abrupt end, with Steve Annear later revealing that the lanky rider had been psyched out by some off-track mates.

On the night, Bobby Eldridge was indebted to the home camp, as announcer Dave Stallworthy gave him a lift down from Bristol, and Ken Westaway, a good friend to St Austell Speedway, helped him out in the pits. There really was no end of help from the friendly Cornish club to their opposition, as they also loaned Mark Phillips to the Wizards as one of their reserves!

There was due to be a £200 challenge in the second half, sponsored by Ivan Kessell Garages, but unfortunately it didn't take place due to the rain and mist that had again descended over the circuit. Looking at the programme, local author and enthusiast Jeremy Jackson made reference to the British Masters Grass-track Championship at Skegness, which Kelvin Tatum had won the previous week. Two of the competitors were top Gulls Wayne Barrett and Steve Bishop, neither of whom disgraced themselves, with Wayne scoring 21 points, while 'Bish' totalled 19.

The following Monday saw the two sides exchange tracks, with the Gulls making the trip across The Solent to race at the 392 metre Smallbrook Stadium raceway. Despite the vast difference in the two circuits, the St Austell boys acquitted themselves well, before going down to a 35-43 defeat. Scoring a solid paid 12 points, Jason Prynne led the Gulls' scoring, while Steve Bishop chipped in with 11. Meanwhile, the Wizards were best served by paid maximums (14+1) from Bobby Eldridge and Gavin Hedge.

Ready for the parade. From left to right: Darren Matthews, Wayne Barrett, Steve Bishop, Chris Bennett and Jason Prynne.

On 26 August, the re-scheduled match against runaway league leaders Peterborough Thundercats took place, having originally been washed out in June. This turned out to be one of the very best meetings ever seen at the Moto Parc and the atmosphere created by an estimated 3,000 crowd was absolutely electric. The visitors, managed by Peter Oakes, took a 3-2 lead in a re-run opening heat after David Howe had defeated Wayne Barrett. There were only two riders in the re-start as Freddie Stephenson had been excluded for falling, while Darren Matthews had been omitted, as he wasn't under power at the time of the stoppage. The Gulls took the lead in the second heat and held a narrow advantage right up to heat eleven when the score stood at 34-31. Courtesy of Jason Bunyan and Simon Stead, Peterborough then inflicted a maximum points win over Jason Prynne and Darren Matthews to enter the final heat 36-35 ahead. Then the tension went up a notch for the last race, and although Steve Bishop dashed to victory in typical fashion, David Howe and Simon Stead filled the middle positions ahead of Jason Prynne to give the Thundercats a 39-38 success.

The Gulls might have been beaten, but they certainly weren't disgraced as the visitors undoubtedy possessed the best young side in the league. It is worth recording their line-up that night, for it was jam packed with talent, as follows: David Howe; Freddie Stephenson; Simon Stead; Ross Brady; Oliver Allen; Jason Bunyan. Meanwhile, the reserve was Carl Wilkinson, and although he didn't get a ride, he would of course go on and develop his talents elsewhere, before linking up with Newport in 2002. Top of the pile on their visit to Cornwall was David Howe, who scored 12 points, while Simon Stead was paid for 12. In Steve Bishop, St Austell still boasted the best individual performer on the night, as that final heat victory completed what had become an almost routine 15 point maximum. The meeting had been so enjoyable that the Gulls actually challenged the Thundercats to a re-match, but this was politely declined.

The evening's entertainment was completed by a couple of second half races, which both resulted in wins for Richard Ford over Chris Bennett, Mike Bowden and Carl Wilkinson. The programme insert contained an advert for an interesting social evening at St.Blazey Football Club on 5 September, with 1960s-style music supplied by a group called Dry Ice. Of course, the event had a speedway connection, as the proceeds would be going towards a new track spare.

A trip to Swindon was next on the agenda, when the galloping Gulls faced the M4 Raven Sprockets and they stole away with a 40-38 victory under their wings. The match first swung one way and then the other, with St Austell moving into a 2 point lead after heat nine. It was an advantage they would maintain until the end, and despite Steve Bishop suffering an engine failure in the final heat, 'Mr Reliable' Wayne Barrett took the flag to seal the victory. That win took Wayne's tally to 13 points, while 'Bish' finished with a round dozen, although it would have been another 15 pointer, but for those mechanical gremlins. For Steve, it had been a return to his old stomping ground, for he had made his British League debut for Swindon way back in 1981, before going on to serve Exeter, Stoke, Arena-Essex and Long Eaton among others. Rounding off the meeting, the home club were best served on the night by the future St Austell Gull and Trelawny Tiger Gary Phelps, who garnered a paid 12 point return, while John Jefferies gave solid support with 11 points.

There was more away action the following day, when the Gulls appeared at the well-appointed home of Mildenhall for another league encounter. Although Steve Bishop netted 15 points from six starts, he had little support and the Gulls slipped to a 30-48 defeat. For the home side, Geoff 'Big Leggy' Powell secured a fine 12 point maximum in his own inimitable style, while Nathan Morton (11 points) and Garry Sweet (paid 11) made telling contributions. The Gulls' performance was best summed up by team manager Andy Annear 'Having won at a big track like Swindon, we were disappointed to lose 30-48 at Mildenhall, but it was a sombre day anyway because of the death of Diana, Princess of Wales, and our performance matched it.'

Back at the amazing Longstone Pit raceway, the next meeting saw a good field assembled to battle it out in the Cornish Grand Prix on 2 September. The start time had been brought forward to 7pm for the last match, against Peterborough, but in view of the nights drawing in, this one began at 6.45pm. Another large crowd were in place for the meeting, and it proved to be another memorable one, although not necessarily for the right reasons. Not only did it get dark early on, but it also rained, with several of the heats being run in atrocious conditions. Indeed, announcer Dave Stallworthy had to cross the track after the meeting in order to do the presentations and he literally sank into the pudding-like mix that the track had turned into! In spite of the difficulties, the riders were to be applauded, for just getting on with the job without a single complaint. Amazingly, with no respite from the elements, those in attendance also proved to be hardy souls as they stood and watched without showing the slightest inclination of wanting to leave.

The meeting had been scheduled for fifteen heats, plus a grand final involving the top four scorers, however, it was slightly curtailed in view of the weather, with the last three qualifying races being deleted. As an added incentive for the riders, local supporter Fred Paul, who had quickly become a good friend of the Gulls, put up a £100 prize for the fastest time of the night. The bonus was subsequently scooped by Steve Bishop, who made light of the conditions and circumnavigated the 230 metre circuit in a new record time of 56.22 seconds when taking heat 2.

After the qualifying heats, Mark Simmonds jointly led the way with 'Bish', both having scored 11 points, while Roger Lobb had accumulated 10 and Wayne Barrett 8. It was 'Simmo' who swept to victory in the final and the Cornishman was a popular winner, having suffered a nasty injury the previous year. Mark actually missed a huge chunk of the 1997 campaign, but had regained his fitness by practising at the Clay Country Moto Parc, before linking with the Isle of Wight late in the season. Anyway, back to the Cornish Grand Prix, and second place in the final was filled by Steve Bishop, with Wayne Barrett beating Roger Lobb for third position on the podium.

Such was Steve Bishop's dominance at the clay raceway, he had been retitled as the 'King of St Austell' by announcer Dave Stallworthy. Aside from engine failures, 'Bish' had not yet suffered defeat by an opponent on the circuit. However, the Cornish Grand Prix marked a turning point as Roger Lobb beat him in heat four, before Mark Simmonds repeated the feat in the grand final of course.

The final home league match took place the following week, when Mildenhall were the visitors for the encounter that should originally have been staged on 5 August. Yet again the mini-track and its sweeping bends served up some thrilling racing, with St Austell just shading a 40-38 success. The scores were close throughout and going into the last heat, the Gulls only held a slender two point advantage. It was Steve Bishop who subsequently raced to the flag from Gavin Hedge and Dean Garrod, thereby securing another win for the men in the famous blue and white race-jackets. 'Bish' had earlier suffered another rare defeat, when former Glasgow rider Geoff Powell got the better of a terrific track battle in heat eight. The defeat was actually caused by Steve's unselfishness, as he was team-riding with Mark Phillips at the time and 'Big Leggy' took advantage to sneak through on the inside of the third bend.

There was an interesting occurrence at the end of heat five, when a winning time of 73.85 seconds was announced for 'Bish', and it was only then that it became obvious the riders had in fact completed 5 laps! The meeting was followed by a firework display, which was brilliant amidst the wonderful lunar landscape setting of the Clay Country Moto Parc. As usual, there was no expense spared by promoter Brian Annear, with £2,000 worth of fireworks illuminating the night sky.

The Gulls completed their league fixtures at King's Lynn on 13 September, when they faced the Anglian Angels. There was a surprising one-match return by Dean Garton and things couldn't possibly have started any better for the Gulls, as Dean and Wayne Barrett swept to maximum points in a re-run opening heat, after home man Matt Read had fallen on the second turn and been excluded. With Steve Bishop revelling in the wide-open spaces of the Saddlebow Road circuit and thundering to yet another 15 point full house, it was no surprise that the Gulls ran out comfortable 44-34 victors. The opening heat duo supplied 'Bish' with great backing as Dean recorded a paid 10 point return, while Wayne notched a paid 9 total. Dean's remarkable performance had a lot to do with the team spirit that was prevalent in the Gulls' camp, for he was actually mounted on a brand new machine, which had been loaned to him by Chris Harris' father! Meanwhile, for the vanquished Angels, Gary Corbett netted a paid 12 tally, with Matt Read recovering well from his heat one misfortune to bag 11 points. The Gulls match formed the first section of a double-header, and the Angels subsequently eked out a narrow 40-38 success over Buxton in the Amateur League fixture that followed.

That completed a twenty-four match league programme for St Austell, which had seen them triumph thirteen times, and suffer defeat on eleven occasions, to yield a highly creditable sixth position in the final table. There are no prizes for guessing that Steve Bishop was perched on top of the Gulls' statistics, having scored 247 (plus 2 bonus) points for a 10.83 average, while also notching 9 maximums (8 full and 1 paid). Wayne Barrett was the only ever-present rider in the squad and he supplied 'Bish' with great support, both at home and on the team's travels, scoring a total of 247 (plus 9 bonus) points for a 9.14 average. Meanwhile, with 157 points and a 7.68 average to his name, Jason Prynne was worthy of a big pat on the back, especially as he had no previous speedway experience prior to the big launch at the Gulls picturesque nest. It would be unfair to leave anyone out, so the final averages for the rest of the team in that historic first year were: Dean Garton 7.00; Darren Matthews 5.52; Mark Phillips 4.56; Chris Bennett 4.49; Mike Bowden 4.14; Simon Phillips 4.00.

Throughout the season, in order to drum up support, promoter Brian Annear gave away large amounts of complimentary tickets, as well as advertising extensively at great cost. Brian openly admitted that he wanted to carry on longer, but to his great disappointment, the season had to be brought to a premature close due to a BSPA ruling that Amateur League tracks could only stage a maximum of 12 meetings. The match against Mildenhall had actually been the 13th meeting to go ahead, and Brian still wanted to bring Colin Hill back with his Exeter side for the previously mooted challenge match. There were conflicting rumours about whether the meeting would be staged or not, but in the end it did go ahead on the afternoon of Sunday 21 September. Having already gone over the permissible fixtures limit, the match was run as a charity event, with supporters allowed in for free, although they could make a donation if they so wished. Among the local charities to benefit from the meeting was the Marie Curie Nursing Service, who were to receive £500. There was great sadness in the week leading up to the match, however, with the news that former Gulls rider and promoter Trevor Redmond had passed away.

The charity meeting saw the Gulls sponsored by the Bruce Wayne Oil Company of Weston-Super-Mare, who afterwards were to back the team right the way through to the end of the 2000 season. So, in what was quite a mouthful to say, the BWOC Gulls took on the Exeter Highfield Coachworks Devon Rangers, who were managed for the occasion by that great collector of speedway memorabilia Robert Doran. The side from Exeter was an interesting one and featured all-action entertainer Frank Smart, as well as Kevin Phillips, Paul Oughton, Andy Carfield, Gary Lobb and Paul

Wayne Barrett.

Jim Collins.

Fudge. Meanwhile, the Gulls tracked Wayne Barrett at no.1, with the rest of the side completed by Simon Phillips, Steve Bishop, Mark Simmonds, Chris Bennett and Bristol-based grass-tracker Jim Collins. There was one other rider who made his first appearance on track at this meeting, and his name was Seemond Stephens, the 10 times Cornish Motocross Champion, who filled the reserve berth for the home side.

The match was a good one, with plenty of thrills and no less than five re-runs, with the Gulls running out winners in the end, by 49 points to 44. The Gulls were losing 21-27 at one point, but thanks to some sporting generosity on the part of the visitors, they introduced Steve Bishop as a golden double tactical substitute in heat nine. The 'King of St Austell' didn't disappoint either, speeding to victory with Mark Simmonds following to give the Gulls an 8-1 advantage, thereby turning the deficit into a 29-28 lead at one fell swoop! 'Bish' was up to his tricks again in heat eleven, circumnavigating the track in 56.22 seconds to equal his own track record, before screaming around in a new best time of 56.14 seconds in heat fifteen. Strangely though, this was never officially recognized as the official track record, probably due to the nature of the meeting.

After the antics of heat nine, St Austell managed to hold their lead and eventually ran out 49-44 winners, with that man 'Bish' top scoring with 18 points, inclusive of that golden double score. Chipping in with good support was tower of strength Wayne Barrett, who scored 12 points, while Mark Simmonds recorded a paid 12. For the visitors, Gary Lobb garnered a paid 13 total, while Frank Smart gave a typical swashbuckling display to glean 11 points. Seemond Stephens did take one ride, when nominated for heat fourteen, and although he ran a last, his promise was there for all to see as he took his first steps on a speedway career that would take him from St Austell to Eastbourne, Swindon, Exeter and eventually back to the Clay Country Moto Parc to line-up for Trelawny in 2002. There was plenty of action for the crowd as a special second half individual event saw three qualifying heats and a twice re-run final that was eventually won by Steve Bishop from Wayne Barrett and Mark Simmonds. Then, the Annear brothers Andy and Steve came out for a match race, which was won by the former, but the piece de resistance was saved until last...

The estimated 2,000 crowd were then treated to the incredible sight of Western Morning News correspondent 'Grizzly' Adams on board a speedway bike for the very first time. In fact, the effervescent reporter had never ridden any sort of bike without stabilizers prior to this, but his effort was worthy of the highest praise as

Paul Adams.

Paul Adams going through his paces.

he was raising money for the Cornwall Air Ambulance charity. Amazingly, the intrepid newshound managed to negotiate four laps of the track without falling off, although he was timed at 93.25 seconds, some 37 seconds outside Steve Bishop's track record!

Promoter Brian Annear was absolutely raving about the season in his programme notes, his opening gambit proclaiming 'Well! What a first season we've had.' He went on to enthuse over the record crowds and thanked the fans for their support, as well as praising the team and pointing out that they had used just nine riders during the course of the league campaign. All that remained was the Gulls' end of season Dinner Dance, which took place at the Cliff Head Hotel, Carlyon Bay on 7 November. A great night was had by all, with the £20 ticket including starter, main meal and dessert. Ray Arthur, the outdoor public address system expert, who supplied the amp and speakers at all Gulls home meetings, was on hand to rig up a radio microphone system. This allowed Dave Stallworthy to go around the room interviewing various people, including all the riders of course.

Guest of honour at the Dinner Dance was David Hughes, who was then the Speedway Control Board manager. There were also some very special trophies distributed, they belonged to Roger Kessell and had originally been won by his late father Ivan, many moons previously, at Rocky Park. The first of these famous old trophies was the Huddy & Kneebone Cup, which was presented to Mark Phillips, who was quite understandably voted the most exciting rider of the year. The Eustace Cup was used as the supporters' rider of the year award and there was no surprise when Steve Bishop was announced as the recipient. Chris Bennett was presented with the W. Vivian Cup for being the highest scorer of bonus points, while top points man Wayne Barrett not only collected the Phillips Cup, but also a brand new trophy, sponsored by BWOC in memory of Chris Julian. Promoter Brian Annear took the microphone and thanked everybody for their overwhelming support throughout the year, while also praising landowners English China Clays International, who played a major part in the Gulls revival. Western Morning News correspondent Paul Adams was also on hand to present Carol Pitman with a £1,000 cheque for the Cornwall Air Ambulance, this being the proceeds from his sponsored track ride. All in all, it was a most enjoyable evening and a fitting way to end what had been a marvellous season.

Tuesday 3 June, 1997 – Amateur League
ST.AUSTELL 'GULLS' 34 WESTERN WARRIORS 41

ST.AUSTELL

Wayne Barrett	3 2 3 3 2 - -	13	
Chris Bennett	0 1'0 1'- - -	2	2
Darren Matthews	2 2 X 2 0 - -	6	
Mark Phillips	1'X X 1 - - -	2	1
Jason Prynne	3 2 1'2 - - -	8	1
Mike Bowden	0 M2 1'- - -	3	1
Simon Phillips	0 - - - - - -	0	

WESTERN WARRIORS

Gary Lobb	2 3 X 3 1 - -	9	
Richard Ford	1'1 3 0 - - -	5	1
Roger Lobb	3 3 3 3 3 - -	15	
Nick Couch	0 0 0 0 - - -	0	
Paul Oughton	2 3 2 2 - - -	9	
Andy Carfield	1'1 1'0 - - -	3	2

PROGRAMME CHANGES:-
Ht 6: S.Phillips replaced Bowden

		Gulls	WW
Ht 1	Barrett, G.Lobb, Ford, Bennett, 61.62 (Track Record)	3	3
Ht 2	R.Lobb, Matthews, M.Phillips, Couch, 58.79 (Track Record)	6	6
Ht 3	Prynne, Oughton, Carfield, Bowden, 61.97	9	9
Ht 4	R.Lobb, Barrett, Bennett, Couch, 58.43 (Track Record)	12	12
Ht 5	(Re-Run) Oughton, Matthews, Carfield, M.Phillips (f,ex), 62.05	14	16
Ht 6	G.Lobb, Prynne, Ford, S.Phillips, Bowden (ex, 2 mins), 61.12	16	20
Ht 7	Barrett, Oughton, Carfield, Bennett, 60.97	19	23
Ht 8	(Re-Run) Ford, Matthews (ex, silencer), G.Lobb (ex, outside assistance), M.Phillips (f,ex), 66.96	19	26
Ht 9	R.Lobb, Bowden, Prynne (f,rem), Couch, 59.54	22	29
Ht 10	(Re-Run) Barrett, Oughton, M.Phillips, Ford, 62.30	26	31
Ht 11	G.Lobb, Matthews, Bowden, Couch, 63.03	29	34
Ht 12	R.Lobb, Prynne, Bennett, Carfield, 60.31	32	37
Ht 13	(Nominated) R.Lobb, Barrett, G.Lobb, Matthews, 59.77	34	41

Tuesday 17 June, 1997 – Amateur League
ST.AUSTELL 'GULLS' 53 SHUTTLE CUBS 25

ST.AUSTELL

Wayne Barrett	2 3 2 2'- - -	9	1
Chris Bennett	1'M1'3 - - -	5	2
Steve Bishop	3 3 3 3 3 - -	15	
Simon Phillips	1 2'1 3 1 - -	8	1
Darren Matthews	2 2 3 2'- - -	9	1
Mark Phillips	1'1 1'M1 - - -	3	2
Mike Bowden	2'2'- - - - -	4	2

SHUTTLE CUBS

Paul Lee	3 3 2 2 2 - -	12	
Nick Simmons	X F 0 1 - - -	1	
Nathan McDonald	F 0 1 0 - - -	1	
Mark Blackwell	2 1 0 0 - - -	3	
Rob Clarence	3 1 3 0 0 - -	7	
Aaron Baker	0 0 0 1 - - -	1	
Neil Cochrane	- - - - - - -	-	

PROGRAMME CHANGES:-
Ht 4: Bowden replaced Bennett;
Ht 9: Bowden replaced M.Phillips

		Gulls	Cubs
Ht 1	(Re-Run) Lee, Barrett, Bennett, Simmons (f,ex), 58.22 (Track Record)	3	3
Ht 2	Bishop, Blackwell, S.Phillips, McDonald (fell), 58.09 (Track Record)	7	5
Ht 3	Clarence, Matthews, M.Phillips, Baker, 62.78	10	8
Ht 4	Barrett, Bowden, Blackwell, McDonald, Bennett (ex, 2 mins), 60.32	15	9
Ht 5	Bishop, S.Phillips, Clarence, Baker, 59.69	20	10
Ht 6	Lee, Matthews, M.Phillips, Simmons (fell), 61.28	23	13
Ht 7	Clarence, Barrett, Bennett, Baker, 61.25	26	16
Ht 8	Bishop, Lee, S.Phillips, Simmons, 58.43	30	18
Ht 9	Matthews, Bowden, McDonald, Blackwell, M.Phillips (ex, 2 mins), 63.82	35	19
Ht 10	S.Phillips, Barrett, Simmons, Clarence, 63.42	40	20
Ht 11	Bishop, Lee, M.Phillips, Blackwell, 59.93	44	22
Ht 12	Bennett, Matthews, Baker, McDonald, 63.89	49	23
Ht 13	(Nominated) Bishop, Lee, S.Phillips, Clarence, 60.04	53	25

Tuesday 24 June, 1997 – Amateur League
ST.AUSTELL 'GULLS' 47 BELLE VUE 'COLTS' 31

ST.AUSTELL			
Wayne Barrett	2 2'3 2 3 - -	12	1
Simon Phillips	T 3 2'3 - - -	8	1
Steve Bishop	3 3 R3 2'- -	11	1
Chris Bennett	1 2'2 1'- - -	6	2
Darren Matthews	R 1'R M- - -	1	1
Mark Phillips	1 2 2 2'- - -	7	1
Mike Bowden	1'1 - - - - -	2	1
BELLE VUE			
Jamie Isherwood	3 3 3 RF - -	9	
Lee Dixon	F X - - - - -	0	
Glenn Furniss	2 1 3 F - - -	6	
Elvis Jones	0 X 1 1 - - -	2	
Scott Donovan	3 X F - - - -	3	
Simon Cartwright	2'1 1 3 2 - -	9	1
Andy Taylor	1 0 1 - - - -	2	

PROGRAMME CHANGES:-
Ht 1: Bowden replaced S.Phillips in the re-run; Ht 8: Taylor replaced Dixon; Ht 10: T/S Cartwright for Donovan; Taylor replaced Dixon; Ht 12: Bowden replaced Matthews

		Gulls	Colts
Ht 1	(Re-Run) Isherwood, Barrett, Bowden, Dixon (fell), S.Phillips (ex, tapes), 59.00	3	3
Ht 2	Bishop, Furniss, Bennett, Jones, 58.00 (Track Record)	7	5
Ht 3	Donovan, Cartwright, M.Phillips, Matthews (ret), 62.00	8	10
Ht 4	(Re-Run) S.Phillips, Barrett, Furniss, Jones (f,ex), 62.44	13	11
Ht 5	(Re-Run) Bishop, Bennett, Cartwright, Donovan (f,ex), 61.09	18	12
Ht 6	(Awarded) Isherwood, M.Phillips, Matthews, Dixon (f,ex), No Time	21	15
Ht 7	Barrett, S.Phillips, Cartwright (f,rem), Donovan (fell), 64.36	26	16
Ht 8	Isherwood, Bennett, Taylor, Bishop (ret), 62.17	28	20
Ht 9	Furniss, M.Phillips, Jones, Matthews (ret), 62.51	30	24
Ht 10	Cartwright, Barrett, Bennett, Taylor, 61.89	33	27
Ht 11	Bishop, M.Phillips, Jones, Isherwood (ret), 59.24	38	28
Ht 12	S.Phillips, Cartwright, Bowden, Furniss (fell), Matthews (ex, 2 mins), 61.08	42	30
Ht 13	(Nominated) Barrett, Bishop, Taylor, Isherwood (fell), 61.46	47	31

Tuesday 1 July, 1997 – Amateur League
ST.AUSTELL 'GULLS' 44 M4 RAVEN SPROCKETS 34

ST.AUSTELL			
Wayne Barrett	2 2 3 3 2'- -	12	1
Simon Phillips	0 1'0 2 - - -	3	1
Steve Bishop	3 3 3 3 3 - -	15	
Jason Prynne	1 2'1 2'- - -	6	2
Chris Bennett	1'3 0 1'- - -	5	2
Mark Phillips	2 0 1 0 - - -	3	
Mike Bowden	- - - - - - -	-	
M4 RAVEN SPROCKETS			
Gary Phelps	3 1'2 3 1'0 -	10	2
Keith Lansley	1 2 0 X - - -	3	
Bobby Eldridge	2 3 2'2 3 1 -	13	1
Rob Cooling	X F - - - - -	0	
Martin Williams	3 1 1'1 - - -	6	1
Ian Clarke	0 0 2 0 - - -	2	
Wayne Holloway	- - - - - - -	-	

PROGRAMME CHANGES:-
Ht 9: T/S Phelps for Cooling; Ht 11: T/S Eldridge for Cooling

		Gulls	M4
Ht 1	Phelps, Barrett, Lansley, S.Phillips, 59.28	2	4
Ht 2	(Awarded) Bishop, Eldridge, Prynne, Cooling (f,ex), No Time	6	6
Ht 3	Williams, M.Phillips, Bennett, Clarke, 59.90	9	9
Ht 4	Eldridge, Barrett, S.Phillips, Cooling (fell), 59.50	12	12
Ht 5	Bishop, Prynne, Williams, Clarke, 59.00	17	13
Ht 6	Bennett, Lansley, Phelps, M.Phillips, 62.25	20	16
Ht 7	Barrett, Clarke, Williams, S.Phillips, 61.25	23	19
Ht 8	Bishop, Phelps, Prynne, Lansley, 58.34	27	21
Ht 9	Phelps, Eldridge, M.Phillips, Bennett, 63.19	28	26
Ht 10	(Awarded) Barrett, Prynne, Williams, Lansley (f,ex), No Time	33	27
Ht 11	Bishop, Eldridge, Phelps, M.Phillips, 60.38	36	30
Ht 12	Eldridge, S.Phillips, Bennett, Clarke, 61.80	39	33
Ht 13	(Nominated) Bishop, Barrett, Eldridge, Phelps, 61.82	44	34

Tuesday 8 July, 1997 – Amateur League
ST.AUSTELL 'GULLS' 37 BUXTON 'HITMEN' 41

ST.AUSTELL

Rider	Scores		
Wayne Barrett	1'2 1 1 - - -	5	1
Chris Bennett	2 1'0 0 - - -	3	1
Steve Bishop	3 3 3 3 3 - -	15	
Jason Prynne	T 0 2'3 2'- -	7	2
Darren Matthews	0 0 2 1 - - -	3	
Mark Phillips	1 2 X X - - -	3	
Mike Bowden	1 - - - - - -	1	

BUXTON

Rider	Scores		
Jamie Young	3 3 R 1'- - -	7	1
Richard Moss	0 1 0 - - - -	1	
Stephen Read	2 3 3 2'- - -	10	1
Simon Tawlks	X 0 1 - - - -	1	
Jon Armstrong	2'2 3 2 1 - -	10	1
Paul Macklin	3 1'2'3 - - -	9	2
Neil Painter	1 2 0 - - - -	3	

PROGRAMME CHANGES:-
Ht 2: Bowden replaced Prynne in the re-run; Ht 8: Painter replaced Moss; Ht 11: Painter replaced Tawlks

		Gulls	Bux
Ht 1	Young, Bennett, Barrett, Moss, 61.47	3	3
Ht 2	(Re-Run Twice) Bishop, Read, Bowden, Tawlks (f,ex), Prynne (ex, tapes), 57.84	7	5
Ht 3	(Re-Run) Macklin, Armstrong, Phillips, Matthews, 60.65	8	10
Ht 4	Read, Barrett, Bennett, Tawlks, 60.38	11	13
Ht 5	Bishop, Armstrong, Macklin, Prynne, 65.00	14	16
Ht 6	Young, Phillips, Moss (f,rem), Matthews (f,rem), 61.22	16	20
Ht 7	Armstrong, Macklin, Barrett, Bennett, 60.66	17	25
Ht 8	(Re-Run) Bishop, Prynne, Painter, Young (ret), 59.72	22	26
Ht 9	(Re-Run) Read, Matthews, Tawlks, Phillips (ex, foul riding), 59.13	24	30
Ht 10	Prynne, Armstrong, Barrett, Moss, 59.44	28	32
Ht 11	(Awarded) Bishop, Painter, Young, Phillips (f,ex), No Time	31	35
Ht 12	Macklin, Read, Matthews, Bennett, 60.13	32	40
Ht 13	(Nominated) Bishop, Prynne, Armstrong, Painter, 57.53 (Track Record)	37	41

Tuesday 15 July, 1997 – Amateur League
ST.AUSTELL 'GULLS' 55 ANGLIAN ANGELS 21

ST.AUSTELL

Rider	Scores		
Wayne Barrett	3 3 3 3 - - -	12	
Chris Bennett	1 R 2'2'- - -	5	2
Steve Bishop	3 R 3 3 - - -	9	
Mark Phillips	2'R 2'2'- - -	6	3
Jason Prynne	3 3 3 3 3 - -	15	
Darren Matthews	2'2'2'2'1 - -	7	3
Dean Garton	1 - - - - - -	1	

ANGLIAN ANGELS

Rider	Scores		
Matt Read	2 1 X 1 2 2 -	8	
Mike Bowden	R 0 1 1 - - -	2	
John Curtis	1 2 0 1 - - -	4	
David Nix	X - - - - - -	0	
Peter Grimwood	1 3 0 0 - - -	4	
Ian Leverington	0 2'1 F - - -	3	1
Martin Matthews	R 0 - - - - -	0	

PROGRAMME CHANGES:-
Ht 9: T/S Read for Nix
Ht 11: M.Matthews replaced Nix

		Gulls	AA
Ht 1	Barrett, Read, Bennett, Bowden, 59.28	4	2
Ht 2	(Re-Run) Bishop, Phillips, Curtis, Nix (f,ex), 57.44 (Track Record)	9	3
Ht 3	Prynne, D.Matthews, Grimwood, Leverington, 61.65	14	4
Ht 4	Barrett, Curtis, Bennett (ret), Nix (ns), 58.90 (3 Riders Only)	17	6
Ht 5	Grimwood, Leverington, Bishop (ret), Phillips (ret), 65.31	17	11
Ht 6	Prynne, D.Matthews, Read, Bowden, 59.13	22	12
Ht 7	Barrett, Bennett, Leverington, Grimwood, 61.90	27	13
Ht 8	Bishop, Phillips, Bowden, Read (ex, crossed white line), 60.25	32	14
Ht 9	Prynne, D.Matthews, Read, Curtis, 59.94	37	15
Ht 10	Barrett, Phillips, Bowden, Grimwood, 59.12	42	16
Ht 11	Bishop, Read, D.Matthews, M.Matthews (ret), 57.81	46	18
Ht 12	Prynne, Bennett, Curtis, Leverington (fell), 60.06	51	19
Ht 13	(Nominated) Prynne, Read, Garton, M.Matthews, 59.95	55	21

Tuesday 22 July, 1997 – Amateur League
ST.AUSTELL 'GULLS' 58 BERWICK 'BORDER RAIDERS' 20

ST.AUSTELL

Wayne Barrett	2'3 1'3 - - -	9	2
Dean Garton	3 2'2 3 - - -	10	1
Steve Bishop	3 3 3 3 - - -	12	
Mark Phillips	1 2'2'2'2 - -	9	3
Jason Prynne	3 3 3 2'- - -	11	1
Darren Matthews	0 2'2'- - - -	4	2
Chris Bennett	2'1'1'- - - -	3	2

BERWICK

Tony Howe	1 1 0 0 - - -	2	
Andrew Swales	0 0 - - - - -	0	
Gareth Martin	0 X 1 F - - -	1	
Malcolm Hogg	2 1 1 1 - - -	5	
David McAllan	1'0 0 1 3 - -	5	1
Peter Johnson	2 1 3 R - - -	6	
Danny Fairburn	X X 1 - - - -	1	

PROGRAMME CHANGES:-
Ht 6: Fairburn replaced Swales; Ht 8: T/S Martin for Swales; Ht 9: Bennett replaced Matthews; Ht 10: Fairburn replaced Swales; Ht 12: Fairburn replaced Martin

		Gulls	Ber
Ht 1	Garton, Barrett, Howe, Swales, 58.04	5	1
Ht 2	Bishop, Hogg, Phillips (f,rem), Martin (fell), 60.65	9	3
Ht 3	(Re-Run) Prynne, Johnson, McAllan, Matthews, 60.33	12	6
Ht 4	(Awarded) Barrett, Garton, Hogg, Martin (f,ex), No Time	17	7
Ht 5	Bishop, Phillips, Johnson, McAllan, 57.85	22	8
Ht 6	(Awarded) Prynne, Matthews, Howe, Fairburn (f,ex), No Time	27	9
Ht 7	Johnson, Garton, Barrett, McAllan, 60.45	30	12
Ht 8	Bishop, Phillips, Martin, Howe, 59.70,	35	13
Ht 9	Prynne, Bennett, Hogg (f,rem), Martin (fell), 60.05	40	14
Ht 10	(Awarded) Barrett, Phillips, McAllan, Fairburn (f,ex), No Time	45	15
Ht 11	Bishop, Matthews, Hogg, Howe, 59.09	50	16
Ht 12	Garton, Prynne, Fairburn, Johnson (ret), 60.48	55	17
Ht 13	(Nominated) McAllan, Phillips, Bennett, Swales, 60.70	58	20

Tuesday 29 July, 1997 – Amateur League
ST.AUSTELL 'GULLS' 53 LATHALLAN 'LIGHTNING' 25

ST.AUSTELL

Wayne Barrett	3 2 1 3 - - -	9	
Dean Garton	2'R 3 1'- - -	6	2
Steve Bishop	3 3 3 3 3 - -	15	
Darren Matthews	1 1 2'- - - -	4	1
Jason Prynne	3 3 3 2 2'- -	13	1
Chris Bennett	1 R 1 - - - -	2	
Simon Phillips	2'2'- - - - -	4	2

LATHALLAN

Paul Taylor	1 1'1 X - - -	3	1
Steven McAllister	0 2 0 1 - - -	3	
Blair Scott	2 3 2 2 3 R-	12	
Mark McIlkenny	0 1 0 1 1 - -	3	
Brian Turner	2 2 0 F - - -	4	
Steven Jones	0 R M - - - -	0	
Iain Milne	0 - - - - - -	0	

PROGRAMME CHANGES:-
Ht 7: T/S Scott for Jones; Ht 8: Phillips replaced Matthews; Ht 11: Phillips replaced Bennett; Ht 12: Milne replaced Jones

		Gulls	Lin
Ht 1	Barrett, Garton, Taylor, McAllister, 59.34	5	1
Ht 2	Bishop, Scott, Matthews, McIlkenny, 57.15 (Track Record)	9	3
Ht 3	Prynne, Turner, Bennett, Jones, 58.72	13	5
Ht 4	Scott, Barrett, McIlkenny, Garton (ret), 59.25	15	9
Ht 5	Bishop, Turner, Matthews, Jones (ret), 58.62	19	11
Ht 6	Prynne, McAllister, Taylor, Bennett (ret), 60.00	22	14
Ht 7	Garton, Scott, Barrett, Turner, 59.53	26	16
Ht 8	Bishop, Phillips, Taylor, McAllister, 61.39	31	17
Ht 9	Prynne, Scott, Bennett, McIlkenny, 59.81	35	19
Ht 10	Barrett, Matthews, McAllister, Turner (fell), 60.00	40	20
Ht 11	(Awarded) Bishop, Phillips, McIlkenny (f,rem), Taylor (f,ex), No Time	45	21
Ht 12	Scott, Prynne, Garton, Milne, Jones (ex, 2 mins), 59.78	48	24
Ht 13	(Nominated) Bishop, Prynne, McIlkenny, Scott (ret), 59.34	53	25

Tuesday 12 August, 1997 – Amateur League
ST.AUSTELL 'GULLS' 43 OXFORD 'CUBS' 11
Meeting abandoned after Heat-9

ST.AUSTELL

Wayne Barrett	2'3 3 - - - -	8	1
Darren Matthews	3 1 2'- - - -	6	1
Steve Bishop	3 3 3 - - - -	9	
Chris Bennett	1 2'2'- - - -	5	2
Jason Prynne	3 3 3 - - - -	9	
Dean Garton	2'2'2'2'- - - -	6	3
Simon Phillips	- - - - - - -	-	

OXFORD

Simon Wolstenholme	1 1 0 - - - -	2	
Gary Fawdrey	0 0 - - - - -	0	
Phil Ambrose	0 2 1 R - - -	3	
Jason McKenna	2 0 1 - - - -	3	
Lee Driver	0 0 0 - - - -	0	
Jason Newitt	1 1 1 - - - -	3	

PROGRAMME CHANGES:-
Ht 8: T/S Ambrose for Fawdrey

Note: Due to heavy rain, this meeting was curtailed after Heat-9, with the result being allowed to stand.

		Gulls	Oxf
Ht 1	Matthews, Barrett, Wolstenholme, Fawdrey, 61.56	5	1
Ht 2	Bishop, McKenna, Bennett, Ambrose, 56.38 (Track Record)	9	3
Ht 3	Prynne, Garton, Newitt, Driver, 60.28	14	4
Ht 4	Barrett, Ambrose, Matthews, McKenna, 60.32	18	6
Ht 5	Bishop, Bennett, Newitt, Driver, 60.38	23	7
Ht 6	Prynne, Garton, Wolstenholme, Fawdrey, 60.65	28	8
Ht 7	Barrett, Matthews, Newitt, Driver, 61.58	33	9
Ht 8	Bishop, Bennett, Ambrose, Wolstenholme, 61.35	38	10
Ht 9	Prynne, Garton, McKenna, Ambrose (ret), 61.93	43	11

Tuesday 19 August, 1997 – Amateur League
ST.AUSTELL 'GULLS' 45 ISLE OF WIGHT 'WIZARDS' 33

ST.AUSTELL

Wayne Barrett	2 3 3 3 3 - -	14	
Darren Matthews	1'1'T 1 1 - - -	3	1
Steve Bishop	3 3 3 3 2'- -	14	1
Chris Bennett	0 X 1 - - - -	1	
Jason Prynne	3 2 2 3 - - -	10	
Dean Garton	0 1'0 T - - -	1	1
Simon Phillips	0 1 1 - - - -	2	

ISLE OF WIGHT

Bobby Eldridge	3 3 F 2 - - -	8	
Colin Crook	0 0 2 R - - -	2	
Greg Daniels	2 2 3 0 - - -	7	
Paul Fudge	1'1'1'1 0 - -	3	2
Paul Lydes-Uings	2 1'0 2 - - -	5	1
Kevin Phillips	1'2 2 2 0 - -	7	1
Mark Phillips	1 - - - - - -	1	

PROGRAMME CHANGES:-
Ht 4: S.Phillips replaced Matthews in the re-run; Ht 8: S.Phillips replaced Bennett; Ht 11: S.Phillips replaced Garton in the re-run

Note: Heat times were only given to one decimal point at this meeting.

		Gulls	IOW
Ht 1	Eldridge, Barrett, Matthews, Crook, 58.0	3	3
Ht 2	Bishop, Daniels, Fudge, Bennett, 56.6	6	6
Ht 3	Prynne, Lydes-Uings, K.Phillips, Garton, 60.4	9	9
Ht 4	(Re-Run) Barrett, Daniels, Fudge, S.Phillips, Matthews (ex, tapes), 59.1	12	12
Ht 5	(Re-Run Twice) Bishop, K.Phillips, Lydes-Uings, Bennett (f,ex), 59.5	15	15
Ht 6	Eldridge, Prynne, Garton, Crook, 59.3	18	18
Ht 7	Barrett, K.Phillips, Matthews, Lydes-Uings, 59.6	22	20
Ht 8	Bishop, Crook, S.Phillips, Eldridge (fell), 58.9	26	22
Ht 9	Daniels, Prynne, Fudge, Garton, 60.0	28	26
Ht 10	Barrett, Lydes-Uings, Bennett, Crook (ret), 59.9	32	28
Ht 11	(Re-Run) Bishop, Eldridge, S.Phillips, Fudge, Garton (ex, tapes), 58.9	36	30
Ht 12	Prynne, K.Phillips, Matthews, Daniels, 60.4	40	32
Ht 13	(Nominated) Barrett, Bishop, M.Phillips, K.Phillips, 57.0	45	33

Tuesday 26 August, 1997 – Amateur League
ST.AUSTELL 'GULLS' 38 PETERBOROUGH 'THUNDERCATS' 39

ST.AUSTELL

Wayne Barrett	2 2 3 R - - -	7	
Darren Matthews	X 1'0 0 - - -	1	1
Steve Bishop	3 3 3 3 3 - -	15	
Mark Phillips	1 0 1 1 - - -	3	
Jason Prynne	3 2 3 1 0 - -	9	
Simon Phillips	0 1'1 1 - - -	3	1
Chris Bennett	- - - - - - -	-	

PETERBOROUGH

David Howe	3 3 2 2 2 - -	12	
Freddie Stephenson	X 0 X 2'- - -	2	1
Simon Stead	2 3 2 2'1'- -	10	2
Ross Brady	0 0 F F - - -	0	
Oliver Allen	2 1'1'3 - - -	7	2
Jason Bunyan	1'2 2 3 - - -	8	1
Carl Wilkinson	- - - - - - -	-	

PROGRAMME CHANGES:-
None!

		Gulls	Pet
Ht 1	(Awarded) Howe, Barrett, Stephenson (f,ex), Matthews (ex, not under power), No Time	2	3
Ht 2	Bishop, Stead, M.Phillips, Brady, 57.56	6	5
Ht 3	Prynne, Allen, Bunyan, S.Phillips, 57.63	9	8
Ht 4	Stead, Barrett, Matthews, Brady, 58.57	12	11
Ht 5	Bishop, Bunyan, Allen, M.Phillips, 57.28	15	14
Ht 6	Howe, Prynne, S.Phillips, Stephenson, 57.69	18	17
Ht 7	Barrett, Bunyan, Allen, Matthews, 59.15	21	20
Ht 8	(Re-Run) Bishop, Howe, M.Phillips, Stephenson (f,ex), 57.25	25	22
Ht 9	Prynne, Stead, S.Phillips, Brady (fell), 59.66	29	24
Ht 10	Allen, Stephenson, M.Phillips, Barrett (ret), 65.36	30	29
Ht 11	Bishop, Howe, S.Phillips, Brady (fell), 57.31	34	31
Ht 12	(Re-Run) Bunyan, Stead, Prynne, Matthews, 60.78	35	36
Ht 13	(Nominated) Bishop, Howe, Stead, Prynne, 58.44	38	39

Tuesday 2 September, 1997
CORNISH GRAND PRIX

Mark Phillips	3 1 1 1 - - -	6
Simon Phillips	2 1 3 1 - - -	7
Mike Bowden	0 2 0 0 - - -	2
Chris Bennett	1 X 1 2 - - -	4
Greg Daniels	1 0 0 - - - -	1
Wayne Barrett	2 1 3 2 - - -	8
Darren Matthews	0 X 1 1 - - -	2
Steve Bishop	3 2 3 3 - - -	11
Gary Lobb	1 3 0 2 - - -	6
Roger Lobb	2 3 2 3 - - -	10
Jason Prynne	0 2 2 R - - -	4
Mark Simmonds	3 3 2 3 - - -	11
Kevin Phillips (Res)	0 0 - - - - -	0

PROGRAMME CHANGES:-
Ht 6: K.Phillips replaced Bennett in the re-run;
Ht 11: K.Phillips replaced Daniels

Note: Heats 13-15 were not run due to worsening weather conditions.

Ht 1	M.Phillips, S.Phillips, Bennett, Bowden, 60.13
Ht 2	Bishop, Barrett, Daniels, Matthews, 56.22 (Track Record)
Ht 3	Simmonds, R.Lobb, G.Lobb, Prynne, 57.72
Ht 4	R.Lobb, Bishop, M.Phillips, Daniels, 59.12
Ht 5	(Awarded) G.Lobb, Bowden, S.Phillips, Matthews (f,ex), No Time
Ht 6	(Re-Run) Simmonds, Prynne, Barrett, K.Phillips, Bennett (f,ex), 58.19
Ht 7	S.Phillips, Prynne, M.Phillips, Daniels, 61.03
Ht 8	Bishop, Simmonds, Matthews, Bowden, 59.03
Ht 9	Barrett, R.Lobb, Bennett, Daniels, 62.81
Ht 10	Bishop, G.Lobb, S.Phillips, Prynne (ret), 59.78
Ht 11	R.Lobb, Bennett, Matthews, K.Phillips, 62.84
Ht 12	Simmonds, Barrett, M.Phillips, Bowden, 61.47
Final	Simmonds, Bishop, Barrett, R.Lobb, 62.13

Tuesday 9 September, 1997 – Amateur League
ST.AUSTELL 'GULLS' 40 MILDENHALL 'FEN TIGERS' 38

ST.AUSTELL

Wayne Barrett	3 3 1 3 F - -	10	
Simon Phillips	1 1 0 0 - - -	2	
Steve Bishop	3 3 2 3 3 - -	14	
Mark Phillips	1 1 1'X - - -	3	1
Jason Prynne	1 3 3 2 - - -	9	
Chris Bennett	0 1 X 1 - - -	2	
Darren Matthews	- - - - - - -	-	

MILDENHALL

Geoff Powell	2 2 3 2 - - -	9	
Jamie Barton	0 0 0 1' - - -	1	1
Garry Sweet	0 0 2 1 - - -	3	
Nathan Morton	2 2 1 F - - -	5	
Dean Garrod	3 M2'2 1 - -	8	2
Gavin Hedge	2'2 3 3 2 - -	12	1
Simon Brown	R - - - - - -	0	

PROGRAMME CHANGES:-
Ht 5: Brown replaced Garrod

		Gulls	Mild
Ht 1	Barrett, Powell, S.Phillips, Barton, 60.88	4	2
Ht 2	Bishop, Morton, M.Phillips, Sweet, 59.44	8	4
Ht 3	Garrod, Hedge, Prynne, Bennett, 60.37	9	9
Ht 4	Barrett, Morton, S.Phillips, Sweet, 59.26	13	11
Ht 5	Bishop, Hedge, M.Phillips, Brown (ret), Garrod (ex, 2 min), 73.85 (5 laps!)	17	13
Ht 6	Prynne, Powell, Bennett, Barton, 59.72	21	15
Ht 7	Hedge, Garrod, Barrett, S.Phillips, 59.75	22	20
Ht 8	Powell, Bishop, M.Phillips, Barton, 60.66	25	23
Ht 9	(Re-Run) Prynne, Sweet, Morton, Bennett (f,ex), 60.25	28	26
Ht 10	(Awarded) Barrett, Garrod, Barton, M.Phillips (f,ex), No Time	31	29
Ht 11	Bishop, Powell, Bennett, Morton (fell), 57.13	35	31
Ht 12	Hedge, Prynne, Sweet, S.Phillips, 59.41	37	35
Ht 13	(Nominated) Bishop, Hedge, Garrod, Barrett (fell), 59.15	40	38

Sunday 21 September, 1997 – Charity Practice Challenge
ST.AUSTELL 'GULLS' 49 EXETER 'DEVON RANGERS' 44

ST.AUSTELL

Wayne Barrett	2 3 2 2 3 - -	12	
Simon Phillips	1'2'0 1 3 - -	7	2
Steve Bishop	3 1 2 6 3 3 -	18	
Jim Collins	0 0 0 F - - -	0	
Mark Simmonds	3 2 2'3 1 - -	11	1
Chris Bennett	X 0 0 1 - - -	1	
Seemond Stephens	0 - - - - - -	0	

EXETER

Frank Smart	3 3 3 2 0 - -	11	
Kevin Phillips	F n 1 1 2 - -	4	
Paul Oughton	2 0 0 2 0 - -	4	
Andy Carfield	1'1 1 1'1' - -	5	3
Gary Lobb	1'3 3 3 2 - -	12	1
Paul Fudge	2 2'1 1 0 2 -	8	1

PROGRAMME CHANGES:-
Ht 6: Fudge replaced K.Phillips, who was unable to partake in the re-run; Ht 9: Golden Double T/S Bishop for Bennett

Note: Steve Bishop's track record time in Heat-15, was not deemed as being official.

		Gulls	Exet
Ht 1	(Re-Run) Smart, Barrett, S.Phillips, K.Phillips (fell), 59.00	3	3
Ht 2	(Re-Run) Bishop, Oughton, Carfield, Collins (15 yds), 58.97	6	6
Ht 3	(Re-Run) Simmonds, Fudge, Lobb, Bennett (f,ex), 59.12	9	9
Ht 4	Barrett, S.Phillips, Carfield, Oughton, 61.42	14	10
Ht 5	Lobb, Fudge, Bishop, Collins, 59.13	15	15
Ht 6	(Re-Run) Smart, Simmonds, Fudge, Bennett, K.Phillips (f,ns), 58.96	17	19
Ht 7	Lobb, Barrett, Fudge, S.Phillips, 59.13	19	23
Ht 8	Smart, Bishop, K.Phillips, Collins, 58.81	21	27
Ht 9	Bishop (GD), Simmonds, Carfield, Oughton, 59.90	29	28
Ht 10	Lobb, Barrett, K.Phillips, Collins (fell), 59.63	31	32
Ht 11	(Re-Run) Bishop, Smart, Carfield, Bennett, 56.22 (Equalled Track Record)	34	35
Ht 12	Simmonds, Oughton, S.Phillips, Fudge, 61.60	38	37
Ht 13	(Nominated) S.Phillips, K.Phillips, Bennett, Oughton, 60.81	42	39
Ht 14	(Nominated) Barrett, Fudge, Carfield, Stephens, 60.18	45	42
Ht 15	(Nominated) Bishop, Lobb, Simmonds, Smart, 56.14 (Track Record)	49	44

2

1998

The season kicked off with a rather different style of press and practice day, which featured the BWOC Gulls facing an Exeter Devon Rangers side in a full 15 heat challenge match on the afternoon of Sunday 19 April. The reason for this unusual occurrence was because the cameras of BBC South West were in attendance. The race action was filmed from various vantage points, including high up on the cliffs, down by the start line and even in the commentary box! The action was subsequently screened on BBC2 as part of the 'Out And About' series on 14 May.

The Gulls team for the match was led by familiar no.1 Wayne Barrett, with the rest of the side completed by Chris Bennett, Steve Bishop, Chris Harris, Jason Prynne and Seemond Stephens. The inclusion of Seemond Stephens was particularly interesting, as he had only appeared on the scene for the last meeting of the previous year, but despite his lack of experience, the local youngster racked up an impressive paid 12 point tally. For those who knew Seemond well, this perhaps was not such a surprise as he had spent many hours practising over the winter months and had even bought a machine from Mark Loram. Having turned 15 at the tail end of 1997, former mascot Chris Harris (or 'Baby Gull' as he was affectionately known) made his first competitive appearance,

1998 Gulls, from left to right: Gary Lobb, Chris Bennett, Steve Bishop, Ryan Dearing, Chris Harris (on bike), Jason Prynne, Jim Collins, Wayne Barrett and Seemond Stephens.

Seemond Stephens.

and he too impressed the sun-drenched crowd of some 500, recording a paid 6 score. The Gulls ran out convincing 53-36 winners, with both Steve Bishop and Wayne Barrett performing as solidly as ever, netting 13 points and paid 12 respectively, while Jason Prynne recorded a paid 11 and Chris Bennett notched paid 6.

Unlike 1997, when Brian Annear had a dearth of riders to make up his side, in 1998, he was spoilt for choice and this was emphasized by the Exeter side, which included many riders vying for a place in the Gulls line-up. These included Gary Lobb, who scorched to a quite brilliant 15 point maximum and Simon Phillips, who finished with a 10 point haul. The rest of the team was made up of Richard Ford, Kevin Phillips, Paul Fudge and Jim Collins, with Chris Dix and Ryan Dearing (son of future promoter Peter) getting some rides as stand-in reserves. Also of interest on the day was the fact that Andy Annear was team manager for the Gulls, with brother Steve in charge of the opposition.

During the season, promoter Brian Annear actually pulled a fast one on the authorities, who wanted clubs to buy racing fuel, more commonly known as either methanol or dope, from designated suppliers. The official dope had a dye put in it, so the powers that be could easily tell if illegal substances were being added to it. However, Brian discovered that it was possible mix ordinary dope with the coloured fuel on a fifty-fifty basis, thereby saving considerable amounts of money, without detection! Of course, Brian didn't let on about this while he was still involved with the running of the track, but he did reveal this little gem during an interview in 2001, when research was being carried out for the production of this book.

One of the changes at the track in 1998 saw the race control caravan replaced by a double-decker bus, which had formerly been used as a mobile restaurant in Wadebridge. Steve Annear actually went to collect the bus and this proved to be eventful in itself, as not only did the bus allegedly have no tax disc, but the brakes inadvertently came on halfway through the journey back! The bus did eventually make it to the Clay Country Moto Parc though, where it was used by the referee and meeting officials.

The Amateur League was retitled the Conference League in 1998, and the Gulls' official start to the season saw them travel up to Newport for their first match on 2 May. It proved to be a bad day at the office for the Gulls though, as they crashed to a 33-53 reverse. Ever-reliable Steve Bishop performed well, garnering 13 points, while both Chris Harris and Seemond Stephens made their debut in league racing – Chris notching paid 5 points, while Seemond scored two. Meanwhile, Newport were led from the front with double-figure returns from the powerful quartet of Jon Armstrong (13+1), Andrew Appleton (12+1), Nick Simmons (9+2) and Roger Lobb (9+1). Despite the disappointing result, there was some good news immediately after the match, when Steve Bishop overcame Andrew Appleton to win the Bronze Helmet.

The Gulls faced their first match in the newly formed British Youth Development League on 11 May at Exeter, when they lost 16-20 to Devon Demons. With 6 points, Seemond Stephens was the top Gull on show, with Paul Oughton's 8 points heading the homesters score-chart. The match formed the second-half of the programme, which had earlier seen Exeter and the Isle of Wight battle out a 45-45 draw in a Premier League Cup fixture. The new Development League had been formed to give youngsters a first step on the speedway ladder, with the six-heat matches mainly being run as the second-half of a major fixture.

Back at their picturesque home on 19 May, St Austell faced Devon Demons in a challenge match and, in his programme notes, Brian Annear revealed that the Gulls brilliant 230 metre raceway had been completely re-laid, with new drainage put in. The Gulls promoter was full of praise for trackman Nigel Prynne, Simpson Plant Hire and Lobb Bros for the many hours work they had put in over the winter. Rodney Simpson was a tremendous supporter and backer of speedway in Cornwall, while Lobb Bros was also a plant hire business, run by the brothers, one of whom was the father of Gary Lobb, with the other being Roger's dad. Brian also explained why the cost of admission had been raised, one of the main reasons being that Conference League matches were run over fifteen heats, as opposed to the thirteen heats in the former Amateur League. St Austell had also entered the British Youth Development League and this meant another six heats of racing, with visiting teams reluctant to travel all the way down to Cornwall unless their travel expenses were met. Other contributory factors were that the promotion had increased the insurance cover for the riders and there was also a possibility that the Gulls might go up a league in 1999, when new riders would obviously have to be purchased.

David Collins penned a piece in the programme entitled 'From The Top Desk', in which he recalled that it was just a year ago that everyone was getting ready for the Gulls first season back after an absence of 34 years, and what a great success it all turned out to be too. 'DC' also explained that the match against Devon signalled the Gulls' first official home match under the sponsorship of BWOC Ltd., who were the leading independent fuel suppliers to the South West. The BWOC oil rig logo had become a regular sight on forecourts in the Cornwall area and obviously everyone connected with St Austell Speedway was greatly appreciative of their involvement.

Anyway, the thirteen heat challenge match against Devon resulted in a narrow 40-37 success for the Gulls, with the main points coming from Steve Bishop (11), Wayne Barrett (10) and Jason Prynne (9+1). Top scorer for the visitors was Paul Oughton, who rode impressively for a 13 point tally, and although Roger Lobb only scored a paid 7, he did have the satisfaction of defeating 'Bish' in the opening race. On a bumper night of action, St Austell also staged their first home match in the British Youth Development League, beating Exeter 22-14, with Chris Harris netting a paid 9 to top the scoring. Talking of 15-year-old Chris, a unique fund raising package had been put together to help the youngster, with the publication of an A4 folded souvenir booklet featuring photographic memories from the Gulls far off days of 1951 and 1952. Chris was pictured on the cover, sitting astride his machine in front of the Rose Vidney Farm Livery Stables, who were providing much needed sponsorship.

To return to the meeting against Devon, Adrian Newman appeared at reserve for the Demons, scoring but a single point. However, he did enough to impress Brian Annear, who promptly signed him at the conclusion of the meeting. The Gulls promoter later explained that Adrian had telephoned him prior to the match to see if there might be the opportunity to have a spin and he subsequently arrived in an old Austin Metro, with his bike literally in bits on the back seat! Adrian hailed from Sunshine in Melbourne, Australia and he soon became a hit with the Gulls supporters, who enjoyed his full-throttle riding style and affectionately nicknamed him 'Skippy'.

Steve Bishop and the Bronze Helmet.

On parade for the Simpson Plant Hire Individual Challenge.

The next racing on the agenda at the Clay Country Moto Parc was an individual challenge on 26 May, sponsored by Simpson Plant Hire. This meeting not only featured Conference League riders from the Devon and Cornwall areas, but also included Mark Simmonds, who rode for Premier League Exeter. Mark had previously won the Cornish Grand Prix in 1997, and he duly stamped his authority all over the meeting to score maximum points from his four rides in the qualifying heats. The man from Indian Queens then went on to win the A final, beating Steve Bishop, Roger Lobb and Wayne Barrett in a new track record time of 55.90 seconds. Prior to that, the Grand Prix style meeting had seen a C final success for Seemond Stephens, with the B final resulting in victory for Paul Oughton.

Promoter Brian Annear was as much his own publicity machine in 1998 as he had been the previous year, with the Gulls receiving regular coverage in several local newspapers, including *The Cornish Guardian*, *The Western Morning News*, *The West Britain* and *The Sunday Independent*. Aside from this, there was an added boost, when *The Cornish Riviera Holiday Times* included a feature on the super shale sport on offer at the Clay Country Moto Parc.

June kicked in with the visit of Newport Mavericks for a Conference League match, with skipper Steve Bishop leading St Austell to a comfortable 57-32 success. The 'King of St Austell' recorded a paid 12 point maximum, while both Wayne Barrett and Jason Prynne plundered paid 13 point tallies from five starts apiece. Meanwhile, new signing Adrian Newman made his debut for the Gulls at reserve, and after winning his first ride, he completed the meeting with a paid 6 point total. For the Mavericks, Roger Lobb gave a magnificent performance, plundering 15 points from six rides, while future Gull Martin Williams chipped in with a paid 9 point return.

One of the big problems of the season had already become all too evident and that was the lack of continuity. Including the Newport match, four home meetings had been staged and aside from the Gulls riders, Richard Ford had ridden in every one, while Paul Oughton, Roger Lobb and Kevin Phillips had each appeared on three occasions.

Following the meeting with the Mavericks, Steve Bishop faced Roger Lobb in his first defence of the Bronze Helmet, with the vast majority of folk expecting another win for 'Bish'. However, in the race, which was sponsored by former track stalwart and character supreme Bert Harkins, things didn't work out as predicted. Roger Lobb drove from the start to lead, with Steve harrying away behind and eventually drawing level on the back straight of lap two. Both riders went into the third turn together and appeared to clash, with Steve spinning out of contention. That left Roger to complete the race unchallenged, but the usually easy going 'Bish' was far from happy at the conclusion of the race, voicing his anger at referee Dave Dowling. Although Steve later apologized for his outburst, the man in control was not amused at the time and actually fined the Gulls skipper. So, Steve's short reign as holder was over, but as things turned out, the helmet remained in the possession of a St Austell rider, for after the meeting, Newport promoter Tim Stone agreed to let Roger Lobb join the Gulls!

It was away action next as St Austell visited the Marsh Lane home of Skegness Braves on the Lincolnshire coastline. Having never previously appeared at the 300-metre raceway, the Gulls adapted brilliantly and raced to a 51-38 success. Riding at no.3, Wayne Barrett gave a colossal display to score paid 17 points from six rides, while 'Bish' lent solid support with a paid 13. The home side were beset with misfortune throughout and suffered no less than seven exclusions, with Simon Wolstenholme (9+1), Jason McKenna (9+1) and Peter Boast (9) doing their utmost to stem the tide.

Back at the Clay Country Moto Parc, the next action was a qualifying round for the Dunlop sponsored Conference League Riders' Championship. Steve Bishop was at his brilliant best for this one, thundering to a full 15-point score to take victory, while 12 points was sufficient for Chris Harris to finish as runner-up. The highlight of the meeting was heat fourteen, when 'Bish' ripped up the track to beat Seemond Stephens, Simon Phillips and Richard Moss in a new track record time of 54.94 seconds.

Around this stage of the season, the Gulls became embroiled in a saga over tyres, which had begun when Brian Annear bought a batch direct from Dunlop. The tyres were described as being like chewing gum, and in fact they were so soft that there were suggestions made of cheating in the St Austell camp! There was nothing of the sort going on of course, as Brian had specifically ordered Conference League tyres and that is what they were sent, complete with the correct stamp on each. Indeed, the tyres had been used at Skegness a week earlier, when referee Dave Dowling had tested and passed them. However, on 14 June, Roger Lobb, Chris Harris and Jason Prynne took some tyres from the same batch to Mildenhall for a qualifying round of the Conference League Riders' Championship, and they failed the test!

There was Conference League action, one week later on 16 June, with the visit of Skegness. The powerful Gulls septet cantered to a 57-32 victory over their beleaguered opposition, who had to borrow Simon Phillips and 15-year-old Ryan Dearing in order to track a full side. Wayne Barrett was again dominant, blasting his way to a 15-point maximum, while both Jason Prynne and Adrian Newman knocked up scores of paid 10. Surprisingly, Steve Bishop only attained 8 points, although his score was restricted by an ultra-rare fall and subsequent exclusion in heat ten. Meanwhile, Roger Lobb made his debut in a Gulls race-jacket, taking victory in his first two rides on the way to an 8-point tally. For the Braves, Peter Boast performed manfully to net paid 9 points, before going on to impressively relieve Roger Lobb of the Bronze Helmet in what was the newest Gulls' first defence of the coveted trophy. Incredibly, Roger's appearance for St Austell completed a hat-trick of teams for the youngster on the Clay raceway in 1998, for he had previously appeared for Devon Demons and Newport Mavericks!

In the programme for the match against Skegness, it was interesting to note that Steve Bishop was still credited with the track record of 55.4 seconds. Although he was correctly credited with establishing the record on 9 June 1998, this must have been a printing error, as Steve's new best time was actually considerably quicker at 54.94 seconds. This error wasn't actually picked up until 2001, when the research was in full swing for the production of this book!

The tyre saga continued to rumble on a sunny evening at Newport on 19 June, when Seemond Stephens appeared in a qualifying round for the Conference League Riders' Championship. Seemond's steed was parked in the hot sunshine and it was later found that the compound of his rear tyre had actually changed! Thankfully, Roger and Gary Lobb subsequently came to Brian Annear's rescue and purchased the batch of tyres for use in the Premier League, where the softer compound was quite legal.

On 23 June, the Reading Ravens flew down to St Austell for a double-header challenge, firstly at Youth Development level and then for Conference League action. The weather on the night was far from ideal and was more like the middle of winter than flaming June. Despite the conditions, the first match was completed and saw the Gulls eke out a narrow 19-17 victory, with Simon Phillips netting a paid 9 points to head the score-chart. For the visitors, a paid 8 points saw Simon Moon finish on top of the pile, while fully-fledged Reading Racer of the future Shane Colvin scored 6 points. The major match got off to a flying start, when Steve Bishop blitzed to victory in 53.43 seconds. Although this record time was announced on the night and subsequently reported in *Speedway Star*, it was later deemed to be inaccurate and was never recognized as being official. There was no let up in the weather as the match continued, and by the time heat six had been completed, a combination of drizzle and fog had made visibility difficult to say the least. Referee Barry Richardson wisely decided to abandon the proceedings, with the Gulls holding a 29-7 advantage at the time. There had been much laughter prior to that though, with photographer John Yeo trying to keep the vision from the bus clear by cleaning the windows with a mop, whilst racing was actually in progress! From inside the bus, there was the humorous sight of a mop bobbing up and down from below, with referee Barry Richardson having to move from side to side so that he could see the track action in between the strokes!

Brian Annear's programme notes gave cause for concern, as he referred to a number of supporters who had complained about the £1 increase in the price of admission.

Ryan Dearing.

Brian explained that most of this was swallowed up due to having to register for VAT. Some folk had also voiced their concern at the lack of league fixtures, and Brian explained that despite offering to pay the travel costs, it was difficult to get teams to visit Cornwall. Brian suggested that the Gulls could have gone into the Premier League, which would have meant a turnstile price of £7, and he wondered whether the fans would have accepted that.

A challenge match against a composite team of Conference League All-Stars was planned for 30 June, but in the event, this was cancelled as it clashed with a certain football match that took place in St Etienne, featuring England against Argentina in the World Cup!

Into July, and the Gulls were on the road again, with a trip to the pleasant West Row home of Mildenhall on Conference League business. Aside from Steve Bishop, the St Austell boys were unable to cope with the firepower possessed by the home side and slumped to a 35-55 reverse. Dean Garrod led the onslaught with a round dozen points, while Garry Sweet backed him up with a solid paid 11. After running a last in his opening ride, 'Bish' recovered well to finish with a respectable 13 points from six starts, but by and large, he fought a lone battle, with Chris Harris and Wayne Barrett next in line on 6 points apiece. The Gulls did fare significantly better in the Youth Development League match that followed, however, racking up a thundering 26-10 victory. Chris Harris brilliantly plundered a three-ride paid maximum, while Jason Prynne (7+1) and Seemond Stephens (7) also gave impressive performances.

Returning to the Clay Country Moto Parc after the break for the World Cup, St Austell entertained Buxton in another league fixture. The visiting Hitmen proved no match for the might of the Gulls, who walloped in eight maximum heat advantages on their way to a 61-29 success. The immaculate Steve Bishop garnered a 15-point maximum, while Roger Lobb produced a dazzling display to rack up a paid full-house from five starts. That wasn't the end of the maximums though, for both Wayne Barrett and the ever-improving Seemond

Chris Harris.

Stephens returned paid dozens. Considering the situation, Jamie Young gave a tremendous showing for the visitors, scoring 11 of his team's points. The Youth Development League match also resulted in a handsome win for the homesters by the score-line of 25-11. Chris Harris again performed well, blasting to a paid 12 point maximum, with Seemond Stephens also remaining unbeaten as he took the chequered flag in all three of his rides.

The programme for the match against Buxton included a letter from Amanda Harris, explaining what a fabulous night out it was to see the speedway at the Nanpean circuit. Enthusiastically, she listed the team members and then went on to extol the virtues of the burgers, chips and ice cream that were always available on race nights. Amanda finished by proclaiming 'Even if you don't enjoy the racing, you'll still enjoy the food! This fab evening out starts at 7pm, so be there or miss out!'

Having already held a qualifying round, everyone in Cornwall was eagerly awaiting the final of the Conference League Riders' Championship at the home of the Gulls on Sunday 12 July, when all the top stars would be taking part. Unfortunately, torrential rain intervened and with the track waterlogged on the Saturday afternoon, the prestigious event was called off in order to save everyone having a wasted journey.

On 14 July, better weather was in evidence for the visit of Newport Mavericks in the first leg of the Knock-Out Cup semi-final. The match took place under new floodlights, and it was imperative for the Gulls to build up as big a lead as possible to take up to Newport for the second leg. However, a bad start saw them lose a 4-2 in the opening heat, with the Mavericks then gaining a 5-1 in the second race. The homesters rallied, however, and after sharing the third heat, they went on the rampage, eventually chalking up a 59-31 victory. The amazing Steve Bishop gave a captain's display, scorching to a paid 18 point maximum, while the fast-starting Seemond Stephens also rode undefeated, gleaning a paid 15 pointer. Steve Bishop's performance included another super-charged effort, when he clocked a winning time of 54.42 seconds in heat ten, thereby establishing another new and officially recognized track record. On a night when the visitors fell away after making such a good start, Andrew Appleton topped the scoring with 10 points. Young Andrew would of course, go on and represent the senior Newport side, before going on to help Oxford lift the Elite League Championship in 2001.

Other news from the time saw the arrival of a second double-decker bus at Clay Country Moto Parc. This was because the original one was also used to tyre pack the track every week, which meant that the electrics for the starting gate and track lighting constantly had to be disconnected and reconnected again! Needless to say, this had become a chore, so the second bus was acquired for use as the race control, with the other one solely used for tyre-packing purposes.

St Austell didn't have long to wait for the second leg of the Knock-Out Cup semi-final, with the trip to Queensway Meadows taking place on 17 July. Newport's no.1, Scott Pegler, opened the meeting in breathtaking fashion, zooming to a new Conference League track record of 61.3 seconds for the 285-metre circuit. The heat was shared though, with Steve Bishop and Chris Harris filling the other points scoring positions. The Gulls then gained a couple of heat advantages and it wasn't until heat ten that the

Brian Annear and Steve Bishop with the Conference League Riders Championship Trophy.

Mavericks actually got their noses in front. It had been a fabulous stonewalling performance by the Cornish side, and although Newport eventually won 52-38, the Gulls had booked their place in the final by 97 points to 83 on aggregate. With a paid 18-point maximum, Andrew Appleton gave a superlative performance for the Welsh side, whereas a paid 14 tally made Roger Lobb the Gulls hero on the day.

Back at the Longstone Pit on 21 July, Brian Annear made a second attempt to stage the final of the Conference League Riders' Championship, and thankfully, the weather was much more favourable. Having battled their way through the qualifying rounds, the meeting featured the cream of the league and included all seven of the regular Gulls. The flamboyant St Austell promoter had paid £500 to bring the event to Cornwall, and in his programme notes, he joked about having to wear a jacket and trousers for the occasion. Brian hoped that he would be spared any witty comments as everyone was so used to seeing him parading around in a pair of natty shorts.

The event was fully backed by local fans and businesses, including Fred Paul, Angela Sleeman, John Yeo, Cornish Ford, Pegasus Printers, Autopaints, Marshalls Motors, T.A.Kittow & Sons, Simpson Plant Hire, Annear's Garage, Lobb Bros, Easy Fit, Hawkins Motors, Boscawen Hotel, Nicholson, St Blazey Motorcycles and BWOC. Prize money was put up by the Claycountry Motorcycle Club, with the winner receiving £100, while the runner-up got £80 and third placed man collected £50. The meeting was run on a twenty-heat format and it was that man 'Bish', who powered his way to a 15-point maximum to take all the plaudits. In effect, the meeting was decided in heat nineteen, when Steve Bishop met and defeated the previously unbeaten Andrew Appleton. The Newport man, therefore had to settle for second place on the podium, with the Gulls' own super Seemond Stephens filling third spot, having notched 12 points. There really did seem to be some confusion over the track record at the time, as Steve Bishop was credited with a new best time of 55.37 seconds in heat six of the meeting, although he had clearly gone faster a week previously, when clocking 54.42 seconds in the KOC match versus Newport!

On 28 July, the Gulls faced Peterborough Thundercats in a challenge match, with the Cornish supporters drooling at the prospect after recalling the thrilling encounter served up by the two sides eleven months previously. Promoter Brian Annear had promised to charge the supporters just £2 for admission and he was true to his word for this meeting. As usual, the jovial Gulls main-man couldn't resist the opportunity of having a quip and in the programme, he stated, 'So, on to tonight's £2 entrance challenge meeting – the one the "Anti-Brian fans" said wouldn't happen!'

The visitors were again managed by Peter Oakes and featured several youngsters who would go on and become household names, including Simon Stead, Oliver Allen, Andrew Moore and Ross Brady. The Thundercats team also included guest rider Andrew Appleton, as well as young Jon Underwood, who sadly lost his life in a motor accident whilst returning to this country from a grass-track meeting on the continent in June 2000. Somewhat surprisingly, the Gulls raced to a fairly comfortable 51-38 victory, with Roger Lobb giving another marvellous display to plunder 17 points and head the scoring. Meanwhile, for the Peterborough boys, only Andrew Appleton revealed anything like true form, scoring 14 points from six rides. It really was a bumper night of speedway for the Clay Country faithful, as a Youth Development League match was also held. This gave Peter Oakes the opportunity to gain revenge and he duly led his young charges to a 20-16 win, with Simon Stead scorching to a three-ride maximum.

With no away fixtures, the Cornish shale fans had to wait another week for the next track action at Nanpean, when Mildenhall Fen Tigers travelled down for a league match. Once again, the power-packed Gulls had little difficulty in posting a 52-38 win, with the main contributions coming from Steve Bishop and Roger Lobb. Both blitzed through the opposition to total 15 points, with Steve capturing a full house and Roger being paid for the lot. The 'men from the fen' were managed by genial microphone man extraordinaire Malcolm Vasey, with their major contributor Geoff 'Big Leggy' Powell plundering 12 points. Three second-half races followed the match, with Simon Phillips taking victory in two, while Seemond Stephens won the other. Two of the races were significant as Mark Phillips was back on track for the first time in 1998, and he rode well to finish second in both. Mark's all-action style had certainly endeared him to supporters in the Gulls first season at the clay raceway, and those present were delighted to see him return to the saddle.

Back on the road, the St Austell men made the journey up to Buxton on 9 August for a double-header of Conference League and Youth Development League racing. The Gulls power proved too much for the inexperienced home side in the first match, with Roger Lobb's outstanding 18-point maximum being the highlight of a 53-36 victory, while Jamie Young fought a lone battle for the Hitmen, notching 14 points. Seemond Stephens' subsequent three-ride full-house took the Gulls to a 23-13 success in the second meeting, with future Sheffield rider Adam Allott heading the Hitmen's scoring on the 7-point mark.

Buxton then faced the daunting prospect of travelling down to St Austell, where the Gulls comfortably raced to a 55-35 win. It was Wayne Barrett's turn to top the Gulls scoring with a paid 14 total, but the undoubted star of the meeting was Simon Stead, who weighed in with a fabulous 17 points from six starts. The youngster, who was destined for great things, put one over on Steve Bishop in heat six and then for good measure, repeated the dose in heat thirteen. In fact, the only time the lad from Sheffield suffered defeat, was in the very last heat, when Wayne Barrett lowered his colours. The second-half featured another Youth Development League match, with the Gulls showing no mercy as they walloped long-distance travellers Glasgow by 26 points to 10. Once again, Seemond Stephens scorched to a three-ride maximum, while Chris Harris was paid for a 9-point total.

With the holiday season in full swing, a bumper crowd was in attendance for the next match at Nanpean, as Belle Vue Colts journeyed down from Manchester. A feast of speedway began with the Gulls scorching to a 59-31 success in a challenge fixture, with Wayne Barrett blasting home a paid 15-point maximum, while Roger Lobb weighed in with a paid 14 tally. For the Belle Vue side, James Birkinshaw gave a great performance to score 13 points, and but for his contribution, it is likely the Gulls would have topped the 70 mark. As it was, the Colts had to borrow Richard Ford in order to track a full side, but the youngster from Exeter had to pull out of the meeting after blowing his only motor in heat three. The Gulls were sympathetic to the problems of their visitors and subsequently allowed them to borrow Simon Phillips. A Youth Development League match followed and the Gulls ran out easy winners by a 24-12 scoreline, with Seemond Stephens again taking victory in all three of his rides. A wonderful evening of entertainment also included four heats of vintage speedway racing, featuring among others, former Gull Adrian Kessell, who again appeared on the 1926 Zenith that his father had ridden at Rocky Park in the 1930s.

A full week passed before the Gulls next action and it was the turn of Norfolk Braves to visit Cornwall for a league encounter on 25 August. The Braves had begun the season at Skegness, but due to problems created by track sharing with stock cars, the venture didn't last long and the team subsequently moved to King's Lynn in June. Unfortunately, the side from Norfolk happened to turn up on a night when every member of the home side hit peak form. The Gulls were absolutely rampant and blitzed through the opposition to win by 71 points to 19. Skipper Steve Bishop ended the night with a full 15 points to his name, having gone through the card with relative ease. However, just to emphasize the Gulls' solidity, it is worth running through the rest of the side's scores:

Seemond Stephens 12+1, Wayne Barrett 10+2, Roger Lobb 10+2, Chris Harris 9+1, Adrian Newman 8+2 and Jason Prynne 7+3. For the beleaguered Braves, only former road racer Peter Boast showed any resistance to the onslaught, notching an 8-point total.

A Youth Development League match was also staged as part of the programme, which saw the Gulls easily defeat the interestingly named King's Lynn Jousters 28-8. Continuing his speedway learning curve, Simon Phillips sped to a fine paid maximum from three starts, while Adrian Newman was also unbeaten.

Brian Annear and Dave Stallworthy.

The sidecar boys, from left to right: Tony Stephens, Phil Williams, Ken Westaway, Adrian Newman, Wayne Westaway and Justin Westaway.

Despite the big winning margin, it was still an entertaining night for the supporters, for not only did they see twenty-one heats of speedway, but also four sidecar speedway races. This was nostalgia at its very best, with the three partaking outfits being Ken Westaway and Adrian Newman (1956 Triumph), Justin and Wayne Westaway (1952 Triumph) plus Phil Williams and Tony Stephens (1937 Ariel). It was a joy to see the vintage machines going through their paces once more, and Phil Williams' winning time for the first heat was an amazing 72.76 seconds, just 14 seconds or so outside the average times clocked by the solo speedway boys on the night. Ken Westaway took victory in the second race, before his sons Justin and Wayne sped to success in races 3 and 4. The results were academic, however, for it brought back so many great memories of bygone days.

As many folk recalled, speedway ended at Par Moor in 1963, but the sidecars had continued on at the venue right up until 1986. The Cornish outfits also made appearances at Plymouth and Exeter, but a real highlight occurred in 1970, when legendary promoter Trevor Redmond featured sidecar speedway at the world famous Wembley Stadium. The drivers who enjoyed that wonderful experience at the spiritual home of speedway included two of men who had thrilled the Moto Parc faithful, Ken Westaway and Phil Williams, with the others being Dave Westaway and Roy Wedlake.

Since then, Ken Westaway and Phil Williams had paraded their outfits at Exeter's Diamond Jubilee meeting in 1989, while the following year, Ken organised demonstrations at Wolverhampton, Swindon and Reading during the England versus World All-

Stars sidecar Test series. These demos were followed by appearances at the Peterborough-staged BMF Rally vintage speedway races in 1991 and 1992, when former Gull Ivor Toms also joined in the racing. Ken Westaway and his partner Carol Pitman had become very much a part of the Cornish speedway scene in 1998, helping out young Australian Adrian Newman, and of course, they were later to look after Czech star Pavel Ondrasik in 2001.

Going back to the meeting on 25 August, the raceday programme featured a lovely cover photograph of Ken Westaway and Phil Pitman, taken at Wolverhampton in 1990. Phil was a racer of note, having recorded many victories in sidecar grass-track racing, including fifth place in the 1995 British Masters Championship. Sadly, Phil had lost his life in a grass-track accident at the Berks Bonanza in 1996, but it was wonderful that he should appear on the programme cover as he would have definitely raced in the meeting.

The Gulls then enjoyed a weekend away, firstly facing the Jousters in a Youth Development League fixture at King's Lynn on Saturday 29 August. The match formed the second part of a double-header that had seen the homesters suffer a 40-50 defeat at the hands of Poole in an Elite League fixture. Unfortunately, the Gulls went down to a narrow 17-19 defeat, despite the efforts of Seemond Stephens, who blitzed around the Saddlebow Road raceway and won all three of his rides. The Gulls were back in action at the very same circuit one evening later, when they faced Norfolk Braves in a Conference League meeting. The super 342-metre circuit served up some great entertainment, with the Gulls going ahead after a second heat maximum from 'Skippy' Newman and Roger Lobb. The home side clawed their way back , taking a 22-20 lead after heat seven, but then the decisive blow was landed by Wayne Barrett and the affectionately titled 'Baby Gull' (Chris Harris) three heats later. A 5-1 result gave St Austell a lead they would hold for the remainder of the contest. The Gulls gradually pulled away thereafter, running out comfortable 51-39 victors, with Roger Lobb completing a remarkable paid 18 point maximum. With a score of paid 14, Steve Bishop lent super support, while future Swindon star Oliver Allen yielded a fine paid 10 to head the Braves score-chart.

September kicked off with Edinburgh Monarchs making the tiring journey down to the Clay Country for a challenge match. Like so many other meetings in 1998, the meeting resulted in a rout as the Gulls cantered to a 69-20 success. Both Steve Bishop and the fast-learning Seemond Stephens romped to paid maximums, with Chris Harris and Adrian Newman also hitting double-figures. For the under-fire visitors, Gateshead born Steven Jones caught the eye with 8 points, but he received scant support from his team-mates. The evening also included a Youth Development League match, which unsurprisingly resulted in a 25-11 success for the Gulls over the Armadale Devils, with both Chris Harris and Seemond Stephens having little difficulty in racking up unbeaten paid 9 point tallies.

Promoter Brian Annear again continued his policy of giving the public full value for money, as the programme also included four heats of moto-speedway. In short, this featured mainly 250cc motocross bikes equipped with speedway tyres, but unlike our beloved shale sport, the machines were fitted with brakes. Among those participating were Brian Annear's sons Andy and Steve, although in the event, neither was to taste

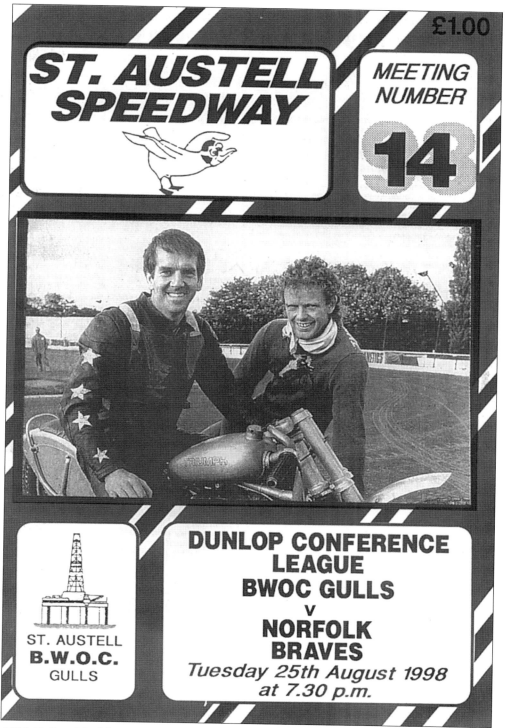

1998 Gulls v. Norfolk programme, featuring Ken Westaway and the late Phil Pitman on the cover.

success. Instead, Jon Orchard enjoyed two victories, while brothers Johnny and Justin Hawkins collected one win apiece. It was certainly interesting to note that the fastest winning time of 64.69 seconds recorded by Justin Hawkins was only about six seconds slower than that of conventional speedway at the Clay raceway.

An advertisement appeared in the programme for the first time for Albert's Private Hire Cars from Penzance, whose proprietor was Albert Poulton. As everyone was soon to learn, Albert proved to be a larger than life character, who would go on and become Chairman of the Gulls Supporters' Club and later on hold a similar position with the Trelawny Tigers Supporters' Club. Albert and his wife have since worked tirelessly behind the scenes, raising money to help keep speedway alive and one simply cannot underestimate the contribution they have made.

Mildenhall beckoned the following Sunday afternoon, when the Gulls appeared on Conference League business. This turned out to be one of the matches of the season as the lead swung one way and then the other, before honours ended even in a 45-45 draw. The sides were level going into the last heat, and at one point it looked as if race leader Ross Brady and the third placed Geoff Powell might snatch a match-winning advantage. There was controversy though, when Powell took evasive action on the back straight and later alleged that Seemond Stephens had turned left in front of him. Referee Mick Bates saw nothing wrong, however, with Seemond and 'Bish' subsequently following Brady home to secure the draw. That took the classy Brady to a 16 point tally for the day, while the Gulls' last heat duo were their undoubted stars, with Steve being paid for 16 points and Seemond garnering a paid 15. Following the match, Steve Bishop had the opportunity of regaining the Bronze Helmet as he challenged holder Ross Brady. It wasn't to be for 'Bish', however, as the talented young Scotsman proved too hot to handle and blazed away to retain the prestigious title.

The return match against Mildenhall was played out in Cornwall two nights later, but the meeting took place in conditions that were far from perfect. The rain and fog, which had appeared in varying degrees throughout the season, again descended over the Clay Country Moto Parc, making life difficult for riders and fans alike. Referee Graham Reeve made an inspection of the track after heat ten, and subsequently brought the interval forward in the hope that the weather might improve. Unfortunately, the rain just got worse, although after consultation with the two captains, the riders came out for heat eleven. Amid poor visibility, a 5-1 from Seemond Stephens and Roger Lobb put the Gulls 46-20 ahead, and with it then being mathematically impossible for the Fen Tigers to win, the meeting was sensibly brought to a premature close. Despite all the difficulties, both Steve Bishop (9) and Roger Lobb (6+3) remained unbeaten, while the impressive Ross Brady had netted 8 points for Mildenhall.

The result against Mildenhall had been sufficient for St Austell to leap-frog Newport and take over top spot in the Conference League table, with just five matches left to run. It was all the more exciting then, that Newport should be the next visitors to Cornwall on 15 September. However, with most people expecting a top-of-the-table clash, the match was effectively over before it started when the Mavericks arrived with only a five-man team. The meeting went ahead with Newport having no rider at either no.2 or no.3, which meant they had to partake in four heats with only one representa-

Wayne Barrett.

tive. The Gulls took full advantage of the situation, opening up with a 4-2, and subsequently thundering to eleven 5-1s on their way to a 70-20 massacre. Roger Lobb gave another fantastic display, scorching to a 15 point maximum and his signing must surely rank as one of the shrewdest moves of the year in British Speedway, for he most certainly turned the Gulls into a power-house outfit. On a night of big scoring, Steve Bishop weighed in with a paid 15-point full-house, while Wayne Barrett and Seemond Stephens returned paid 12-point maximums. Meanwhile, with six-points, the Mavericks best performer on the night was a man very familiar with the marvellous Moto Parc raceway, namely Simon Phillips.

In the programme, an enthusiastic Brian Annear was clearly looking forward to the month ahead, referring to it as probably the most important in the history of Cornish Speedway as the Gulls had a great chance of claiming a brilliant double by winning both the Conference League Championship and the Knock-Out Cup. Later in his column, Brian encouraged the regular 'come rain or shine' supporters to try and persuade one extra person to attend the forthcoming meetings, so that he could gauge support for the possibility of joining the Premier League in 1999.

A number of people thought the team would needed revamping considerably in order to go up a league, but looking at the riders of 1998, this would not necessarily have been the case: Steve Bishop was a rider of great experience and would go on to appear at Premier League level for Swindon in 1999, and Somerset in 2002; Jason Prynne enjoyed an ever-present season at Exeter in 2001; Roger Lobb had appeared for Exeter in 1998, 2000 and 2002, while also spending a year at Arena-Essex in 1999; Seemond Stephens linked with Swindon in 1999, and Exeter in 2000-01, before

Seemond Stephens and Roger Lobb.

returning to the Clay Country Moto Parc with Trelawny in 2002; Adrian Newman had spells with both the Isle of Wight and Workington in 2000; Chris Harris rode for Exeter in 1999 and 2000, prior to returning to the Duchy and Trelawny in 2001-02; Wayne Barrett enjoyed spells with Exeter in both 1999 and 2000. It might not have been Premier League Championship material, but the nucleus was certainly there.

On a huge night for Cornwall, Mildenhall travelled down for the first leg of the Knock-Out Cup final on 22 September. There was bad news prior to the start as Wayne Barrett had been sidelined by a grass-track injury sustained the previous weekend, with Roger Lobb's cousin Gary stepping into the side as a result. The BWOC Gulls started the match very slowly and after six heats, the score stood at 18 points apiece. A 4-2 from Seemond Stephens and Adrian Newman gave the homesters the lead in heat seven, prior to a disastrous heat right, when Gary Lobb suffered a fractured collarbone in an unfortunate track spill. The next two races were shared, before the Gulls landed maximum points, courtesy of Seemond Stephens and Adrian Newman in heat eleven. The Fen Tigers then secured a 4-2 in the following race, before the Gulls finally broke the visitors dogged resistance with three 5-1's on the bounce to close the match with a 53-36 victory. Steve Bishop gave a superb performance with 17 points, only suffering defeat to David 'Magic Man' Mason in heat ten. Meanwhile, Seemond Stephens weighed in a thumping paid 17 return, with the diminutive Mason notching 13 points to head the Fen Tigers scoring. After the match, Bronze Helmet holder Ross Brady had the daunting prospect of facing 'King of St Austell' Steve Bishop in his latest title defence. Amid great expectancy, 'Bish' kept the Gulls supporters happy, zipping to victory and regaining the prized trophy he had initially challenged Roger Lobb for at the start of the campaign.

On another bumper evening of racing at the magical Moto Parc, there was also a meeting against Mildenhall in the Youth Development League. Inspired by a paid 11 total from 'Skippy' Newman and an unbeaten 9 point score from Chis Harris, the homesters were again in the ascendancy, racking up a comfortable 25-11 success. At this point, it is well worth recording the important role that super-fan Fred Paul played throughout the season, as he had sponsored the team oil and fuel for all of the Gulls Development League matches.

More Youth Development League action followed, with a trip to Swindon two evenings later. The Gulls match formed the second half of a double-header, which had earlier seen Swindon's senior side wallop Belle Vue 55-35 in an Elite League fixture. The mini-match that followed was a close affair, but the Gulls just shaded it 19-17, with Seemond Stephens netting an undefeated 9 points and demonstrating the form that was to eventually land him a team spot with the Wiltshire side.

It was around this time that announcer Dave Stallworthy was having trouble juggling his day job with the journey to and from Cornwall, so Graham Hambly was pressed into action to help out. Graham had a tremendous speedway pedigree, for, as well as being a journalist of high regard, he had also been the man on the microphone at Plymouth (1968-70), Exeter (1968-84), Newport (1974-77), Bristol (1977-78) and Swindon (1979-80). So, on the nights when the popular off-the-wall style of Dave Stallworthy was missing, it was safe to say that the job was in very good hands. Graham had been helping out with the radio microphone, but his first match in the box, so to speak, was against Swindon Sprockets on 29 September.

In the programme for the match against the Sprockets, Brian Annear revealed that the attendance for the first leg of the Knock-Out Cup final had been less than 500! The Gulls promoter went on 'This makes any thoughts of going into the Premier League next season just a dream. You must all know who the missing fans are, so please just give them a whisper in their ears and say that if the next three meetings don't bring 1,000 people through the gate each week, there may not even be speedway at the Moto Parc next season.'

It was a sad fact that crowds had fallen away during the second season of racing at the picturesque venue. The 1997 season had been curtailed and the Gulls promoter had wished to build on all that had been achieved, running a full season of meetings, however, there were a number of reasons why things didn't work out satisfactorily. Firstly and most significantly, only five teams participated in the Conference League in 1998, and that meant the same riders appeared in Cornwall all too frequently. Then, there was the increased cost of admission and also the fact that a number of meetings were run in damp conditions during the so-called Summer months. Unfortunately, this proved to be a bad combination and crowd levels fell as a result. Another contributory factor was probably the number of hammerings that were handed out at the clay venue, with many of the Gulls opponents beaten before the tapes went up.

It must be said that in spite of the poor weather at several meetings, the track surface was always in excellent condition. This was due to the sterling efforts of former Cornish

Grass-track Champion Nigel Prynne, who had been on board since the grand opening in 1997. Many times, other tracks might well have considered a postponement to be the only option, but Nigel and his team always did their utmost to make sure that racing could go ahead at the super clay raceway.

Turning back to the track action against Swindon, the evening began with a Youth Development League fixture. The visitors included James Birkinshaw in their quartet and the Sheffield born youngster revealed a penchant for the super 230-metre circuit, winning all three of his rides. Young James failed to receive the necessary support from his team-mates, however, and the Gulls secured a 20-16 success. Chris Harris (8+1) and Seemond Stephens (7) made telling contributions to an exciting encounter, which whetted the appetite for the fifteen-heat challenge match that followed. James Birkinshaw continued in the Swindon side and again collected three wins, including a thrilling success over Steve Bishop in heat six. Unfortunately, it was another night of inclement weather, with the remnants of Hurricane Carl sweeping over the track and reducing the crowd level to only just over 200! With the Gulls holding a 33-27 lead after heat ten, stand-in referee Brian James had no alternative than to abandon the match, which had looked like rising to an exciting climax. At the time of the stoppage, Steve Bishop headed the Gulls score-chart on 8 points, while with a full 9 points to his name, James Birkinshaw looked well capable of going through the card for Swindon.

Brian Annear had been so impressed that he promptly signed young James to replace the injured Gary Lobb! The youngster duly made his Gulls debut on 2 October in a Youth Development League match at Peterborough, scoring 9 points from five starts. Unfortunately, St Austell suffered a 17-19 defeat, but that wasn't bad at all, considering they only had two riders! Aside from 'JB', the other teamster was Seemond Stephens, who notched 8+2 points in the fixture held after Peterborough had earlier defeated Newport 48-40 in a Young Shield match. The reasons for the team shortages were because both Jason Prynne and Adrian Newman were unable to travel due to work commitments, while Chris Harris' van gave up the ghost, after he reached Taunton Dean!

That completed the Gulls programme in the Youth Development League and the final table showed them respectably occupying fourth position out of seventeen teams. The league was run on a percentage basis, with Berwick taking the Championship, having attained 89.29% of their possible points total from 14 matches. Meanwhile, St Austell took part in 15 matches, winning 11 to achieve a percentage of 73.33%. Seemond Stephens did remarkably well, remaining ever-present and thundering to 117 points to top the averages on 10.17. The other regulars were the tigerish Chris Harris, who averaged 9.51, while Adrian Newman achieved a 7.56 figure and Jason Prynne finished on 6.00. The Gulls also had another six riders, who appeared as and when required, namely Simon Phillips, Chris Bennett, Vince Purnell, Mark Phillips, Gary Lobb and James Birkinshaw.

It was a momentous occasion on 3 October, when the Gulls journeyed to Mildenhall for the second leg of the Knock-Out Cup final, defending a 17 point lead. After sharing the opening two races, the Gulls took command of the match, thanks to maximum points from James Birkinshaw and Wayne Barrett. Although the Fen

Mark Simmonds.

Jason Prynne.

Tigers fought hard and managed to draw level after 9 heats, the Gulls were in a determined mood and eventually pulled away to win 52-38, thereby securing a marvellous 105-74 aggregate victory. Geoff Powell (12+1 points) and Ross Brady (9) did their best to stem the tide, but the St Austell boys were so fired-up for the occasion, that victory on the day was never really in doubt. The super Gulls septet were all heroes and it is only right and proper to record the names of those responsible for winning the club's first major silverware in a history stretching right back to 1949. Seemond Stephens was top man on the day, his electric starting ability taking him to a massive paid 16 point tally. Newest recruit James Birkinshaw fully justified Brian Annear's faith, scorching to 13 points, while the always-dependable Steve Bishop knocked up a paid dozen points. Going through the rest of the side, Roger Lobb scored 6+2, Wayne Barrett recorded 4+2, Chris Harris notched 3+2 and last but not least, Jason Prynne chipped in with 1+1. After the match, Steve Bishop had little difficulty in retaining the Bronze Helmet, racing to a comfortable victory from Fen Tigers representative Dean Garrod.

So, with the cup safely in the bag, it was a night of celebration back at the Clay Country Moto Parc on 6 October, when the Gulls entertained Premier League side Exeter Falcons in a full 15 heat challenge match. Although Exeter had visited previously, they had been under the guise of the Devon Rangers, which was basically a junior team. Indeed, the Gulls and the Falcons hadn't actually locked horns since a Provincial League encounter at Par Moor on 18 June 1963, when St Austell won 41-37. Sadly, Steve Bishop missed the meeting due to a dose of flu, with the Gulls operating the rider replacement facility in his place. The absence of 'Bish' certainly didn't help the homesters cause, and the greater experience of the opposition proved too much as they slumped to a 30-59 defeat. At least the meeting had caught the imagination of the good folk from Devon and Cornwall, for there was a much-improved attendance. James Birkinshaw again gave a great display, heading the Gulls scoring with a paid 11 points, but on a night when the visitors dominated, he was the only home man to reach double-figures. Meanwhile, for the Falcons, the swashbuckling style of Frank Smart was a pure joy to watch as he plundered a paid 15-point maximum, with Michael Coles (11+1) and Graeme Gordon (10+2) supplying brilliant backing.

The Gulls completed their Championship charge five nights later at Buxton, emphatically winning 53-36 to complete a glorious double. Simon Stead was the home side's mainstay, accumulating 16 points, while the super St Austell seven simply ran riot on the wonderful 240-metre circuit. Leading the way were Wayne Barrett and Seemond Stephens with paid 11 point tallies, while the fit-again Steve Bishop eased his way to a 10 point total. James Birkinshaw would almost certainly have recorded a maximum, but suffered a tapes exclusion in his first outing, prior to reeling off three successive victories. It really was a day of joy for the Gulls, with the only setback occurring after the match, when the highly talented Simon Stead relieved Steve Bishop of the Bronze Helmet.

Back at the Longstone Pit raceway on 13 October, the Gulls were scheduled to race against an England Under-19 side, which included David Howe, Matt Read, Oliver Allen, Chris Harris, Simon Stead, Rob Clarence and Chris Neath in their ranks. There was a great deal of anticipation for the match and a big crowd was expected, but once again the weather played havoc as thick fog descended and forced referee Barry Richardson to postpone the match.

The final home meeting of the season took place the following week, with the staging of the Cornish Grand Prix, when Exeter's Mark Simmonds was happy to try and defend the title he had won the previous September. A good crowd was in place for this one, and a great line-up also included all the double-winning Gulls, plus David Howe and Peter Jeffery. The meeting was run over fifteen heats, with the highest four scorers going through to the grand final. A 12-point tally was sufficient for Mark Simmonds to top the scoring, with David Howe close behind on 11. However, with three riders recording 10 points, a run-off was required to settle the remaining two slots in the final. This eventually saw Steve Bishop win from Wayne Barrett, with Seemond Stephens being the unlucky rider to miss out. So, to the grand final and super 'Simmo' reiterated his position as the no.1 rider in Cornwall, blasting to the chequered flag ahead of David Howe and Steve Bishop, with Wayne Barrett at the rear.

As usual, a full programme of entertainment had been laid on for the supporters, with four heats of vintage speedway also taking place. The six enthusiasts who partook were John Stallworthy, Jim Gregory, Terry Stone, Tom Richardson, Alan Patis and the amazing Adrian Kessell. A range of machines from the late 1920s and early '30s were used, with the riders resplendent in the famous old body colours of Plymouth, Wimbledon, Rayleigh, New Cross and West Ham, as well as the original St Austell design from Par Moor. These races proved as popular as ever with the supporters, before the curtain was brought down on the season's racing with another of Brian Annear's wonderful firework displays. It really was a great way to end an incredible season, with the home of the Gulls resembling a war zone as the wind got hold of the fireworks and sent them crashing down to earth in the car park next to the pits.

The Presentation Evening was next on the agenda, taking place at St Stephen Community Centre on 23 October, with the majority of the riders were in attendance, although James Birkinshaw and Gary Lobb were unable to make it. A representative from the team sponsor BWOC came along and presented the awards, with cult hero Steve Bishop again being voted rider of the year and collecting the Eustace Cup. Meanwhile, Adrian Newman picked up the Huddy & Kneebone Cup and super Seemond Stephens won two awards, taking home the W. Vivian Cup and the Cornwall Motorcycle Dealers' Trophy. Another rider whose whole-hearted efforts were greatly appreciated was Roger Lobb and he also received two awards, collecting the Phillips Cup and the BWOC Memorial Trophy in memory of Chris Julian.

With the home schedule and the presentation evening wrapped up for the year, there was just one outstanding away league fixture at Newport on 25 October. Having already wrapped up the title, the Gulls could have been forgiven for taking life easy, but they wanted to end the season on a high and slaughtered the Mavericks by 54 points to 35. The scores were level at 18 points apiece after six heats, before the St Austell boys started to fire on all cylinders and ran away with the match. The home side were best served by Chris Neath and Scott Pegler, who each netted 12 points, while the Gulls top men were Roger Lobb (14+1) and Steve Bishop (12+1). Following the match, Roger

Lobb ended the season as the winter holder of the Bronze Helmet after defeating the highly talented Chris Neath.

The final league table showed St Austell sitting pretty in pole position, having won 13 and drawn one of their 16 matches. The Gulls had totally dominated their sphere of racing, having also won the Knock-Out Cup of course, whilst skipper Steve Bishop had lifted the Conference League Riders' Championship. Not only that, but 'Bish' was also the highest scorer in the entire league, having brilliantly racked up 196 points. When the Knock-Out Cup matches were added on, the Gulls' immaculate skipper totalled 246 points for a wonderful 10.36 average. On top of all that, Steve also joined forces with Wayne Barrett to lift the British Best Pairs Grass-track Championship. What a fantastic season for the brilliant Bristolian! Shrewd early season signing Roger Lobb was next in line for the Gulls, rattling up 180 points for a 9.63 average, while Wayne Barrett clocked up 160 points for an 8.82 figure. In what was a very solid outfit indeed, Seemond Stephens achieved an 8.49 average, while Adrian Newman (6.30), Chris Harris (6.03) and Jason Prynne (5.67) always gave of their best in the engine room of the team. In what was the Gulls' greatest ever year, it wouldn't be fair to exclude the other riders who played a part, with Simon Phillips, Jim Collins, Kevin Phillips, Gary Lobb and James Birkinshaw all helping the cause in varying degrees.

Long after the season had ended, there was an extra meeting at the Clay Country arena on Monday 28 December, when the British Sporting Sidecar Association promoted an event billed as Motorcycle Track Racing. The composite event featured a full programme of over 30 races and included speedway, grass-track, moto-cross and quads. When the points were totted up, the speedway section resulted in victory for Seemond Stephens, with Simon Phillips finishing as runner-up ahead of Les Rowlands. A Gulls rider was also victorious in the grass-track competition, with first place going to Wayne Barrett from Chris Bennett, while Jason Prynne filled third spot. It was an interesting way to end the year, and the winter chill most certainly blew away some of the cobwebs!

Sunday 19 April, 1998 – Press Day Challenge Match
ST.AUSTELL 'GULLS' 53 EXETER 'DEVON RANGERS' 36

ST.AUSTELL

Wayne Barrett	2 2 3 3 1¹- -	11	1
Chris Bennett	0 1¹1 0 2¹- -	4	2
Steve Bishop	2 3 3 3 2 - -	13	
Chris Harris	1¹X 0 1 3 - -	5	1
Jason Prynne	2¹1 1¹2 3 - -	9	2
Seemond Stephens	3 3 2 2¹1 - -	11	1

EXETER

Simon Phillips	3 2 2 1 2 0 -	10	
Richard Ford	1 0 1¹- - - -	2	1
Gary Lobb	3 3 3 3 3 - -	15	
Kevin Phillips	0 R 0 - - - -	0	
Paul Fudge	0 2 2 2 - - -	6	
Jim Collins	1 X X 1 - - -	2	
Ryan Dearing	0 0 0 - - - -	0	
Chris Dix	1 0 - - - - -	1	

PROGRAMME CHANGES:-
Ht 10: Dearing replaced Ford;
Ht 11: Dearing replaced K.Phillips

Note: Steve Bishop's track record time for Heat-2, was not deemed as being official.

		Gulls	Exe
Ht 1	S.Phillips, Barrett, Ford, Bennett, 57.31	2	4
Ht 2	Lobb, Bishop, Harris, K.Phillips, 55.53 (Track Record)	5	7
Ht 3	Stephens, Prynne, Collins, Fudge, 58.69	10	8
Ht 4	Lobb, Barrett, Bennett, K,Phillips (ret), 57.24	13	11
Ht 5	(Re-Run) Bishop, Fudge, Harris (f,ex), Collins (f,ex), 56.90	16	13
Ht 6	Stephens, S.Phillips, Prynne, Ford, 56.88	20	15
Ht 7	(Awarded) Barrett, Fudge, Bennett, Collins (f,ex), No Time	24	17
Ht 8	Bishop, S.Phillips, Ford, Harris, 56.56	27	20
Ht 9	Lobb, Stephens, Prynne, K.Phillips, 56.91	30	23
Ht 10	Barrett, Fudge, Harris, Dearing, 56.78	34	25
Ht 11	Bishop, Stephens, S.Phillips, Dearing, 58.41	39	26
Ht 12	Lobb, Prynne, Collins, Bennett, 58.31	41	30
Ht 13	(Nominated) Harris, Bennett, Dix, Dearing, 59.71	46	31
Ht 14	(Nominated) Prynne, S.Phillips, Stephens, Dix, 57.91	50	33
Ht 15	(Top Scorers) Lobb, Bishop, Barrett, S.Phillips, 57.09	53	36

Tuesday 19 May, 1998 – Challenge Match
ST.AUSTELL 'GULLS' 40 DEVON 'DEMONS' 37

ST.AUSTELL

Steve Bishop	2 3 3 3 - - -	11	
Chris Harris	1¹0 2¹1 1 - -	5	2
Wayne Barrett	2 0 3 3 2 - -	10	
Seemond Stephens	1¹2 R T - - -	3	1
Jason Prynne	M 3 2 3 1¹- -	9	1
Simon Phillips	1 X - - - - -	1	
Chris Bennett	0 0 1 - - - -	1	

DEVON

Roger Lobb	3 1¹X 2 - - -	6	1
Richard Ford	0 2 0 2 - - -	4	
Paul Oughton	3 2 2 3 3 - -	13	
Chris Courage	0 2¹1¹1 X - -	4	2
Kevin Phillips	3 3 1 2 0 - -	9	
Adrian Newman	T 1 R R - - -	1	

PROGRAMME CHANGES:-
Ht 3: Bennett replaced Prynne; Courage replaced Newman in the re-run; Ht 9: Bennett replaced S.Phillips, Ht 10: Harris replaced Stephens in the re-run; Ht 11: Bennett replaced S.Phillips

Note: A six heat British Youth Development League match was also run, which saw St.Austell defeat Devon 22-14. The points scorers were: (St.Austell) Chris Harris 7+2; Seemond Stephens 7+1; Jason Prynne 6; Chris Bennett 2; (Devon) Paul Oughton 7+1; Roger Lobb 5; Richard Ford 1; Chris Courage 1

		Gulls	Dev
Ht 1	Lobb, Bishop, Harris, Ford, 58.69	3	3
Ht 2	Oughton, Barrett, Stephens, Courage, 57.21	6	6
Ht 3	(Re-Run) K.Phillips, Courage, S.Phillips, Bennett, Newman (ex, tapes), Prynne (ex, 2 mins), 57.21	7	11
Ht 4	Bishop, Oughton, Courage, Harris, 58.09	10	14
Ht 5	K.Phillips, Stephens, Newman, Barrett, 60.01	12	18
Ht 6	(Re-Run) Prynne, Oughton, Lobb, S.Phillips (f,ex), 58.82	15	21
Ht 7	Bishop, Harris, K.Phillips, Newman (ret), 58.13	20	22
Ht 8	Barrett, Ford, Lobb (ex, foul riding), Stephens (ret), 58.26	23	24
Ht 9	Oughton, Prynne, Courage, Bennett, 58.32	25	28
Ht 10	(Re-Run) Bishop, K.Phillips, Harris, Ford, Stephens (ex, tapes), 58.60	29	30
Ht 11	Barrett, Lobb, Bennett, Courage (ex), 58.42	33	32
Ht 12	Prynne, Ford, Harris, Newman (ret), 58.77	37	34
Ht 13	(Nominated) Oughton, Barrett, Prynne, K.Phillips (f,rem), 58.53	40	37

Tuesday 26 May, 1998
SIMPSON PLANT HIRE INDIVIDUAL CHALLENGE

Steve Bishop	3 2 3 X - - -	8
Chris Harris	1 1 1 1 - - -	4
Wayne Barrett	2 2 2 2 - - -	8
Seemond Stephens	F 1 T 0 - - -	1
Jason Prynne	2 3 F 2 - - -	7
Mark Simmonds	3 3 3 3 - - -	12
Roger Lobb	1 3 3 3 - - -	10
Chris Bennett	0 0 0 2 - - -	2
Richard Ford	R 0 1 0 - - -	1
Kevin Phillips	3 1 2 1 - - -	7
Paul Oughton	2 X 2 3 - - -	7
Adrian Newman	1 2 1 1 - - -	5
Chris Dix (Res)	0 - - - - - -	0

PROGRAMME CHANGES:-
Ht 9: Dix replaced Stephens in the re-run

1st MARK SIMMONDS;
2nd STEVE BISHOP; 3rd ROGER LOBB

Ht 1	Bishop, Barrett, Harris, Stephens (fell), 57.72
Ht 2	Simmonds, Prynne, Lobb, Bennett, 57.50
Ht 3	Phillips, Oughton, Newman, Ford (ret), 61.25
Ht 4	Prynne, Bishop, Phillips, Bennett, 58.87
Ht 5	Lobb, Barrett, Harris, Ford, 57.32
Ht 6	(Re-Run) Simmonds, Newman, Stephens, Oughton (f,ex), 57.94
Ht 7	Bishop, Oughton, Harris, Prynne (fell), 58.40
Ht 8	Lobb, Barrett, Newman, Bennett, 57.09
Ht 9	(Re-Run) Simmonds, Phillips, Ford, Dix, Stephens (ex, tapes), 56.44
Ht 10	Oughton, Bennett, Harris, Ford, 59.66
Ht 11	Lobb, Prynne, Phillips, Stephens, 57.50
Ht 12	(Awarded) Simmonds, Barrett, Newman, Bishop (f,ex), No Time
Ht 13	(C Final) Stephens, Bennett, Harris, Ford (ret), 58.97
Ht 14	(B Final - Awarded) Oughton, Phillips, Prynne, Newman (f,ex), No Time
Ht 15	(A Final) Simmonds, Bishop, Lobb, Barrett, 55.90 (Track Record)

Tuesday 2 June, 1998 – Conference League
ST.AUSTELL 'GULLS' 57 NEWPORT 'MAVERICKS' 32

ST.AUSTELL

Steve Bishop	3 2'3 2'- - -	10	2
Chris Harris	2'3 2 1 - - -	8	1
Wayne Barrett	3 2'2 3 2 - -	12	1
Seemond Stephens	1 3 1'2 - - -	7	1
Jason Prynne	3 2 3 3 1'- -	12	1
Kevin Phillips	2'R F 1'- - -	3	2
Adrian Newman	3 0 1'1 - - -	5	1

NEWPORT

Paul Oughton	1 2 1 2 1 - -	7	
Richard Ford	R 0 0 1'0 - -	1	1
Roger Lobb	2 3 2 2 3 3 -	15	
Graig Gough	R M- - - - -	0	
Martin Williams	X 1'1 3 3 0 -	8	1
Andy Carfield	1 0 0 X R - -	1	
Andrew Appleton R/R	- - - - - - -	-	

PROGRAMME CHANGES:-
Ht 2: R/R Williams; Ht 4: R/R Oughton; Ht 8: R/R Williams; Ht 10: Carfield replaced Gough; Ht 13: Ford replaced Williams; Ht 14: R/R Lobb

Note: Graig Gough was a non-starter in Heat-14, and was not replaced

		Gulls	New
Ht 1	Bishop, Harris, Oughton, Ford (ret), 59.00	5	1
Ht 2	(Re-Run) Newman, Phillips, Carfield, Williams (f,ex), 60.44	10	2
Ht 3	Barrett, Lobb, Stephens, Gough (ret), 60.20	14	4
Ht 4	Prynne, Oughton, Williams, Newman, 60.87	17	7
Ht 5	Stephens, Barrett, Oughton, Ford, 60.04	22	8
Ht 6	Harris, Bishop, Williams, Carfield, 60.00	27	9
Ht 7	Lobb, Prynne, Phillips (ret), Gough (ex, 2 mins), 59.00 (3 Riders Only)	29	12
Ht 8	Williams, Harris, Newman, Ford, 58.06	32	15
Ht 9	Williams, Barrett, Stephens, Carfield, 58.02	35	18
Ht 10	(Awarded) Bishop, Lobb, Harris, Carfield (f,ex), No Time	39	20
Ht 11	Prynne, Oughton, Ford, Phillips (fell), 59.71	42	23
Ht 12	Barrett, Lobb, Newman, Carfield (ret), 59.00	46	25
Ht 13	Prynne, Bishop, Oughton, Ford, 60.62	51	26
Ht 14	Lobb, Stephens, Phillips, 57.56 (3 Riders Only)	54	29
Ht 15	(Nominated) Lobb, Barrett, Prynne, Williams, 58.12	57	32
	Bronze Helmet: Lobb, Bishop (fell), 58.10		

Tuesday 9 June, 1998
CONFERENCE LEAGUE RIDERS' CHAMPIONSHIP Q/R

Rider	Scores	Total
Lee Dixon	1 3 1 3 3 - -	11
Steve Bishop	3 3 3 3 3 - -	15
Chris Harris	2 3 1 3 3 - -	12
Garry Sweet	0 1 2 1 0 - -	4
Wayne Barrett	2 2 2 R 1 - -	7
Chris Bennett	F 1 2 2 2 - -	7
Paul Macklin	3 X 3 0 0 - -	6
Seemond Stephens	X 3 X 2 2 - -	7
Jason Prynne	1 F 2 3 2 - -	8
Richard Ford	3 2 R 1 1 - -	7
Simon Phillips	2 2 0 1 2 - -	7
Mark Thompson	0 T 1 1 1 - -	3
Richard Moss	0 1 1 0 0 - -	2
Adrian Newman	3 0 3 2 3 - -	11
Kevin Phillips	1 M - - - - -	1
Paul Oughton	2 2 3 2 1 - -	10
Ryan Dearing (Res)	1 0 F 0 0 - -	1

PROGRAMME CHANGES:-
Ht 7: Dearing replaced K.Phillips; Ht 8: Dearing replaced Thompson in the re-run; Ht 10: Dearing replaced K.Phillips; Ht 16: Dearing replaced K.Phillips; Ht 17: Dearing replaced K.Phillips

1st STEVE BISHOP 15-pts;
2nd CHRIS HARRIS 12-pts; =3rd LEE DIXON & ADRIAN NEWMAN 11-pts

Ht 1	Bishop, Harris, Dixon, Sweet, 56.88
Ht 2	(Awarded) Macklin, Barrett, Bennett (fell), Stephens (ex, foul riding), No Time
Ht 3	Ford, S.Phillips, Prynne, Thompson, 59.77
Ht 4	Newman, Oughton, K.Phillips, Moss, 60.19
Ht 5	Dixon, Barrett, Moss, Prynne (fell), 58.37
Ht 6	Bishop, Ford, Bennett, Newman (f,rem), 56.69
Ht 7	(Re-Run) Harris, S.Phillips, Dearing, Macklin (f,ex), K.Phillips (ex, 2 mins), 57.10
Ht 8	(Re-Run) Stephens, Oughton, Sweet, Dearing, Thompson (ex, tapes), 59.22
Ht 9	Oughton, Bennett, Dixon, S.Phillips, 59.27
Ht 10	Bishop, Barrett, Thompson, Dearing (fell), 59.83
Ht 11	(Re-Run) Newman, Prynne, Harris, Stephens (f,ex), 56.42
Ht 12	Macklin, Sweet, Moss, Ford (ret), 60.69
Ht 13	Dixon, Newman, Thompson, Macklin, 58.13
Ht 14	Bishop, Stephens, S.Phillips, Moss, 54.94 (Track Record)
Ht 15	Harris, Oughton, Ford, Barrett (ret), 57.17
Ht 16	Prynne, Bennett, Sweet, Dearing, 60.96
Ht 17	Dixon, Stephens, Ford, Dearing, 60.17
Ht 18	Bishop, Prynne, Oughton, Macklin, 58.55
Ht 19	Harris, Bennett, Thompson, Moss, 57.64
Ht 20	Newman, S.Phillips, Barrett, Sweet, 58.18

Tuesday 16 June, 1998 – Conference League
ST.AUSTELL 'GULLS' 57 SKEGNESS 'BRAVES' 32

ST.AUSTELL

Rider	Scores	Total	Bonus
Steve Bishop	3 2 X 3 - - -	8	
Chris Harris	1 1 1'0 3 - - -	5	1
Wayne Barrett	3 3 3 3 3 - - -	15	
Seemond Stephens	X 0 2'3 - - -	5	1
Jason Prynne	2'2'3 1 0 - -	8	2
Adrian Newman	2'3 1 2'- - -	8	2
Roger Lobb	3 3 2 0 - - -	8	

SKEGNESS

Rider	Scores	Total	Bonus
Peter Boast	2 2 1 0 2 1'-	8	1
Simon Phillips	0 1'1 2 1 - -	5	1
Lee Dixon	2 R R 2 - - -	4	
Ryan Dearing	1' R - - - - -	1	1
Simon Wolstenholme	1 3 R 2 0 - -	6	
Freddie Stephenson	1 0 1 1 1'2 -	5	1
Gavin Hedge	R 0 3 - - - -	3	

PROGRAMME CHANGES:-
Ht 7: Boast replaced Dearing; Ht 10: Wolstenholme replaced Dearing; Ht 14: Phillips replaced Hedge

Heat	Result	Gulls	Skeg
Ht 1	Bishop, Boast, Harris, Phillips, 55.62	4	2
Ht 2	Lobb, Newman, Stephenson, Hedge (ret), 58.16	9	3
Ht 3	(Re-Run) Barrett, Dixon, Dearing, Stephens (f,ex), 58.50	12	6
Ht 4	Lobb, Prynne, Wolstenholme, Hedge, 58.59	17	7
Ht 5	Barrett, Boast, Phillips, Stephens, 57.34	20	10
Ht 6	Wolstenholme, Bishop, Harris, Stephenson, 58.03	23	13
Ht 7	Newman, Prynne, Boast, Dixon (ret), 58.97	28	14
Ht 8	Hedge, Lobb, Phillips, Harris, 57.88	30	18
Ht 9	Barrett, Stephens, Stephenson, Wolstenholme (ret), 57.72	35	19
Ht 10	(Re-Run) Harris, Wolstenholme, Dixon (ret), Bishop (f,ex), 58.31	38	21
Ht 11	Prynne, Phillips, Newman, Boast, 58.72	42	23
Ht 12	Barrett, Dixon, Stephenson, Lobb, 57.81	45	26
Ht 13	Bishop, Boast, Prynne, Wolstenholme, 55.81	49	28
Ht 14	Stephens, Newman, Phillips, Dearing (ret), 59.04	54	29
Ht 15	(Nominated) Barrett, Stephenson, Boast, Prynne, 58.16	57	32
	Bronze Helmet: Boast, Lobb, 57.08		

Tuesday 23 June, 1998 – Conference League
ST.AUSTELL 'GULLS' 29 READING 'RAVENS' 7
Meeting abandoned after Heat-6

ST.AUSTELL

Steve Bishop	3 3 - - - -	6	
Chris Harris	2'1 - - - -	3	1
Wayne Barrett	3 3 - - - -	6	
Seemond Stephens	2'2'- - - -	4	2
Jason Prynne	2'- - - - -	2	1
Adrian Newman	2'- - - - -	2	1
Roger Lobb	3 3 - - - -	6	

READING

Shane Colvin	1 1 1 - - -	3	
Steve Targett	0 F - - - -	0	
Peter Collyer	0 - - - - -	0	
Simon Moon	1 - - - - -	1	
Chris Courage	R 2 - - - -	2	
Geoff Batt	1 0 - - - -	1	
Delwyn Rowe	0 - - - - -	0	

PROGRAMME CHANGES:-
Ht 4: Colvin replaced Rowe

Note: A six heat British Youth Development League match was also run, which saw St.Austell defeat Reading 19-17. The points scorers were: (St.Austell) Simon Phillips 7+2; Chris Harris 7; Seemond Stephens 5; Vince Purnell 0; (Reading) Simon Moon 7+1; Shane Colvin 6; Peter Collyer 3+1; Delwyn Rowe 1+1

		Gulls	Read
Ht 1	Bishop, Harris, Colvin, Targett, 53.43 (Track Record)	5	1
Ht 2	Lobb, Newman, Batt, Rowe, 55.09	10	2
Ht 3	Barrett, Stephens, Moon, Collyer, 59.03	15	3
Ht 4	Lobb, Prynne, Colvin, Courage (ret), 59.58	20	4
Ht 5	Barrett, Stephens, Colvin, Targett (fell), 58.47	25	5
Ht 6	Bishop, Courage, Harris, Batt, 57.15	29	7

This match was abandoned after six heats due to thick fog, which had descended over the track.

The track record set by Steve Bishop in Heat-1, was later deemed to be inaccurate and was not recognised as being official.

Tuesday 7 July, 1998 – Conference League
ST.AUSTELL 'GULLS' 61 BUXTON 'HITMEN' 29

ST.AUSTELL

Steve Bishop	3 3 3 3 3 - -	15	
Chris Harris	1 1 0 2'- - -	4	1
Wayne Barrett	3 2'3 2'- - -	10	2
Seemond Stephens	2'3 2'3 - - -	10	2
Jason Prynne	2'1 2 0 - - -	5	1
Kevin Phillips	2'0 1'0 - - -	3	2
Roger Lobb	3 3 3 3 2'- -	14	1

BUXTON

Jamie Young	2 1 3 3 2 - -	11	
Paul Burnett	0 0 - - - - -	0	
Chris Moorcroft	F 0 - - - - -	0	
Phil Pickering	1 2'1 2 1 - -	7	1
Phil Knowles	0 2 1'1 R 1'-	5	2
Nathan McDonald	1 0 0 R - - -	1	
Paul Macklin	R 1 2 1 1'R -	5	1

PROGRAMME CHANGES:-
Ht 7: Young replaced Moorcroft; Ht 8: Knowles replaced Burnett; Ht 10: Macklin replaced Pickering; Ht 11: Knowles replaced Burnett; Ht 12: Pickering replaced Moorcroft

Note: A six heat British Youth Development League match was also run, which saw St.Austell defeat Buxton 25-11. The points scorers were: (St.Austell) Chris Harris 11+1; Seemond Stephens 9; Adrian Newman 4+2; Vince Purnell 1; (Buxton) Phil Pickering 5; Chris Moorcroft 3+2; Paul Burnett 3; Michael Pickering 0

		Gulls	Bux
Ht 1	Bishop, Young, Harris, Burnett, 56.98	4	2
Ht 2	Lobb, Phillips, McDonald, Macklin (ret), 59.24	9	3
Ht 3	Barrett, Stephens, Pickering, Moorcroft (fell), 57.68	14	4
Ht 4	Lobb, Prynne, Macklin, Knowles, 58.06	19	5
Ht 5	Stephens, Barrett, Young, Burnett, 59.19	24	6
Ht 6	Bishop, Knowles, Harris, McDonald, 57.84	28	8
Ht 7	Young, Pickering, Prynne, Phillips, 59.20	29	13
Ht 8	Lobb, Macklin, Knowles, Harris, 59.53	32	16
Ht 9	Barrett, Stephens, Knowles, McDonald, 58.40	37	17
Ht 10	Bishop, Harris, Macklin, Moorcroft, 56.00	42	18
Ht 11	Young, Prynne, Phillips, Knowles (ret), 57.53	45	21
Ht 12	Lobb, Barrett, Pickering, McDonald (ret), 58.47	50	22
Ht 13	Bishop, Young, Knowles, Prynne, 57.84	53	25
Ht 14	Stephens, Pickering, Macklin, Phillips, 59.28	56	28
Ht 15	(Nominated) Bishop, Lobb, Pickering, Macklin (ret), 56.87	61	29

Tuesday 14 July, 1998 – Knock-Out Cup Semi-Final, 1st Leg
ST.AUSTELL 'GULLS' 59 NEWPORT 'MAVERICKS' 31

ST.AUSTELL

Steve Bishop	3 2'3 3 3 3 -	17	1
Chris Harris	1 3 1 0 - - -	5	
Wayne Barrett	R 1 2'1 - - -	4	1
Seemond Stephens	3 3 3 3 2'- -	14	1
Jason Prynne	1 2'0 1 - - -	4	1
Adrian Newman	F 2 2'- - - -	4	1
Roger Lobb	T 3 3 2'3 - -	11	1

NEWPORT

Scott Pegler	2 2 1 R 2 F -	7	
Andy Carfield	0 0 M- - - -	0	
Andrew Appleton	2 3 2 2 1 - -	10	
Paul Oughton	1'0 1'0 1 - -	3	2
Chris Neath	0 1 2 1 0 - -	4	
Martin Williams	2'0 0 - - - -	2	1
Richard Ford	3 1 1 0 - - -	5	

PROGRAMME CHANGES:-
Ht 2: Prynne replaced Lobb in the re-run; Ht 7: Pegler replaced Oughton; Ht 8: Oughton replaced Carfield; Neath replaced Ford; Ht 11: Bishop replaced Prynne; Lobb replaced Newman; Ford replaced Carfield; Ht 12: Oughton replaced Williams

Note: Newport subsequently won the second leg 52-38, but it was the Gulls who progressed to the final by an aggregate score of 97-83.

		Gulls	New
Ht 1	Bishop, Pegler, Harris, Carfield, 55.72	4	2
Ht 2	(Re-Run) Ford, Williams, Prynne, Newman (fell), Lobb (ex, tapes), 60.13	5	7
Ht 3	Stephens, Appleton, Oughton, Barrett (ret), 57.41	8	10
Ht 4	Lobb, Prynne, Ford, Neath, 56.88	13	11
Ht 5	Stephens, Pegler, Barrett, Carfield, 58.03	17	13
Ht 6	Harris, Bishop, Neath, Williams, 57.28	22	14
Ht 7	Appleton, Newman, Pegler, Prynne, 55.84	24	18
Ht 8	Lobb, Neath, Harris, Oughton, 57.94	28	20
Ht 9	Stephens, Barrett, Neath, Williams, 56.82	33	21
Ht 10	Bishop, Appleton, Oughton, Harris, 54.42 (Track Record)	36	24
Ht 11	Bishop, Lobb, Ford, Pegler (ret), 57.38	41	25
Ht 12	Lobb, Appleton, Barrett, Oughton, 58.28	45	27
Ht 13	Bishop, Pegler, Prynne, Neath, 58.29	49	29
Ht 14	Stephens, Newman, Oughton, Ford, 58.34	54	30
Ht 15	(Nominated) Bishop, Stephens, Appleton, Pegler (fell), 58.25	59	31

Tuesday 21 July, 1998
CONFERENCE LEAGUE RIDERS' CHAMPIONSHIP

Seemond Stephens	2 3 2 2 3 - -	12
Martin Williams	0 0 0 R 1 - -	1
Andrew Appleton	3 3 3 3 2 - -	14
Wayne Barrett	1 3 3 2 1 - -	10
Adrian Newman	2 2 3 2 2 - -	11
Steve Bishop	3 3 3 3 3 - -	15
Dean Garrod	1 0 2 3 2 - -	8
Paul Macklin	F 2 X 1 F - -	3
Jason Prynne	1 1 2 1 3 - -	8
Roger Lobb	3 2 1 1 2 - -	9
Peter Boast	2 1 1 3 3 - -	10
Paul Lydes-Uings	0 1 2 1 R - -	4
Kevin Phillips	R 0 R 2 1 - -	3
Richard Ford	2 1 1 0 0 - -	4
Chris Neath	3 2 1 0 1 - -	7
Chris Harris	1 - - - - - -	1
Vince Purnell (Res)	0 0 0 0 - - -	0

PROGRAMME CHANGES:-
Ht 8: Purnell replaced Harris; Ht 9: Purnell replaced Harris; Ht 15: Purnell replaced Harris; Ht 18: Purnell replaced Harris

1st STEVE BISHOP 15-pts
2nd ANDREW APPLETON 14-pts; 3rd SEEMOND STEPHENS 12-pts

Ht 1	Appleton, Stephens, Barrett, Williams, 56.54
Ht 2	Bishop, Newman, Garrod, Macklin (fell), 56.58
Ht 3	Lobb, Boast, Prynne, Lydes-Uings, 59.38
Ht 4	(Re-Run) Neath, Ford, Harris, Phillips (ret), 57.84
Ht 5	Stephens, Newman, Prynne, Phillips, 57.78
Ht 6	Bishop, Lobb, Ford, Williams, 55.37
Ht 7	Appleton, Neath, Boast, Garrod, 56.56
Ht 8	Barrett, Macklin, Lydes-Uings, Purnell, 57.22
Ht 9	Bishop, Stephens, Boast, Purnell, 55.62
Ht 10	Newman, Lydes-Uings, Neath, Williams, 59.38
Ht 11	(Re-Run) Appleton, Prynne, Ford, Macklin (f,ex), 57.94
Ht 12	Barrett, Garrod, Lobb, Phillips (ret), 59.13
Ht 13	Garrod, Stephens, Lydes-Uings, Ford, 59.13
Ht 14	Boast, Phillips, Macklin, Williams (ret), 59.13
ht 15	Appleton, Newman, Lobb, Purnell, 56.66
Ht 16	Bishop, Barrett, Prynne, Neath, 57.47
Ht 17	Stephens, Lobb, Neath, Macklin (fell), 59.87
Ht 18	Prynne, Garrod, Williams, Purnell, 59.27
Ht 19	Bishop, Appleton, Phillips, Lydes-Uings (ret), 56.22
Ht 20	Boast, Newman, Barrett, Ford, 58.28

Tuesday 28 July, 1998 – Challenge Match
ST.AUSTELL 'GULLS' 51 PETERBOROUGH 'THUNDERCATS' 38

ST.AUSTELL

Steve Bishop	2 2 3 2¹- - -	9	1
Chris Harris	0 0 1 0 - - -	1	
Wayne Barrett	2¹3 0 2¹- - -	7	2
Seemond Stephens	3 2¹1 3 F - -	9	1
Jason Prynne	R 0 1¹- - - -	1	1
Adrian Newman	1¹2 2 2¹- - -	7	2
Roger Lobb	2 3 3 3 3 3 -	17	

PETERBOROUGH

Simon Stead	1¹0 2 3 1 1¹-	8	2
Jon Underwood	1 1 0 1¹0 0 -	3	1
Oliver Allen	T 1 2 1 - - -	4	
Andrew Moore	X - - - - - -	0	
Ross Brady	2 1 3 2¹X 1 -	9	1
Andrew Appleton	3 3 3 3 0 2 -	14	
Paul Oughton	0 R - - - - -	0	

PROGRAMME CHANGES:-
Ht 1: Appleton replaced Stead; Ht 3: Oughton replaced Allen in the re-run; Ht 4: Stead replaced Oughton; Ht 7: Brady replaced Moore; Ht 8: Stead replaced Oughton; Ht 10: Underwood replaced Moore; Ht 13: Lobb replaced Prynne; Ht 14: Underwood replaced Moore; Brady replaced Oughton

A six heat British Youth Development League match was also run, which saw St.Austell lose 16-20 to Peterborough. The points scorers were: (St.Austell) Seemond Stephens 7; Chris Harris 3+2; Adrian Newman 3+1; Jason Prynne 3; (Peterborough) Simon Stead 9; Oliver Allen 5+1; Andrew Moore 4; Jon Underwood 2

		Gulls	Pet
Ht 1	Appleton, Bishop, Underwood, Harris, 56.68	2	4
Ht 2	Appleton, Lobb, Newman, Oughton, 57.03	5	7
Ht 3	(Re-Run Twice) Stephens, Barrett, Oughton (ret), Moore (f,ex), Allen (ex, tapes), 62.00	10	7
Ht 4	Lobb, Brady, Stead, Prynne (ret), 56.82	13	10
Ht 5	Barrett, Stephens, Underwood, Stead, 60.75	18	11
Ht 6	Appleton, Bishop, Brady, Harris, 58.03	20	15
Ht 7	Brady, Newman, Allen, Prynne, 61.69	22	19
Ht 8	Lobb, Stead, Harris, Underwood, 56.69	26	21
Ht 9	Appleton, Brady, Stephens, Barrett, 59.44	27	26
Ht 10	Bishop, Allen, Underwood, Harris, 58.84	30	29
Ht 11	Stead, Newman, Prynne, Underwood, 59.32	33	32
Ht 12	Lobb, Barrett, Allen, Appleton (f,rem), 57.63	38	33
Ht 13	(Re-Run) Lobb, Bishop, Stead, Brady (f,ex), 58.97	43	34
Ht 14	Stephens, Newman, Brady, Underwood, 59.60	48	35
Ht 15	(Nominated) Lobb, Appleton, Stead, Stephens (fell), 59.03	51	38

Tuesday 4 August, 1998 – Conference League
ST.AUSTELL 'GULLS' 52 MILDENHALL 'FEN TIGERS' 38

ST.AUSTELL

Steve Bishop	3 3 3 3 3 - -	15	
Chris Harris	M 3 0 0 1 - -	4	
Wayne Barrett	2¹3 3 0 - - -	8	1
Seemond Stephens	T 1 0 2 - - -	3	
Jason Prynne	0 0 1¹2 1 - -	4	1
Adrian Newman	1 2 0 1¹- - -	4	1
Roger Lobb	3 3 3 3 2¹- -	14	1

MILDENHALL

Geoff Powell	2 2 3 3 2 - -	12	
Jamie Barton	1¹R - - - - -	1	1
David Osborn	0 0 - - - - -	0	
Mark Thompson	1 0 0 F - - -	1	
Ross Brady	2 2 1¹2 2 R -	9	1
Dean Garrod	2 1¹1¹2 1¹1 -	8	3
Paul Lydes-Uings	0 1¹2 1 3 - -	7	1

PROGRAMME CHANGES:-
Ht 1: Prynne replaced Harris; Ht 3: Harris replaced Stephens in the re-run; Ht 7: Powell replaced Osborn; Ht 8: Brady replaced Barton; Ht 10: Garrod replaced Thompson; Ht 11: Lydes-Uings replaced Barton; Ht 12: Brady replaced Osborn

		Gulls	Mild
Ht 1	Bishop, Powell, Barton, Prynne, Harris (ex, 2 mins), 55.91	3	3
Ht 2	Lobb, Garrod, Newman, Lydes-Uings, 58.03	7	5
Ht 3	(Re-Run) Harris, Barrett, Thompson, Osborn, Stephens (ex, tapes), 57.05	12	6
Ht 4	Lobb, Brady, Lydes-Uings, Prynne, 57.17	15	9
Ht 5	Barrett, Powell, Stephens, Barton, 57.53	19	11
Ht 6	Bishop, Brady, Garrod, Harris, 56.38	22	14
Ht 7	Powell, Newman, Prynne, Thompson, 57.25	25	17
Ht 8	Lobb, Lydes-Uings, Brady, Harris, 58.37	28	20
Ht 9	Barrett, Brady, Garrod, Stephens, 56.91	31	23
Ht 10	Bishop, Garrod, Harris, Osborn, 57.00	35	25
Ht 11	Powell, Prynne, Lydes-Uings, Newman, 56.71	37	29
Ht 12	Lobb, Brady, Garrod, Barrett, 57.50	40	32
Ht 13	Bishop, Powell, Prynne, Brady (ret), 56.18	44	34
Ht 14	Lydes-Uings, Stephens, Newman, Thompson, 58.66	47	37
Ht 15	(Nominated) Bishop, Lobb, Garrod, Thompson (fell), 58.62	52	38

Tuesday 11 August, 1998 – Conference League
ST.AUSTELL 'GULLS' 55 BUXTON 'HITMEN' 35

ST.AUSTELL

Steve Bishop	3 2 3 2 1 - -	11
Jason Prynne	0 1'1'1 - - -	3 2
Wayne Barrett	2'3 2 3 3 - -	13 1
Seemond Stephens	3 2'2 R 2'- -	9 2
Chris Harris	1'1'1 3 0 - - -	5 2
Adrian Newman	2'2 X 3 - - -	7 1
Roger Lobb	3 2 T 2'- - -	7 1

BUXTON

Jamie Young	2 1 2 1 - - -	6
Daniel Hodgson	1'0 R 1'- - -	2 2
Adam Allott	0 3 0 0 0 - -	3
Phil Pickering	1 0 2 1 0 - -	4
Simon Stead	3 3 3 3 3 2 -	17
Mark McIlkenny	F R - - - - -	0
Paul Taylor	1 0 1 1 - - -	3

PROGRAMME CHANGES:-
Ht 8: Stead replaced Taylor; Stephens replaced Lobb in the re-run; Ht 9: Taylor replaced McIlkenny; Ht 12: Pickering replaced McIlkenny

A six heat British Youth Development League match was also run, which saw St.Austell defeat Glasgow 26-10. The points scorers were: (St.Austell) Seemond Stephens 9; Chris Harris 7+2; Simon Phillips 6+1; Mark Phillips 4+2; (Glasgow) Paul Taylor 5; Mark McIlkenny 4+1; Iain Macaulay 1; Gary Flint 0

		Gulls	Bux
Ht 1	Bishop, Young, Hodgson, Prynne, 55.34	3	3
Ht 2	Lobb, Newman, Taylor, McIlkenny (fell), 58.72	8	4
Ht 3	Stephens, Barrett, Pickering, Allott, 57.21	13	5
Ht 4	Stead, Lobb, Harris, Taylor, 58.16	16	8
Ht 5	Barrett, Stephens, Young, Hodgson, 55.91	21	9
Ht 6	Stead, Bishop, Prynne, McIlkenny (ret), 58.25	24	12
Ht 7	Allott, Newman, Harris, Pickering, 58.50	27	15
Ht 8	(Re-Run) Stead, Stephens, Prynne, Hodgson (ret), Lobb (ex, tapes), 55.56	30	18
Ht 9	Stead, Barrett, Taylor, Stephens (ret), 56.43	32	22
Ht 10	Bishop, Pickering, Prynne, Allott, 56.75	36	24
Ht 11	(Re-Run) Harris, Young, Hodgson, Newman (f,ex), 55.62	39	27
Ht 12	Barrett, Lobb, Pickering, Allott, 57.87	44	28
Ht 13	Stead, Bishop, Young, Harris, 55.50	46	32
Ht 14	Newman, Stephens, Taylor, Pickering, 58.41	51	33
Ht 15	(Nominated) Barrett, Stead, Bishop, Allott, 56.84	55	35

Tuesday 18 August, 1998 – Challenge Match
ST.AUSTELL 'GULLS' 59 BELLE VUE 'COLTS' 31

ST.AUSTELL

Roger Lobb	3 2 2 2'2'2'- -	11 3
Jason Prynne	2'1'1'1'3 - - -	7 3
Wayne Barrett	2'3 3 3 3 - -	14 1
Chris Harris	3 X 2'3 - - -	8 1
Seemond Stephens	3 3 1'3 - - -	10 1
Adrian Newman	2 X 2 1 - - -	5
Kevin Phillips	1'F 2 1 - - -	4 1

BELLE VUE

Elvis Jones	1'0 1 1 - - -	3 1
Neil Robinson	R 2 0 0 - - -	2
Jamie Isherwood	1 1'0 - - - -	2 1
Richard Ford	R - - - - - -	0
Lee Dixon	1'3 F - - - -	4 1
Paul Burnett	1 0 0 1 0 - -	2
James Birkinshaw	3 2 3 3 2 F -	13
Simon Phillips	2 1 2 F - - -	5

PROGRAMME CHANGES:-
Ht 1: Burnett replaced Jones; Ht 7: S.Phillips replaced Ford; Ht 10: S.Phillips replaced Ford; Ht 11: Birkinshaw replaced Robinson; Ht 12: S.Phillips replaced Isherwood; Ht 13: Robinson replaced Dixon; Ht 14: S.Phillips replaced Ford

A six heat British Youth Development League match was also run, which saw St.Austell defeat Belle Vue 24-12. The points scorers were: (St.Austell) Seemond Stephens 9; Simon Phillips 7+1; Chris Harris 4+2; Jason Prynne 4+1; (Belle Vue) Lee Dixon 6; Jamie Isherwood 4; Elvis Jones 1; Neil Robinson 1

		Gulls	BV
Ht 1	Lobb, Prynne, Burnett, Robinson (ret), 58.75	5	1
Ht 2	Birkinshaw, Newman, K.Phillips, Burnett, 58.40	8	4
Ht 3	Harris, Barrett, Isherwood, Ford (ret), 58.22	13	5
Ht 4	Stephens, Birkinshaw, Dixon, K.Phillips (fell), 58.75	16	8
Ht 5	(Re-Run) Barrett, Robinson, Jones, Harris (f,ex), 57.32	19	11
Ht 6	Dixon, Lobb, Prynne, Burnett, 59.56	22	14
Ht 7	(Awarded) Stephens, S.Phillips, Isherwood, Newman (f,ex), No Time	25	17
Ht 8	Birkinshaw, K.Phillips, Prynne, Robinson, 58.56	28	20
Ht 9	Barrett, Harris, Burnett, Dixon (fell), 59.09	33	21
Ht 10	Prynne, Lobb, S.Phillips, Isherwood, 60.09	38	22
Ht 11	Birkinshaw, Newman, Stephens, Jones, 59.06	41	25
Ht 12	Barrett, S.Phillips, K.Phillips, Burnett, 58.91	45	27
Ht 13	Stephens, Lobb, Jones, Robinson, 58.62	50	28
Ht 14	Harris, Birkinshaw, Newman, S.Phillips (fell), 58.28	54	30
Ht 15	(Nominated) Barrett, Lobb, Jones, Birkinshaw (fell), 59.32	59	31

Note: Richard Ford blew his only motor in Heat-3, and St.Austell subsequently allowed Belle Vue to borrow Simon Phillips in order to cover his remaining rides.

Tuesday 25 August, 1998 – Conference League
ST.AUSTELL 'GULLS' 71 NORFOLK 'BRAVES' 19

```
ST.AUSTELL
Steve Bishop        3 3 3 3 3 - -    15
Jason Prynne        2'1 2'2'- - -     7  3
Wayne Barrett       2'3 3 2'- - -    10  2
Chris Harris        3 1 2'3 - - -     9  1
Seemond Stephens    3 3 3 2'1 - -    12  1
Adrian Newman       3 2'1 2'- - -     8  2
Roger Lobb          2'2'3 3 - - -    10  2

NORFOLK
Peter Boast         1 2 2 1 2 - -     8
Luke Clifton        0 0 0 0 - - -     0
Darren Smith        1 1 R R - - -     2
Carl Wilkinson      0 0 1 1 - - -     2
Mark Blackwell      0 0 1 R - - -     1
Freddie Stephenson  1 2 F 1 0 - -     4
Jamie Smith         0 1 1 R - - -     2

PROGRAMME CHANGES:-
None!
```

A six heat British Youth Development League match was also run, which saw St.Austell defeat King's Lynn 'Jousters' 28-8. The points scorers were: (St.Austell) Simon Phillips 8+1; Seemond Stephens 7+1; Chris Harris 7+1; Adrian Newman 6+3; (King's Lynn) Freddie Stephenson 6; Luke Clifton 2; Darren Smith 0; Carl Wilkinson 0

		Gulls	KL
Ht 1	Bishop, Prynne, Boast, Clifton, 56.59	5	1
Ht 2	Newman, Lobb, Stephenson, Smith, 57.54	10	2
Ht 3	Harris, Barrett, Smith, Newman, 57.59	15	3
Ht 4	Stephens, Lobb, Smith, Blackwell, 57.96	20	4
Ht 5	Barrett, Boast, Harris, Clifton, 56.91	24	6
Ht 6	Bishop, Stephenson, Prynne, Blackwell, 57.85	28	8
Ht 7	Stephens, Newman, Smith, Wilkinson, 58.56	33	9
Ht 8	Lobb, Prynne, Smith, Clifton, 57.61	38	10
Ht 9	Barrett, Harris, Blackwell, Stephenson (fell), 59.19	43	11
Ht 10	Bishop, Prynne, Wilkinson, Smith (ret), 58.47	48	12
Ht 11	Stephens, Boast, Newman, Clifton, 58.83	52	14
Ht 12	Lobb, Barrett, Stephenson, Smith (ret), 58.69	57	15
Ht 13	Bishop, Stephens, Boast, Blackwell (ret), 57.79	62	16
Ht 14	Harris, Newman, Wilkinson, Smith (ret), 59.87	67	17
Ht 15	(Nominated) Bishop, Boast, Stephens, Stephenson, 57.29	71	19

Tuesday 1 September, 1998 – Challenge Match
ST.AUSTELL 'GULLS' 69 EDINBURGH 'MONARCHS' 20

```
ST.AUSTELL
Steve Bishop        3 3 3 3 2'- -    14  1
Jason Prynne        2'2'2'2'F - - -   6  3
Wayne Barrett       2'3 2'M - - -     7  2
Chris Harris        3 2'3 2'- - -    10  2
Seemond Stephens    3 3 3 2'3 - -    14  1
Adrian Newman       2'1 1 3 3 - -    10  1
Roger Lobb          3 1 3 1 - - -     8

EDINBURGH
Paul Taylor         1 1 2 F - - -     4
Scott Courtney      0 X 1 0 R R -     1
Steven Jones        1 2 2 2 1 - -     8
Jitendra Duffill    0 0 1'R - - -     1  1
Steven McAllister   2 R 1 1 - - -     4
Iain Milne          0 1 0 0 - - -     1
Derek Sneddon       1 F X - - - -     1

PROGRAMME CHANGES:-
Ht 12: Newman replaced Barrett
Ht 14: Courtney replaced Sneddon
```

A six heat British Youth Development League match was also run, which saw St.Austell defeat Armadale 25-11. The points scorers were: (St.Austell) Chris Harris 8+1; Seemond Stephens 8+1; Gary Lobb 6; Vince Purnell 3; (Armadale) Derek Sneddon 5+1; Steven Jones 4; Paul Taylor 2; Jitendra Duffill 0

		Gulls	Edin
Ht 1	Bishop, Prynne, Taylor, Courtney, 57.31	5	1
Ht 2	Lobb, Newman, Sneddon, Milne, 57.81	10	2
Ht 3	Harris, Barrett, Jones, Duffill, 58.15	15	3
Ht 4	Stephens, McAllister, Lobb, Sneddon (fell), 57.41	19	5
Ht 5	(Re-Run) Barrett, Harris, Taylor, Courtney (f,ex), 58.44	24	6
Ht 6	Bishop, Prynne, Milne, McAllister (ret), 57.88	29	7
Ht 7	Stephens, Jones, Newman, Duffill, 58.81	33	9
Ht 8	(Awarded) Lobb, Prynne, Courtney, Sneddon (f,ex), No Time	38	10
Ht 9	Harris, Barrett, McAllister, Milne, 58.10	43	11
Ht 10	Bishop, Jones, Duffill, Prynne (fell), 57.63	46	14
Ht 11	Stephens, Taylor, Newman, Courtney, 57.47	50	16
Ht 12	Newman, Jones, Lobb, Milne, Barrett (ex, 2 mins), 59.88	54	18
Ht 13	Bishop, Stephens, McAllister, Taylor (fell), 57.06	59	19
Ht 14	Newman, Harris, Duffill (ret), Courtney (ret), 58.90	64	19
Ht 15	(Nominated) Stephens, Bishop, Jones, Courtney (ret), 57.18	69	20

Tuesday 8 September, 1998 – Conference League
ST.AUSTELL 'GULLS' 46 MILDENHALL 'FEN TIGERS' 20
Meeting abandoned after Heat-11

ST.AUSTELL			
Steve Bishop	3 3 3 - - - -	9	
Jason Prynne	1 1 1'2'- - -	5	2
Wayne Barrett	2 3 2'- - - -	7	1
Chris Harris	1'2'3 - - - -	6	2
Seemond Stephens	2 3 3 - - - -	8	
Gary Lobb	2'2'2'- - - -	6	3
Roger Lobb	3 R 2 - - - -	5	
MILDENHALL			
Chris Sweet	0 - - - - - -	0	
Jamie Barton	2 X 0 R - - -	2	
Garry Sweet	3 1 X 1 - - -	5	
Mark Thompson	0 1 0 1 - - -	2	
Ross Brady	3 2 3 X - - -	8	
Dean Garrod	1 0 1 - - - -	2	
Simon Brown	0 1 - - - - -	1	

PROGRAMME CHANGES:-
Ht 5: G.Sweet replaced C.Sweet; Ht 8: Brady replaced Brown; Ht 11: Thompson replaced C.Sweet.

Fog descended over the Clay Country Moto Parc, with referee Graham Reeve having little option but to abandon the proceedings. However, as St.Austell held an unassailable lead at the time, the result was allowed to stand.

		Gulls	Mild
Ht 1	Bishop, Barton, Prynne, C.Sweet, 56.25	4	2
Ht 2	R.Lobb, G.Lobb, Garrod, Brown, 57.97	9	3
Ht 3	G.Sweet, Barrett, Harris, Thompson, 58.30	12	6
Ht 4	Brady, Stephens, Brown, R.Lobb (ret), 58.34	14	10
Ht 5	(Awarded) Barrett, Harris, G.Sweet, Barton (f,ex), No Time	19	11
Ht 6	Bishop, Brady, Prynne, Garrod, 56.57	23	13
Ht 7	Stephens, G.Lobb, Thompson (f,rem), G.Sweet (ex, crossed white line), 59.75	28	14
Ht 8	Brady, R.Lobb, Prynne, Barton, 57.50	31	17
Ht 9	(Re-Run) Harris, Barrett, Garrod, Brady (f,ex), 57.50	36	18
Ht 10	Bishop, Prynne, G.Sweet, Thompson, 57.69	41	19
Ht 11	Stephens, G.Lobb, Thompson, Barton (ret), 58.97	46	20

Tuesday 15 September, 1998 – Conference League
ST.AUSTELL 'GULLS' 70 NEWPORT 'MAVERICKS' 20

ST.AUSTELL			
Steve Bishop	3 3 3 3 2'- -	14	1
Jason Prynne	1 2'1 2'- - -	6	2
Roger Lobb	3 3 3 3 3 - -	15	
Chris Harris	2'M 1 - - -	5	2
Seemond Stephens	2'3 3 2'- - -	10	2
Adrian Newman	2'2'2'X 3 - -	9	3
Wayne Barrett	3 3 3 2'- - -	11	1
NEWPORT			
Chris Neath	2 1 R M 1 1 -	5	
No Rider	- - - - - -	-	
No Rider	- - - - - -	-	
Martin Williams	1 1 0 2 1 - -	5	
Simon Phillips	1 1 2 1 0 1 -	6	
Chris Courage	1 0 0 1'0 0 -	2	1
Richard Ford	0 0 2 0 - - -	2	

PROGRAMME CHANGES:-
Ht 5: Newman replaced Harris; Ht 8: Neath filled the absent rider slot; Ht 10: Phillips filled the absent rider slot; Ht 11: Courage filled the absent rider slot; Williams replaced Neath; Ht 12: Neath filled the absent rider slot; Ht 14: Phillips replaced Williams

Note: Newport arrived with a depleted five-man side, with no rider appearing in either a No.2 or No.3 race-jacket. Consequently, Newport tracked only one rider in Heats-1, 3, 5 and 7.

		Gulls	New
Ht 1	Bishop, Neath, Prynne, 56.56 (3 Riders Only)	4	2
Ht 2	Barrett, Newman, Courage, Ford, 56.78	9	3
Ht 3	Lobb, Harris, Williams, 58.19 (3 Riders Only)	14	4
Ht 4	Barrett, Stephens, Phillips, Ford, 58.16	19	5
Ht 5	Lobb, Newman, Neath, Harris (ex, 2 mins), 58.53 (3 Riders Only)	24	6
Ht 6	Bishop, Prynne, Phillips, Courage, 59.06	29	7
Ht 7	Stephens, Newman, Williams, 59.81 (3 Riders Only)	34	8
Ht 8	Barrett, Ford, Prynne, Neath (ret), 57.38	38	10
Ht 9	Lobb, Phillips, Harris, Courage, 58.15	42	12
Ht 10	Bishop, Prynne, Phillips, Williams, 58.78	47	13
Ht 11	(Re-Run) Stephens, Williams, Courage, Newman (f,ex), Neath (ex, 2 mins), 58.98	50	16
Ht 12	Lobb, Barrett, Neath, Courage, 58.00	55	17
Ht 13	Bishop, Stephens, Neath, Phillips, 57.28	60	18
Ht 14	Newman, Harris, Phillips, Ford, 58.85	65	19
Ht 15	(Nominated) Lobb, Bishop, Williams, Courage, 57.66	70	20

Tuesday 22 September, 1998 – Knock-Out Cup Final, 1st Leg
ST.AUSTELL 'GULLS' 53 MILDENHALL 'FEN TIGERS' 36

ST.AUSTELL			
Steve Bishop	3 3 3 2 3 3 -	17	
Jason Prynne	0 X 1'- - - -	1	1
Roger Lobb	2 1 2 2 3 2'-	12	1
Chris Harris	0 1'0 - - - -	1	1
Seemond Stephens	1'3 3 3 2'2'-	14	3
Adrian Newman	1'1 2'- - - -	4	2
Gary Lobb	2 2 X - - - -	4	
MILDENHALL			
Geoff Powell	2 2 R 1 - - -	5	
Jamie Barton	1'0 R 1 - - -	2	1
David Mason	3 2 3 3 1 1 -	13	
Mark Thompson	1 0 - - - - -	1	
Ross Brady	3 2 3 R R R -	8	
Dean Garrod	3 1'0 1 - - -	5	1
Paul Lydes-Uings	0 0 2 0 - - -	2	

PROGRAMME CHANGES:-
Ht 5: Bishop replaced Harris; Ht 8: Stephens replaced Prynne; Ht 10: Brady replaced Thompson; Ht 12: Harris replaced G.Lobb; Ht 14: R.Lobb replaced Harris; Stephens replaced Newman; Mason replaced Thompson

Note: St.Austell subsequently won the second leg of the KOC Final at Mildenhall by 52-points to 38, giving them a crushing aggregate success of 105-74

A six heat British Youth Development League match was also run, which saw St.Austell defeat a three-man Mildenhall side 25-11. The points scorers were: (St.Austell) Chris Harris 9; Adrian Newman 8+3; Seemond Stephens 6; Vince Purnell 2+1; (Mildenhall) Paul Lydes-Uings 6; Simon Brown 4; Jamie Barton 1+1

		Gulls	Mild
Ht 1	Bishop, Powell, Barton, Prynne, 55.72	3	3
Ht 2	Garrod, G.Lobb, Newman, Lydes-Uings, 59.72	6	6
Ht 3	Mason, R.Lobb, Thompson, Harris, 57.00	8	10
Ht 4	Brady, G.Lobb, Stephens, Lydes-Uings, 57.55	11	13
Ht 5	Bishop, Powell, R.Lobb, Barton, 57.50	15	15
Ht 6	(Awarded) Bishop, Brady, Garrod, Prynne (f,ex), No Time	18	18
Ht 7	Stephens, Mason, Newman, Thompson, 57.40	22	20
Ht 8	(Awarded) Stephens, Lydes-Uings, Barton (ret), G.Lobb (f,ex), No Time	25	22
Ht 9	Brady, R.Lobb, Harris, Garrod, 56.85	28	25
Ht 10	Mason, Bishop, Prynne, Brady (ret), 57.56	31	28
Ht 11	Stephens, Newman, Barton, Powell (ret), 58.06	36	29
Ht 12	Mason, R.Lobb, Garrod, Harris, 57.50	38	33
Ht 13	Bishop, Stephens, Powell, Brady (ret), 57.25	43	34
Ht 14	R.Lobb, Stephens, Mason, Lydes-Uings, 58.16	48	35
Ht 15	(Nominated) Bishop, R.Lobb, Mason, Brady (ret), 56.30	53	36
	Bronze Helmet: Bishop, Brady, 57.34		

Tuesday 29 September, 1998 – Challenge Match
ST.AUSTELL 'GULLS' 33 SWINDON 'SPROCKETS' 27
Meeting abandoned after Heat-10

ST.AUSTELL			
Steve Bishop	3 2 3 - - - -	8	
Jason Prynne	2'0 2 1 - - -	5	1
Roger Lobb	3 3 1 - - - -	7	
Chris Harris	2'2'0 - - - -	4	2
Seemond Stephens	2 3 - - - - -	5	
Adrian Newman	2 F - - - - -	2	
Kevin Phillips	1'1'F - - - -	2	2
SWINDON			
Simon Paget	1 0 - - - - -	1	
Martin Williams	0 1 1 - - - -	2	
Glen Phillips	1 1'0 - - - -	2	1
Andy Carfield	X 2 2 - - - -	4	
James Birkinshaw	3 3 3 - - - -	9	
Simon Phillips	3 1 3 2'- - -	9	1
Ray Dickson	F 0 - - - - -	0	

PROGRAMME CHANGES:-
Ht 8: S.Phillips replaced Dickson

Note: With the remnants of Hurricane Carl shedding an awful lot of wet stuff over the Clay Country Moto Parc, referee Brian James had no alternative than to abandon this meeting prior to Heat-11.

A six heat British Youth Development League match was also run, which saw St.Austell defeat Swindon 20-16. The points scorers were: (St.Austell) Chris Harris 8+1; Seemond Stephens 7; Adrian Newman 3+2; Jason Prynne 2+1; (Swindon) James Birkinshaw 9; Andy Carfield 4+1; Martin Williams 2; Simon Paget 1+1

		Gulls	Swin
Ht 1	Bishop, Prynne, Paget, Williams, 59.86	5	1
Ht 2	S.Phillips, Newman, K.Phillips, Dickson (fell), 59.93	8	4
Ht 3	(Re-Run) Lobb, Harris, G.Phillips, Carfield (f,ex), 59.10	13	5
Ht 4	Birkinshaw, Stephens, K.Phillips, Dickson, 58.90	16	8
Ht 5	Lobb, Harris, Williams, Paget, 59.69	21	9
Ht 6	Birkinshaw, Bishop, S.Phillips, Prynne, 58.28	23	13
Ht 7	Stephens, Carfield, G.Phillips, Newman (fell), 59.44	26	16
Ht 8	S.Phillips, Prynne, Williams, K.Phillips (fell), 60.28	28	20
Ht 9	(Re-Run) Birkinshaw, S.Phillips, Lobb, Harris, 60.72	29	25
Ht 10	Bishop, Carfield, Prynne, G.Phillips, 58.85	33	27

Tuesday 6 October, 1998 – Challenge Match
ST.AUSTELL 'GULLS' 30 EXETER 'FALCONS' 59

ST.AUSTELL

Rider		Total	
Steve Bishop R/R	- - - - - -	-	
Wayne Barrett	0 1'R 0 - - -	1	1
Roger Lobb	1 1'1 2 1'2 -	8	2
Adrian Newman	2 0 F 1'0 - -	3	1
James Birkinshaw	2 3 2 1 1 1'-	10	1
Seemond Stephens	1 2 T 0 0 2 -	5	
Jason Prynne	0 0 1 2 - - -	3	

EXETER

Rider		Total	
Frank Smart	3 3 2'3 3 - -	14	1
Graeme Gordon	2'2'3 3 - - -	10	2
Peter Jeffery	R 2 1 3 - - -	6	
Mark Simmonds	3 X 3 3 - - -	9	
Michael Coles	3 3 3 2'R - -	11	1
Kevin Phillips	2'0 0 F - - -	2	1
Simon Phillips	3 1 2'1 - - -	7	1

PROGRAMME CHANGES:-
Ht 1: R/R Lobb; Ht 6: R/R Stephens; Ht 7: T/S Newman for Stephens, after his tapes exclusion; Ht 10: R/R Birkinshaw; Ht 13: R/R Stephens

		Gulls	Exet
Ht 1	Smart, Gordon, Lobb, Barrett, 56.47	1	5
Ht 2	S.Phillips, K.Phillips, Stephens, Prynne, 72.66 (5 laps!)	2	10
Ht 3	(Re-Run) Simmonds, Newman, Lobb, Jeffery (ret), 56.44	5	13
Ht 4	Coles, Birkinshaw, S.Phillips, Prynne (f,rem), 57.47	7	17
Ht 5	Smart, Gordon, Lobb, Newman, 56.04	8	22
Ht 6	(Re-Run Twice) Coles, Stephens, Barrett, K.Phillips (f,rem), 56.31	11	25
Ht 7	(Re-Run Twice) Birkinshaw, Jeffery, Newman (fell), Simmonds (ex, foul riding), Stephens (ex, tapes), 57.53	14	27
Ht 8	Gordon, S.Phillips, Prynne, Barrett (ret), 56.38	15	32
Ht 9	Coles, Lobb, Newman, K.Phillips, 57.18	18	35
Ht 10	Simmonds, Birkinshaw, Jeffery, Barrett, 58.58	20	39
Ht 11	Gordon, Smart, Birkinshaw, Stephens, 59.59	21	44
Ht 12	Jeffery, Prynne, Lobb, K.Phillips (fell), 59.20	24	47
Ht 13	Smart, Coles, Birkinshaw, Stephens, 57.56	25	52
Ht 14	Simmonds, Stephens, S.Phillips, Newman, 57.32	27	56
Ht 15	(Nominated) Smart, Lobb, Birkinshaw, Coles (ret), 56.25	30	59

Tuesday 20 October, 1998
CORNISH GRAND PRIX

Rider		Total
Mark Simmonds	3 2 3 2 2 - -	12
David Howe	2 1 2 3 3 - -	11
Roger Lobb	1 3 X 3 2 - -	9
Adrian Newman	0 2 2 2 1 - -	7
Steve Bishop	3 R 1 3 3 - -	10
Jason Prynne	1 1 1 R M - -	3
Kevin Phillips	2 0 1 1 2 - -	6
Seemond Stephens	X 3 3 1 3 - -	10
Wayne Barrett	3 2 3 2 0 - -	10
James Birkinshaw	2 1 R - - - -	3
Chris Harris	0 X 0 0 R - -	0
Peter Jeffery	1 3 2 1 1 - -	8

PROGRAMME CHANGES:-
None!

Notes: After fouling the tapes in Heat-1, Adrian Newman went from a 20-yard handicap in the re-run; Jamie Birkinshaw was a non-starter in Heats-11 & 13, and was not replaced in either. Steve Bishop, Seemond Stephens and Wayne Barrett had to partake in a run-off to determine the last two places in the final.

1st MARK SIMMONDS;
2nd DAVID HOWE; 3rd STEVE BISHOP

Ht 1	(Re-Run) Simmonds, Howe, Lobb, Newman (20-yards), 56.59
Ht 2	(Re-Run Thrice) Bishop, Phillips, Prynne, Stephens (f,ex), 56.04
Ht 3	Barrett, Birkinshaw, Jeffery, Harris, 57.42
Ht 4	(Re-Run) Stephens, Simmonds, Birkinshaw, Bishop (ret), 57.50
Ht 5	Lobb, Barrett, Howe, Phillips (f,rem), 57.06
Ht 6	(Re-Run) Jeffery, Newman, Prynne, Harris (f,ex), 58.11
Ht 7	Simmonds, Howe, Bishop, Harris, 57.06
Ht 8	(Re-Run) Stephens, Jeffery, Phillips (f,rem), Lobb (ex, foul riding), 58.61
Ht 9	Barrett, Newman, Prynne, Birkinshaw (ret), 57.16
Ht 10	Howe, Barrett, Stephens, Harris, 56.11
Ht 11	Bishop, Newman, Phillips, 56.92 (3 Riders Only)
Ht 12	Lobb, Simmonds, Jeffery, Prynne (ret), 58.52
Ht 13	Howe, Phillips, Prynne (ex, 2 mins), 56.68 (2 Riders Only)
Ht 14	Bishop, Lobb, Newman, Harris (ret), 57.07
Ht 15	Stephens, Simmonds, Jeffery, Barrett, 58.85
Ht 16	(Run-Off) Bishop, Barrett, Stephens, 57.02
Ht 17	(Grand Final) Simmonds, Howe, Bishop, Barrett, 56.51

3

1999

Prior to the season, both Adrian Newman and Chris Harris cheered the Gulls' faithful, with 'Skippy' taking second place in the indoor World Cup ice-racing series in America. Meanwhile, Chris travelled to Sittingbourne on 28 February for the Under-16 Championship and produced a stunning display to win the event. This was a tremendous achievement for the 'Bomber' as the line-up featured some real up and coming racers, including Andrew Moore, Chris Schramm, Jason King, Glen Phillips and Jamie Smith. St Austell's plans for the season ahead were soon knocked sideways, however, when Chris opted for a season of racing at Premier League level with Exeter.

The Gulls were dealt a further blow before they had turned a wheel, when the ultra-popular Steve Bishop was offered the chance of a run in the Premier League with parent club Swindon. The Robins had been hit by an early injury to Gary Phelps, and had initially drafted in 'Bish' to plug the gap. However, the top man in the Conference League had produced a wonder show in his first match back in the Robins colours, notching a paid 18 points from seven rides against Sheffield on 1 April. Following that,

A winter snow scene at the Clay Country Moto Parc.

Gulls v. England Under-19s programme, 1999.

it was quite natural that Swindon would want to retain his services for the remainder of the season, and to his eternal credit, 'Bish' always kept the Gulls management informed of the situation. In an effort to find a winning combination, Swindon were to also snap up the services of Seemond Stephens at the beginning of May, but the Cornishman was to remain with the Gulls, while doubling-up for the Robins.

The season in Cornwall started with something a little bit different, namely the White Gold Charity Motorcycle Show scheduled for the weekend of 8 & 9 May. The event was organized by Clay Country Moto Parc timekeeper Terry Hooke, and apart from speedway, numerous other motorcycle events were planned. Unfortunately, on the Saturday, the rain came down with a vengeance and everything was completely washed out. Terry Hooke went away and burned the midnight oil, re-scheduling the full programme of events in the hope of fitting everything in on the Sunday. Thankfully, the rain cleared overnight and racing got underway in the morning, with the staging of a four-team tournament featuring St Austell, Bristol, Exeter and Plymouth. A variety of riders partook in this event, including most of the Gulls, plus Michael Coles and his father Bob, who rode an old-style upright machine. In the event, the meeting only got as far as the seventh heat of sixteen, and was subsequently abandoned after Greg Daniels had suffered an awkward-looking fall. The Cornwall Air Ambulance was called into action and it was quite a sight to see the helicopter come through the cliffs, before landing on the centre green. Greg was duly whisked off to hospital to receive expert

The Cornwall Air Ambulance lands at the Moto Parc.

Jason Prynne.

attention and thankfully, he wasn't too badly injured as things turned out. The scores at the time of the abandonment showed Exeter in the lead with 16 points, while St Austell had 11, Plymouth 10, and Bristol 4.

The sparse crowd were treated to other forms of motorcycle racing throughout the rest of the day, including sidecars, grass-track, quads, vintage speedway and classic speedway, but the main event was the White Gold GT Motorcycles Solo Masters. The twenty-heat competition saw Mark Simmonds continue his dominance at the Moto Parc, as he went through the card to win with a five-ride maximum. It proved to be an Exeter one-two-three on the rostrum, with Michael Coles finishing as runner-up on 14 points, while the diminutive Chris Harris was third on 13 points. The rain returned by the mid-point of the meeting, and although it left the track in a slippery condition, it had stopped in time for the heat twenty showdown. That was when title contenders Mark Simmonds, Michael Coles and Chris Harris all came to the line, having each taken victory in their first four rides. Super 'Simmo' duly came out on top after getting the better of a wheel-to-wheel battle with 'Colesey', while Chris Harris occupied third spot ahead of Adrian Newman. Of the Gulls contingent in the line-up, Gary Lobb came out on top, scoring 11 points, with Wayne Barrett also in double-figures on the 10 point mark.

The sidecar event deserves particular mention, as it was the first time that the modern 1000cc machines had appeared at the Moto Parc. Top boys Ivor Matthews, Richard Moore, Bob Radley, Craig Cheetham, Justin Westaway and Roy Spreadbury took part, with some of the starts being handicapped to allow all six to race at the same time. A total of five heats were held, with Roy Spreadbury and Ivor Matthews taking a couple of wins apiece, while Craig Cheetham gained a solitary success.

Running through some of the other events, Paul Fudge collected two wins in the vintage speedway section, with Jim Gregory victorious in the other race that was staged. Meanwhile, Mike Cooke, mounted on a Jawa, took victory in all three classic speedway races and Robert Barnard proved to be top man in the quad racing, winning each of the four heats that were run. In a link with the past, Eric Martyn, a former rider at Par Moor in 1962-63, was on hand to help out behind the scenes. Later in the season, Eric would become more involved, standing in as relief announcer on the occasions when Dave Stallworthy was unavailable.

The Gulls swung back into action on 25 May, when the previous season's rained off international challenge against the England Under-19 side was finally restaged. A healthy crowd turned up to watch the action, with the England side of David Howe, Paul Lee, Chris Neath, Simon Stead, Nick Simmons and Chris Harris making for particularly attractive opposition. England had also planned to track Marc Norris, but he had picked up an injury, so they utilized the rider replacement facility in his place. Steve Bishop had hoped to ride for St Austell, but he was unable to attend as his father was ill. Roger Lobb stepped in to lead the homesters at no.1, but it turned up to be a rare Gulls appearance for the 'Lobbster' as he spent the season racing in the Premier League with Arena-Essex. Roger knocked up 11 points in the match, while Seemond Stephens gained a well-taken 10+2, but on the night, the England boys simply ran riot to win 54-36. The sensational Simon Stead led the way with 13 points, while Nick Simmons (9+2), Chris Neath (9+1), David Howe (9) and Chris Harris (7+4), provided fabulous backing.

It was destination Mildenhall on 30 May, as St Austell began their Conference League programme at the well-appointed West Row raceway. Having lost Steve Bishop, Roger Lobb and Chris Harris from the super side of '98, the Gulls had an interesting new look for the match. Seemond Stephens took over the no.1 race-jacket, with the remainder of the side being made up by Martin Williams, Gary Lobb, Jason Prynne, Wayne Barrett, Kevin Phillips and Richard Ford. Another notable non-starter was Adrian Newman, who hadn't realised that he needed to renew his racing licence! The match was close throughout, but St Austell edged ahead in heat twelve, before running out 48-42 victors. Barrie Evans did his utmost to keep the home side in contention, netting a paid 13 points, while the Gulls were best served by a dozen points apiece from Gary Lobb and Wayne Barrett. The Gulls had been due to face Rye House in a second match on the bill, but shortly after the completion of the first meeting, the heavens opened and quickly rendered the circuit unfit for further racing.

Returning to the lunar landscape of the Moto Parc, it was individual action on 1 June, with the second staging of the Simpson Plant Hire Individual Challenge. Unfortunately, the rain was again in evidence and made conditions very difficult for the riders, with referee Graham Reeve being full of praise for their courageous efforts to put on a show for the public. The meeting was run along Grand Prix lines, with A, B and C finals scheduled, although the two minor finals were subsequently scrapped in view of the tricky state of the track. The A final did go ahead, however, when the top scorers met, but it was bad luck for Seemond Stephens, who had notched maximum points in the heats, when he fell and was excluded. At the time of the stoppage, Jason Prynne wasn't under power, so he was also excluded, leaving Adrian Newman (complete with new licence) and Wayne Barrett to engage in a match race to decide the outcome. The re-run saw Wayne zip ahead, only to drift off-line in the slimy conditions, with the all-action 'Skippy' sweeping through to claim a popular victory.

Brian Annear continued his policy of providing extra entertainment, with the first round of the Express Factors Cornish Quad Championship also forming part of the programme. Robert Barnard, who had been so impressive in the White Gold Charity meeting, again showed his liking for the circuit, taking victory in all three heats to score 30 points. However, the six-lap grand final ended in farce, when Alan Ewart finished alone to claim double points (i.e. 20 points), but as he had only notched 8 points in the heats, overall victory still went to Robert Barnard.

The programme for the Simpson Plant Hire meeting included an interesting note thanking a gentleman from Liskeard, who had paid Poole Speedway £1,000 + VAT to release Wayne Barrett from his contract. The keen Gulls supporter then presented Wayne to Exeter promoter Colin Hill, who agreed that St Austell could use the popular rider as and when they wished, with no charge involved. The article also explained that Wayne had been allowed to join Exeter because Conference League tracks were not permitted to own riders.

A week passed before the Gulls next track action, when Mildehall journeyed down to Cornwall on league business. Yet again, a meeting was affected by mist and rain, although thanks to Nigel Prynne's superb track preparation, the meeting was completed satisfactorily. The visitors certainly launched themselves into the action and immediately took the lead, courtesy of a 4-2 from Garry Sweet and Mark Thompson. A see-saw battle developed as the score swung one way and then the other, before the Gulls took, and held, the lead in heat thirteen. The final result was 47-43 and it had been a classic encounter for those lucky enough to witness the event. Seemond Stephens gave his best-ever display thus far, superbly claiming six wins to score an 18-point maximum, with Wayne Barrett chipping in with a more than useful paid 13-point tally. For the battling Fen Tigers, both Garry Sweet and Dean Garrod produced solid showings to garner 11 points apiece. The Bronze Helmet was up for grabs after the match, and as winter holder Roger Lobb had moved on to the Premier League, two challengers faced each other for the coveted prize. After his fabulous performance in the match, there was no denying Seemond his crack, while Dean Garrod got the nod as the other challenger. The electric starting technique of Seemond quickly ended the challenge, however, with the Cornishman delightedly going on to take the chequered flag.

On 15 June, the Moto Parc played host to a Best Pairs meeting, sponsored by Fred Paul, a great friend of St Austell Speedway. As the meeting format comprized a lower number of races than usual, promoter Brian Annear was very fair and reduced the admission prices accordingly. Usual announcer Dave Stallworthy wasn't in the box for this meeting, which allowed Eric Barnes from Upper Seagry, near Chippenham, Wiltshire, to fulfil a lifetime ambition and take the microphone. Eric also did some pit side interviews for Re-Run Videos, but prior to that, he hadn't realized that he was actually being filmed while getting the hang of the microphone. Poor Eric's efforts later found their way on to the end of season 'Crashes and Cock-ups' tape, and jolly amusing

Martin Williams.

they were too! It was probably the worst possible meeting to make your bow as an announcer for instead of the normal points scoring system of 3-2-1-0, the pairs event utilized a 4-3-2-0 structure. Needless to say, this caused the intrepid debut announcer a lot of problems on the night. Another thing that didn't help Eric was the fact that Wayne Barrett missed the meeting and rider replacement was operated for him, with members of the other pairings confusingly taking his outings in turn! Eventually, the meeting was completed following semi-finals and a grand final, with Jason Prynne and Richard Ford emerging triumphant from Seemond Stephens and Ray Dickson. Although there were fewer races than usual, the crowd did receive compensation with the lower admission and were also treated to some vintage sidecar speedway, courtesy of Ken Westaway and his crews.

The Gulls hit the road the following Sunday, with a trip up to the quaint Buxton Raceway in Derbyshire. The home side tore into the match, hitting St Austell with successive 5-1 results in the first two heats. However, the Gulls were made of strong stuff, bouncing straight back with two maximum advantages of their own to level the scores at 12 points apiece. Buxton strained every sinew to pull away thereafter, but could never get more than six points ahead, with the Gulls determinedly coming back to force a 45-45 draw at the death. Top performer for the homesters was James Mann with a paid 12 points, while the gallant BWOC Gulls were led by a faultless 15 point full house from super Seemond Stephens. The Cornishman duly completed a perfect personal afternoon by seeing off the challenge from James Mann to retain the Bronze Helmet.

With the season in full swing, the reformed Rye House Rockets paid their first-ever visit to the full-throttle St Austell circuit on 22 June, with league points at stake. Having previously had three tough league encounters, this meeting was considerably easier as the Gulls thundered to a 67-23 victory. Seemond Stephens again went through the card for 15 points, while Martin Williams (11+4), Wayne Barrett (11), Gary Lobb (9+2) and Richard Ford (7+3) were all paid for double-figures. Riding at no.1, the experienced Simon Wolstenholme yielded 10 points for the under-fire visitors, but he was given little support, and also became Seemond Stephens' latest victim in the Bronze Helmet. Two modern 1000cc sidecar speedway races were also staged for the public's entertainment, when Justin Westaway and Matthew Tyrell went through their paces and gave a thrilling demonstration. In fact it was quite alarming, as Matthew screamed up the home straight, spraying shale at the double-decker bus, with one window after another shattering and the meeting officials having to dive for cover! Following this frightening experience, the inventive Ken Westaway came up with a special sidecar dirt deflector to ensure there wasn't a repeat performance.

The following week, St Austell entertained Bristol Bulldogs in a challenge match for the Southern Shield. The meeting signalled the return of the Bristol born Steve Bishop, who was happy to skipper the visitors at the track where he had attained cult status in its first two seasons of operation. Needless to say 'Bish' received a tremendous reception from the Gulls supporters, prior to producing a wonder show, blitzing to a paid 20 points from six starts. Steve actually took a golden double tactical substitute ride in heat eight, when he surged from behind to record 6 points. 'Bish' had earlier been beaten by Seemond Stephens in heat five, but that turned out to be the only time he was beaten by a Gull as he again demonstrated his zest for the 230-metre raceway. It really was an entertaining match for the spectators, with the Bulldogs eventually taking victory by 49 points to 44. The victors were not just helped by 'Bish' though, for Roger Lobb weighed in with a paid 19 point tally and Frank Smart plundered 10. Although the Gulls possessed strength in depth, only Seemond Stephens was any real match for the visitors devastating heat-leader trio, notching a well-taken 13 point total. The evening's events also included the second round of the Express Factors Cornish Quad Championship, with Simon Butler coming out on top with a total of 56 points, ahead Peter Pollard (38), Alan Ewart (22), Justin Annear (10) and Nigel Polkinghorn (2).

The Gulls had a week of inactivity, before their next track action matched them up against Linlithgow Lightning in their fifth league fixture of the campaign. The meeting resulted in a routine 59-31 success for St Austell, with Seemond Stephens gaining another five ride maximum, while Gary Lobb also rode extremely well to net a paid 15 pointer. Gateshead born Steven Jones was the undoubted star for the Scottish team, netting 12 points and earning the right to challenge Seemond for the Bronze Helmet. Quick reflexes at the start saw the Cornishman roar clear, before sailing off into the night air to retain the trophy he had quickly made his own. The visiting side included a young Scott Courtney, and of course nobody knew it then, but his father Mark would be a regular at the Moto Parc in 2001, representing Trelawny.

Somerset Rebels came visiting on 13 July for a match that was originally scheduled to be a Knock-Out Cup tie, however, with the Highbridge side not finally opening until 2000, the meeting went ahead as a challenge for the West Country Cup. The match day programme opened with news that funds were being raised to purchase a new track spare. Adrian Newman had used the old steed the previous week and it was described as being 'far too slow, old and bent to be of use'. The article went on, '… if anybody would like to purchase the original "Team Pigeon" as a collector's item, it will probably be worth thousands in years to come!'

So, to the meeting, which saw Greg Daniels return to the Moto Parc as team manager of a Rebels side that included Gary Phelps, Jay Stevens, Danny Bird, Glen Phillips, Chris Harris, plus brothers Mark and Simon Phillips. Amazingly, Seemond Stephens swept to another 15 point maximum as he led the Gulls to a 50-40 success. 'Skippy' Newman backed his flying colleague with a paid 14-point tally, while Somerset's best were Danny Bird (11) and Glen Phillips (10+2). Also on the bill, a sidecar speedway challenge match again pitched the Gulls against the Bulldogs. The five heat encounter was close throughout, but it was the home side who just shaded it, winning 15-14. Wayne Westaway notched 10 points for the homesters, with Justin Westaway netting the other five. Justin's passenger was a fellow called Mark Courtney, but this wasn't the famous speedway ace, but a local Cornish chap with the same name! Meanwhile, for the Bristol side, Steve Courtney scored 8 points and Matthew Tyrell scored six.

As previously mentioned, Rye House had reformed in 1999, and despite having no home track, they had joined the Conference League with a view to trying to get back into their old Hoddesdon venue. In the meantime, the Rockets used King's Lynn,

Club Cradley Heath on parade.

Eastbourne and Mildenhall for their 'home' matches, and it was to the latter that St Austell travelled on 18 July for the re-scheduled league match that have fallen victim to rain on 30 May. The meeting formed the second part of a double-header, which also saw Mildenhall defeat King's Lynn 52-38 in a Knock-Out Cup tie. When the Gulls took to the 260-metre circuit, they showed Rye House no mercy, ripping to a staggering 62-28 success. It was Wayne Barrett's turn to record a 15-point maximum, with powerful support coming from Seemond Stephens (11+1), Gary Lobb (11), Adrian Newman (10+1) and Martin Williams (8+4). As he had done a month previously in Cornwall, Simon Wolstenholme gleaned 10 points and easily headed the Rye House scoring. The leading Rocket then challenged Seemond for the Bronze Helmet, but the Gulls no.1 again blasted to victory, with Wolstenholme suffering mechanical problems and retiring from the race.

Back at home the next match saw the Gulls face King's Lynn Braves in more Conference League action. Despite the fact that Wayne Barrett was missing as he was appearing for Exeter at the Isle of Wight, the meeting resulted in another big win for St Austell, by 61 points to 29. In a powerhouse performance, Seemond Stephens dashed to yet another 15-point maximum, while Adrian Newman plundered 12+3 from six starts. Meanwhile, Martin Williams (11+2), Jason Prynne (11+1) and Richard Ford (8+2) all made telling contributions. Freddie Stephenson (11) and Luke Clifton (10+1) topped the pile for the battle-scarred Braves, but they received scant support from their colleagues. After the match, Luke Clifton challenged Seemond for the Bronze Helmet, but he went the way of all the previous challengers as the fast-starting Cornishman took victory for the sixth successive time. Three second-half races were also staged featuring hopefuls Adrian Rowe, Dominic Walsh-Newton, Les Rowlands and Jamie Holmes, with the latter impressively speeding to victory each time.

The programme for the match against King's Lynn featured a full-page advert for the forthcoming Cornish Ford Ka 3 Eclipse Classic on 10 August. This was expected to be one of the highlights of the season, when a quality field would battle it out for individual honour. Ever conscious of involving the public, Brian Annear came up with the idea of special race jackets for the event, which could be sponsored at £20 a time, and received after the meeting.

The Gulls were quickly back in action at the Moto Parc on the afternoon of Sunday 25 July, when they entertained Club Cradley Heath in the J & A Supporters' Trophy. The regular spectators had become used to wet and misty weather, but for this meeting, the sun was beating down and the arena was like an oven. In fact, it was so hot that almost 5,000 gallons of water were put down on the track from 11am onwards! A coach load of fans came down from Cradley, with Brian Annear boarding the vehicle as it arrived and presenting each and every Heathens supporter with a souvenir Gulls badge. Brian also gave some air horns to the travelling fans and his old-fashioned showman style of promotion was greatly appreciated by everyone.

For the match, the Heathens employed former St Austell favourite Chris Harris, and he certainly didn't let them down, racking up a massive 18 points from seven rides.

1999 Gulls, from left to right, back row: Seemond Stephens, Wayne Barrett, Adrian Newman, Gary Lobb, Jason Prynne, Richard Ford and Martin Williams. Front (on bike): Gerrry Sims (mascot).

Steve Camden also chipped in with ten points for the visitors, but the performances from their top two wasn't sufficient to stop the Gulls from securing a 49-41 win. Gary Lobb headed the homesters score-chart with 14 points, while Seemond Stephens was as impressive as ever, notching 13+1.

The following Tuesday, St Austell staged their third home meeting in a week, when Mildenhall were back in town for the first leg of the Knock-Out Cup semi-final. The Gulls seemed to be up for this one, getting their cup defence off to a super start with a 52-38 success. The visiting Fen Tigers certainly made life difficult in the early stages though, and it wasn't until heat five that the men in blue and white actually pulled ahead. Seemond Stephens raced to a paid maximum (14+1), while the successes of Gary Lobb (14) and Jason Prynne (9+3) effectively gave the homesters a three-pronged attack. Meanwhile, Steve Camden performed heroically from the no.7 berth for Mildenhall, keeping them in the contest with a stunning 17-point tally. Following the match, Seemond kept his marvellous run of success going, zipping to the chequered flag ahead of Barrie Evans to retain his grip on the Bronze Helmet.

A busy programme also included the third round of the Express Factors Cornish Quad Championship, with only three riders contesting the five heats. As he had done in the second round on 29 June, Simon Butler again steamed to victory with 52 points, with Peter Pollard (42) and Ben Whitehouse (26) being the other two competitors.

A glance at the Conference League table showed the Gulls occupying first position on 13 points, with Newport just one point behind in second position. It was therefore a mouth-watering prospect when the Welsh side arrived at the Longstone Pit raceway for a league match on 3 August. This meeting turned out to be a totally different ball game to the Mavericks' previous visit on 15 September 1998, when they only tracked a five-man team. Unlike that occasion, when the Gulls racked up a 70-20 victory, this crucial fixture ended in a 47-43 triumph for the visitors. Both sides raced neck and neck, with the scores locked at 36 points apiece after heat twelve. However, Chris Neath then inflicted a rare defeat on Seemond Stephens, and with Bobby Eldridge finishing third, the Mavericks moved into the lead. A penultimate heat 5-1 from Andrew Appleton and Graig Gough sealed St Austell's fate, before Seemond Stephens and Gary Lobb gained a consolation 4-2 in the last race. Chris Neath (12+1), Bobby Eldridge (11+1) and Graig Gough (9+2) were the Newport heroes, while Seemond Stephens (12) and Adrian Newman (11+2) worked manfully for the defeated Gulls. Super Seemond made sure the day wasn't a complete disaster though, when he swept to a further Bronze Helmet victory over Bobby Eldridge after the main match.

So, to 10 August, and what was the biggest meeting of the year at the Moto Parc, namely the Cornish Ford Ka Eclipse Classic. There was a large crowd in attendance for this one, as record numbers of people had journeyed down to the Duchy in readiness for the following morning, when the moon passed before the sun to create a total eclipse. Anyway, back to important speedway matters and a top field had been assembled for the meeting, with James Birkinshaw, Adam Allott, Shane Colvin and Chris Harris all expected to do well. The Cornish Guardian gave a tremendous account of the night, reporting, 'In anticipation of a large turnout, the St Austell Gulls promotion pulled out all the stops to put on a show to remember. The selected cast assembled for this prestigious individual event provided an enthralling evening's entertainment for the largest crowd of the season.'

Unfortunately, 'Clay Country King' Seemond Stephens missed the meeting as he was racing to a paid 11 score for Swindon in a Premier League encounter on the Isle of Wight. Despite his absence, it was still a great spectacle, as the *Cornish Guardian* had quite rightly reported, with Jason Prynne riding brilliantly to net 14 points and lead the top four scorers into the grand final. Joining Jason for the thrilling climax were Adrian Newman (13), Wayne Barrett (12) and Chris Harris (12), while Gary Lobb also notched a 12 point tally, but unluckily missed out due to recording less race wins. The final took two attempts to complete, with the initial effort ending when Jason Prynne and Adrian Newman fell after Wayne Barrett's machine had deposited a large amount of oil on the track. Referee Ronnie Allan excluded both Wayne and Jason, however, after lengthy consultation with the promotion and riders, he allowed all-four riders back for the re-start. It must be said that announcer Dave Stallworthy also encouraged the crowd to cheer if they thought all the riders should be allowed back in and no doubt, this also helped to sway the official's change of heart. Amid a carnival atmosphere, 'Bomber' Harris jetted clear in the re-run and charged on to collect the first prize of £200, with Jason finishing as a most popular runner-up ahead of 'Skippy'.

A funny incident occurred after the meeting, when Dave Stallworthy was interviewing Chris Harris for the video, down by the pit gate. All of a sudden, the track lights went out and a firework display commenced, leaving the ever-chatty Dave to compete with the cracking and banging as he concluded the conversation in darkness! As with previous firework displays at the venue, this was as spectacular as ever, and was a splendid way to end what had been a fabulous night.

Mildenhall hosted the prestigious Conference League Riders' Championship on 14 August, when the Gulls representatives were Adrian Newman and Martin Williams. Unfortunately, things didn't go favourably from a St Austell point of view, with 'Skippy' collecting just a single race win on his way to a 7-point tally, whilst Martin could only muster a couple of points and ended a disappointing night with a 2-minute exclusion. At the other end of the scale, Linlithgow's Jonathan Swales gave an awesome display to take victory with a 15-point full house, and it was a double celebration for the Scottish side as Lightning team-mate Scott Courtney finished third on 11 points. Meanwhile, providing the sandwich filling on the rostrum was Mildenhall man Steve Camden, who netted a 13-point tally.

Team action was back on the menu the following Tuesday, when Buxton landed at the Cornish raceway for a Conference League fixture. The rider replacement facility was operated for Wayne Barrett in this meeting as he had become a regular in the Exeter line-up and it had become difficult to combine riding for both the Gulls and the Falcons, as well as holding down a regular job. Seemond Stephens was back for this one, however, and he was simply devastating as he thundered to a six-ride maximum. Meanwhile, Adrian Newman supplied plenty of thrills on his way to a paid 17 haul as the Gulls collected a 49-41 success over a determined Hitmen outfit. Indeed, the visitors contained several youngsters, who would go on and grace the Premier League, including leading scorer Aidan Collins (12 points), as well as Adam Allott, Lee Smethills

Richard Ford.

and former Coventry mascot Mark Steel. The match was followed by another Bronze Helmet victory for Seemond, who hung on to defeat Aidan Collins after awkwardly locking up in mid-race.

A weekend of away action followed, beginning with a trip up to Heathersfield Stadium, the home of Linlithgow Lightning. The Scottish side had only gained two league points from eight matches, and the Gulls supporters probably expected a fairly comfortable success. However, it was to prove a day of difficulty and frustration for everyone connected with St Austell Speedway. Team manager Andy Annear had set off at 9.30am the day before, accompanied by Jason Prynne, Gary Lobb and Adrian Newman. The foursome went via Arena-Essex as Gary was riding for Exeter in a Knock-Out Cup match at the Purfleet circuit. After the match, the party reached their hotel, somewhere near Wolverhampton, at 3.30am. Following a short snooze, they set off again at 7.30am, but having got near to Preston on the M6, the van misfired and spluttered to a halt. It then took several hours to get the problem sorted, before they were on the road again. Andy worked out that they wouldn't reach Linlithgow until 3.30pm – an hour and a half after the scheduled start time, so he made some frantic calls to Lightning promoter Alan Robertson and meeting referee Jim McGregor.

It was decided that the meeting would have to go ahead, with the Gulls represented by four regulars who had made it, namely Seemond Stephens, Gary Phelps, Richard Ford and Martin Williams, with the addition of local juniors Gary Flint and Neil Stevenson. The rider replacement facility was operated for Gary Lobb, with Scottish Speedway enthusiast Jimmy McIntyre standing in as team manager. Despite their problems, the Gulls started well and held a narrow advantage all the way through until the latter stages. Perhaps the writing was on the wall after heat eleven, when home reserve Scott Courtney brilliantly cut through from the back to win after passing both 'Phelpsy' and Seemond. St Austell still held a 35-31 lead after that, but following a tapes exclusion for Rob Grant, the lively Scott Courtney then combined with David McAllan to inflict a maximum points win over Richard Ford and Gary Flint.

After early leader Seemond Stephens had tumbled out of heat thirteen, the overworked Courtney grabbed the crucial third spot behind Jonathan Swales and Gary Phelps to give the homesters the lead. Amazingly, Courtney then took a fourth consecutive ride and dashed to victory from Martin Williams, but with Derek Sneddon collecting the odd-point, Linlithgow took a four-point lead into the last heat. St Austell could still force a draw and the chance of that increased when David McAllan took a nasty fall and was excluded. It was at this point that Andy Annear and the boys finally arrived to find a car on the track, surrounded by riders and bystanders. 'Skippy' thought David McAllan had been the victim of some kind of road rage incident, but in actual fact, the ambulance was unable to get on the track, so the car was used to transport the injured rider back to the pits. Eventually, the re-run saw Seemond zip to victory, but with recently crowned Conference League Riders' Champion Jonathan Swales holding out Gary Phelps for second place, Linlithgow claimed a narrow 46-44 success. To compound a torrid day for the Gulls, Jonathan Swales then sped to victory over season-long Bronze Helmet holder Seemond, having taken the lead on the first turn.

So, it was immediately back on the road for Andy Annear and his intrepid crew, with the next stop being a hotel in Birmingham. After a good night's sleep, it was off to Mildenhall for the second leg of the Knock-Out Cup semi-final, and thankfully, there were no hiccups, with a full complement of riders making it to West Row in good time for the 3.30pm start. Seemond and 'Fordy' got the match underway with a 4-2, but there was controversy in the second heat, when Steve Camden was excluded for foul riding after Jason Prynne had ended up tangling with the pit bend fence. 'Prynner' and the Fen Tiger then became embroiled in an altercation, but after a bit of pushing and shoving, tempers cooled and racing was able to continue. After drawing level in heat seven, the homesters took the lead, but the Gulls dug deep and squared the match at 39 points apiece, courtesy of maximum points from Seemond and Gary Phelps in heat thirteen. Two shared races followed to leave a final score of 45-45, with St Austell progressing through to the final thanks to an aggregate victory by 97 points to 83. A magnificent 17 points from Barrie Evans headed the Fen Tigers challenge, while Garry Sweet scored a round dozen. Meanwhile for the Gulls, super Seemond returned a magical 15-point maximum, and Adrian Newman plundered 14+1 from a marathon seven ride stint. Having done all the hard work, the St Austell boys were then able to relax and watch the second half of the meeting, which saw Rye House beat Southampton 48-42 in a challenge match.

It was 50 years since speedway arrived at Par Moor, and Gulls promoter Brain Annear had hoped to stage a Golden Jubilee meeting on 24 August. The event was to feature vintage and classic speedway, vintage and 1000cc sidecar speedway, plus a stars of tomorrow event, however, morning rain showed no sign of abating and the celebration was unfortunately called off at lunchtime.

The following Saturday, it was on the road again as St Austell travelled up to Newport for a very important Conference League match. Having lost at home to the Welsh side at the beginning of the month, it was imperative that the Cornish boys produced the goods if they were to stand any chance of retaining the title they had won in 1998. A 4-2 from Seemond and Richard Ford was the perfect start, but the scores were level by heat three, after which the Mavericks moved ahead with maximum points from Graig Gough and Bobby Eldridge. Although the Gulls dug deep, they couldn't get back on terms and Newport ran out winners by 48 points to 42. In fairness, the Mavericks merited their success, as they possessed a super heat-leader trio in Chris Neath (13 points), Andrew Appleton (13) and Bobby Eldridge (10+2). As ever, the Gulls main scoring source was Seemond, who ended up with a 16 point tally from six starts. Newport's win left them on top of the league table, having attained a maximum 16 points from eight matches. Meanwhile, St Austell occupied second spot with 15 points, but having completed eleven meetings, their bid to retain the League Championship was lying in tatters.

August ended with Southampton Saints appearing at the Moto Parc for a challenge match. The famous old Saints had lost their Banister Court home at the close of the 1963 season, and they were appearing in a number of challenge matches throughout the year, with a view to possibly finding a new home base in the future. The match quickly developed into something of a one-sided affair, with the Gulls sweeping to a 58-

Wayne Barrett.

31 success led by 'Skippy' (14) and Seemond (13+1). For the welcome visitors, Chris Courage knocked up a useful 11 points, while both Chris Harris and Jay Stevens returned eight apiece.

On 5 September, a number of the Gulls partook in a charity grass-track meeting, held in memory of local sidecar racer Phil Pitman. Staged at South Tregleath Farm, Washaway, Bodmin, the event was organized by Carol Pitman and the Par 90 Grass-track Club, with the prime aim being to raise money for the Cornwall Air Ambulance. The meeting proved to be very successful, with popular Exeter speedway ace Mark Simmonds eventually emerging as the solo winner. Not only was the racing a roaring success, but, the charity also benefited greatly as a total of £2,500 was raised.

The Gulls were back in speedway action at the clay raceway on 7 September, when the Devon Demons returned for another challenge match. This was an altogether different proposition than the previous home meeting with Southampton, for the visitors' line-up was bolstered by the inclusion of Wayne Barrett, Chris Harris and Gary Phelps. Meanwhile, the Gulls utilized the rider replacement facility for Gary Lobb and gave juniors Adrian Rowe and Dominic Walsh-Newton their first run-out in the side. The match was always close and exciting, with never more than four-points separating the sides and a thrilling finish saw it end with honours even at 45-45. With a four-ride maximum, Seemond Stephens topped the homesters score-chart, while the Demons were ably led by 'Bomber' Harris (13+1) and Wayne Barrett (12). At the lower end of the Gulls scoring, neither Adrian Rowe or Dominic Walsh-Newton enjoyed the best of fortune, each suffering a fall on their way to paid 3 and paid 2 respectively. The meeting was followed by a match-race for the West Country Bronze Helmet, which saw Chris Harris scorch to victory from Martin Williams.

A week of inactivity followed, before the Moto Parc played host to the prestigious Cornish Grand National. The event had previously been known as the Cornish Grand Prix, but Brian Annear was no longer allowed to use the term 'Grand Prix'. The meeting was run over fifteen heats, plus a grand final and featured a dozen top stars, including Exeter Falcons' Michael Coles, Mark Simmonds, Wayne Barrett, Chris Harris and Peter Jeffery. Having won the event in 1997 and 1998, Mark Simmonds was very much the pre-meeting favourite, however, he surprisingly failed to make the final. Having scored 8 points from his first four rides, 'Simmo' fell and suffered exclusion in his last ride, thereby rendering him a spectator for the final. Meanwhile, with a 15-point maximum, Michael Coles sailed through, as did Seemond Stephens with an 11-point tally. A run-off was necessary to determine the last two slots, however, with Peter Jeffery and Roger Lobb subsequently progressing at the expense of Wayne Barrett. The first attempt to run the final was halted when both Seemond and 'Colesey' rolled into the tapes, with the Gulls favourite being deemed at fault and put back 15 yards. The Falcons top man made the most of his second chance, cantering to glory from the gate, with Roger Lobb passing Peter Jeffery in mid-race to claim the runner-up spot.

Having been postponed in August, the Golden Jubilee spectacular did go ahead on its rescheduled date of 21 September, when a whole host of events took place in celebration of the first speedway meeting at Par Moor in 1949. Top referee Graham Reeve was the man on the button for this one, and with such a lot to get through, he did a brilliant job at keeping things moving swiftly. The action packed evening saw Peter Clarke, mounted on a 1930 Rudge, take victory in the vintage speedway class, while top speedway race-jacket supplier Jock Davidson won the classic speedway event. Four heats of vintage sidecar speedway resulted in two wins for Justin Westaway, while Phil Williams and Ken Westaway each won a race apiece. There were also four heats of 1000cc sidecar speedway, with St Austell slipping to a 9-15 defeat at the hands of Bristol. On the conventional speedway front, a mini 'Stars of Tomorrow' tournament took place over seven heats, with a grand final for the top scorers. Jamie Holmes put together a tremendous display, winning all four of his heats, prior to taking victory in the final from Darren Hatton, Dominic Walsh-Newton and Adrian Rowe.

There was more racing at the Moto Parc on 26 September, with the staging of junior style challenge match between St Austell and Plymouth. Unfortunately, the meeting only got as far as the third heat, before heavy rain set in and the racing was brought to a premature close with the visitors holding a 12-6 advantage. It is worth noting that the Gulls line-up included Brian Bedford, who was the son of Stan, a former rider with Liverpool (1949-50), St Austell (1951), Plymouth (1953) and Rye House (1954-55).

A quiet period followed, before the Gulls returned to action at Newport on 16 October, in the first leg of the Knock-Out Cup final. The Mavericks had already wrapped up the Conference League Championship, so everyone was well aware of how difficult a task the tie was going to be. St Austell were bolstered by the inclusion of Wayne Barrett though, and it was something of an irony that the Cornishman's last Gulls appearance had been against Newport at the Moto Parc on 3 August. The Gulls were helped no end, when Chris Neath fell in the opening heat, with Seemond and 'Prynner' taking advantage to secure a 4-2. Newport had drawn level by heat three, before Bobby Eldridge and Jamie Holmes put them ahead in an eventful fourth race. Adrian Newman had been comfortably occupying second place, but a bold effort to snatch victory on the last bend, ended with the Aussie spectacularly mounting the safety fence. From then on, it was a case of the Gulls digging deep to restrict the Mavericks scoring as best they could. The homesters eventually managed to eke out a 52-38 success, but would their 14 point advantage be enough to defend in the second leg showdown? Andrew Appleton was the undoubted star of the afternoon, sweeping to a superlative 15 point full house for the Mavericks, while Nick Simmons (10+1), Bobby Eldridge (9+2) and Chris Neath (9) all chipped in with useful contributions. Meanwhile, as had become pretty much the norm in 1999, Seemond Stephens again topped the Gulls scoring with 14 points.

The St Austell boys were back on track the following afternoon, when they journeyed across country to King's Lynn for their last league match of the campaign. The home side were rooted at the foot of the table and although the Gulls guarded against complacency, they were extremely hopeful of an away win. Surprisingly, Peter Boast and David Nix gave the Braves a first heat 4-2, and they didn't actually fall behind until heat eight, when Adrian Newman and Jason Prynne combined to put the Gulls 25-23 to the good. Following that, it was fairly plain sailing as the Cornish side raced on to a 53-37 success, with Wayne Barrett thundering to an outstanding 16 point tally. Both 'Skippy' (13+2) and Seemond (13+1) also weighed in with telling contributions for the victors, while the Braves relied on Peter Boast (10+1) and Carl Wilkinson (9+1) for the bulk of their scoring. On a busy afternoon of racing, a second match pitched the Braves against Linlithgow, but matters didn't improve for the home side as they suffered another defeat by 44 points to 46.

There was great anticipation leading up to the second leg of the cup final against Newport, which took place on Sunday 24 October, with a 3pm start time. The Gulls put together their strongest possible side for the match, which meant no place for the previously ever-present Richard Ford. However, there was drama before the meeting, when Martin Williams failed to arrive and referee Barry Richardson would not permit the Gulls to utilize the rider replacement facility. In a bizarre twist of fate, the gap was plugged by Richard Ford, and the Devonian quickly proved he was the man for the job by following Seemond Stephens over the line for maximum points in heat one. The Gulls really meant business and by heat five, they had completely wiped out the advantage Newport brought into the contest.

The visitors produced some dogged resistance though, with the aggregate advantage fluctuating one way and then the other as the tie balanced on a knife's edge. However, maximum points from Seemond Stephens and flying reserve Adrian Newman in the tenth heat put the Gulls back in front by two-points on aggregate. The tension mounted as each of the next three heats were shared, before 'Skippy' was brought into the penultimate heat as a reserve replacement for Jason Prynne. The move worked a treat as Adrian sped to victory, and with Bobby Eldridge tumbling down on the third lap, Gary Phelps swept through to complete a cup winning 5-1. The final heat was purely academic, but a win for Seemond left a final result of 55-35, with the Gulls taking the aggregate victory by 93 points to 87. Helped and inspired by Ken Westaway in the pits, spectacular Aussie Adrian Newman was the hero of the hour, with his thrilling riding taking him to an astounding paid 19-point total. There was no doubting the wonderful contribution of 'Skippy', but it could have been a completely different story if his heat four antics in the first leg had ended in serious injury. All the Gulls were worthy of praise though, as with the match so closely contested each and every point was vital. The rest of the scorers were Seemond Stephens 14, Gary Phelps 8+2, Jason Prynne 5+1, Gary Lobb 4+1, Richard Ford 3+2 and Wayne Barrett 3+2. Great credit was due to the losing side, for they made it a wonderful tie overall and their tenacity in the second leg provided the crowd with real edge-of-the-seat excitement. The Mavericks main men on the day were the talented young duo of Chris Neath and Andrew Appleton, who notched 13 points and 12+1 respectively.

With the season completed, a look at the final Conference League table showed St Austell as the runners-up, with a record of eight wins and one draw from their twelve matches. With the inclusion of Knock-Out Cup matches, both Seemond Stephens and Richard Ford were ever-present in the Gulls sixteen official fixtures, and the former was streets ahead in the side's scoring stakes, storming to an incredible total of 226 points for an average of 10.90. Seemond also weighed in with 7 full and 2 paid maximums, but it wasn't all about the fast-starting no.1, as three other riders boasted averages in excess of eight, namely Wayne Barrett (8.39), Adrian Newman (8.33) and Gary Lobb (8.07).

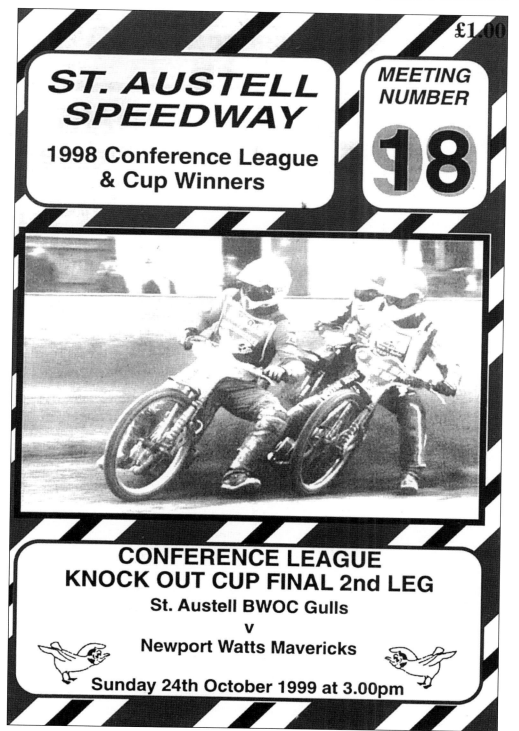

£1.00

ST. AUSTELL SPEEDWAY
1998 Conference League & Cup Winners

MEETING NUMBER 18

CONFERENCE LEAGUE
KNOCK OUT CUP FINAL 2nd LEG
St. Austell BWOC Gulls
v
Newport Watts Mavericks
Sunday 24th October 1999 at 3.00pm

1999 Knock-Out Cup final programme, v. Newport.

With figures like those, it was baffling that St Austell failed to lift the Championship, but it was those two defeats at the hands of Newport that proved crucial.

Of the other lads who proudly donned a Gulls race-jacket, Gary Phelps was the most impressive and did well to attain a 7.52 average from six late-season appearances. Nicknamed 'Millhouse' by promoter Brian Annear, Gloucester youngster Martin Williams produced several top-notch performances, including a paid maximum at home to Rye House and posted a useful 6.69 figure. Truro born Jason Prynne plugged away throughout the campaign for a 5.67 average; incredibly this was exactly the same figure he had achieved the previous year! Richard Ford averaged 4.76 and chipped in with several useful contributions, exemplified by that heat one ride in the home leg of the cup final. Three other riders contributed to the season, with Kevin Phillips making four appearances as and when required, while Gary Flint and Neil Stevenson helped to plug the gaps in the side as mentioned previously at Linlithgow.

Off track, things improved crowd-wise, although local folk obviously preferred the cut and thrust of league and cup matches, compared with the filler-type challenge

The Gulls celebrate their Knock Out Cup success. From left to right, back row: Wayne Barrett, Richard Ford, Gary Lobb, Andy Annear (team manager), Jason Prynne, Gary Phelps and Adrian Newman. Front row: Gerry Sims (mascot) and Seemond Stephens.

meetings. Crowds had been huge in 1997, and dipped alarmingly the following year, but in 1999 they were generally much healthier. The usual rumours did the rounds about the possibility of Premier League racing at the Moto Parc, but with the added cost of admission and wages being generally low in Cornwall, this was set to remain an unrealistic dream, at least until 2001....

The Presentation Evening again took place at St Stephen Community Centre, although much later in the year than previously, on 26 November, when Dave Stallworthy was again in place as the Master of Ceremonies. After his terrific track exploits throughout the season, Seemond Stephens deservedly ended the night with a treble of trophies, for having been voted rider of the year and collecting the Eustace Cup, he was also presented with the BWOC Memorial Trophy and the Phillips Cup. Meanwhile, for the second successive year, Adrian Newman picked up the Huddy & Kneebone Cup for being the most exciting rider, and in a popular double triumph, the Australian also took the W. Vivian Cup. That left the Cornwall Motorcycle Dealers' Trophy and in recognition of his wholehearted efforts, Jason Prynne was presented with the award.

Sunday 9 May, 1999 – ECCI White Gold Four Team Tournament
ST.AUSTELL 11, BRISTOL 4, EXETER 16, PLYMOUTH 10
Meeting abandoned after Heat-7

ST.AUSTELL

Wayne Barrett	3 - - - - -	3
Jason Prynne R/R	- - - - - -	-
Richard Ford	2 2 - - - -	4
Simon Phillips	2 2 - - - -	4

BRISTOL

Jamie Holmes	0 1 - - - -	1
Gavin Horsborough	F 0 - - - -	1
Greg Daniels	2 X - - - -	2
Ray Dickson	1 - - - - -	1

EXETER

Mark Simmonds	3 3 - - - -	6
Gary Lobb	1 1 3 - - -	5
Chris Harris	3 - - - - -	3
Kevin Phillips	2 - - - - -	2

PLYMOUTH

Adrian Newman	1 3 - - - -	4
Michael Coles	3 - - - - -	3
Martin Williams	2 1 - - - -	3
Bob Coles	0 X - - - -	0

PROGRAMME CHANGES:-
None!

Note: Rained off from the previous day, this meeting was abandoned after Heat-7, due to an injury sustained by Greg Daniels. Following a track crash, Daniels was subsequently flown to hospital by air ambulance.

		S.A	Br	Ex	Pl
Ht 1	M.Coles, S.Phillips, Lobb, Holmes, 57.68	2	0	1	3
Ht 2	Harris, Ford, Newman, Horsborough (fell), 56.94	4	0	4	4
Ht 3	Simmonds, Williams, Dickson, 57.41 (3 Riders Only)	4	1	7	6
Ht 4	Barrett, Daniels, Lobb, B.Coles, 59.25	7	3	8	6
Ht 5	(Awarded) Simmonds, S.Phillips, Holmes, B.Coles (ex, obstructing track), No Time	9	4	11	6
Ht 6	Lobb, Ford, Williams, Horsborough, 58.12	11	4	14	7
Ht 7	(Re-Run Awarded) Newman, K.Phillips, Daniels (f,ex), No Time (3 Riders Only)	11	4	16	10

Despite operating rider-replacement for Jason Prynne, St.Austell did not track a rider in either Heat-3 or 7

Sunday 9 May, 1999
WHITE GOLD/G.T.MOTORCYCLES SOLO MASTERS

Wayne Barrett	3 2 2 1 2 - -	10
Jason Prynne	2 2 1 1 2 - -	8
Richard Ford	0 2 1 2 3 - -	8
Adrian Newman	1 3 2 3 R - -	9
Michael Coles	3 3 3 3 2 - -	14
Bob Coles	0 1 1 1 - - -	3
Martin Williams	1 1 3 0 3 - -	8
Gary Lobb	2 2 2 2 3 - -	11
Ray Dickson	1 1 0 0 - - -	2
Gavin Horsborough	0 0 1 X 0 - -	1
Chris Harris	3 3 3 3 1 - -	13
Simon Phillips	2 R 2 2 2 - -	8
Jamie Holmes	1 0 0 0 X - -	1
Mark Simmonds	3 3 3 3 3 - -	15
Kevin Phillips	2 0 0 2 1 - -	5
Greg Daniels	- - - - - - -	-

PROGRAMME CHANGES:-
None!

Notes: With Scheduled riders Roger Lobb, Andy Carfield and Chris Dix not partaking, meeting reserves Gavin Horsborough and Jamies Holmes moved into the main meeting, with Bob Coles also stepping in. As a result, following Greg Daniels' accident in the 4-Team Tournament, there was no replacement for any of his rides, while Ray Dickson (Heat-18) and Bob Coles (Heat-19) also missed rides without replacement.

1st MARK SIMMONDS 15-pts;
2nd MICHAEL COLES 14-pts; 3rd CHRIS HARRIS 13-pts

Ht 1	Barrett, Prynne, Newman, Ford, 57.84
Ht 2	M.Coles, Lobb, Williams, B.Coles, 57.82
Ht 3	Harris, S.Phillips, Dickson, Horsborough, 56.97
Ht 4	Simmonds, K.Phillips, Holmes, 56.69 (3 Riders Only)
Ht 5	M.Coles, Barrett, Dickson, Holmes, 57.20
Ht 6	Simmonds, Prynne, B.Coles, Horsborough, 57.94
Ht 7	Harris, Ford, Williams, K.Phillips, 56.90
Ht 8	Newman, Lobb, S.Phillips (ret), 59.35 (3 Riders Only)
Ht 9	Harris, Barrett, B.Coles, 59.16 (3 Riders Only)
Ht 10	M.Coles, S.Phillips, Prynne, K.Phillips, 58.25
Ht 11	Simmonds, Lobb, Ford, Dickson, 58.07
Ht 12	Williams, Newman, Horsborough, Holmes, 58.50
Ht 13	Simmonds, S.Phillips, Barrett, Williams, 57.56
Ht 14	(Re-Run) Harris, Lobb, Prynne, Holmes, 58.60
Ht 15	(Awarded) M.Coles, Ford, Horsborough (f,ex), No Time (3 Riders Only)
Ht 16	Newman, B.Coles, K.Phillips, Harris, 61.56
Ht 17	Lobb, Barrett, K.Phillips, Horsborough, 58.12
Ht 18	Williams, Prynne, 59.69 (2 Riders Only)
Ht 19	(Awarded) Ford, S.Phillips, Holmes (f,ex), No Time (3 Riders Only)
Ht 20	Simmonds, M.Coles, Harris, Newman (ret), 59.37

Tuesday 25 May, 1999 – International Challenge Match
ST.AUSTELL 'GULLS' 36 ENGLAND UNDER-19's 54

ST.AUSTELL

Rider	Scores	Total
Roger Lobb	2 3 1 3 2 - -	11
Kevin Phillips	0 0 F 0 - - -	0
Gary Lobb	3 2 1 3 - - -	9
Jason Prynne	1 0 0 1 - - -	2
Wayne Barrett	0 1 1 1 - - -	3
Adrian Newman	1 0 0 0 - - -	1
Seemond Stephens	3 1 3 2'1'- -	10 2

ENGLAND U-19's

Rider	Scores	Total
David Howe	3 3 3 R - - -	9
Marc Norris R/R	- - - - - - -	-
Paul Lee	2 2'3 0 - - -	7 1
Chris Neath	1 0 3 2'3 R -	9 1
Simon Stead	3 2 3 2 3 - -	13
Nick Simmons	2 1 1'2 2'1 -	9 2
Chris Harris	X 2'1'2'2'- -	7 4

PROGRAMME CHANGES:-
Ht 1: R/R Neath; Ht 5: R/R Simmons; Ht 8: R/R Simmons; Ht 11: R/R Harris

	Gulls	Eng
Ht 1 Howe, R.Lobb, Neath, Phillips, 55.41	2	4
Ht 2 (Re-Run) Stephens, Simmons, Newman, Harris (ex, foul riding), 56.90	6	6
Ht 3 G.Lobb, Lee, Prynne, Neath, 58.22	10	8
Ht 4 Stead, Harris, Stephens, Barrett, 56.00	11	13
Ht 5 Howe, G.Lobb, Simmons, Prynne, 55.05	13	17
Ht 6 R.Lobb, Stead, Simmons, Phillips, 56.80	16	20
Ht 7 Neath, Lee, Barrett, Newman, 57.30	17	25
Ht 8 Stephens, Simmons, Harris, Phillips (fell), 56.78	20	28
Ht 9 Stead, Simmons, G.Lobb, Prynne, 56.19	21	33
Ht 10 Lee, Neath, R.Lobb, Phillips, 56.97	22	38
Ht 11 Howe, Harris, Barrett, Newman, 56.07	23	43
Ht 12 G.Lobb, Stephens, Simmons, Lee, 57.60	28	44
Ht 13 R.Lobb, Stead, Barrett, Howe (ret), 56.60	32	46
Ht 14 Neath, Harris, Prynne, Newman, 58.13	33	51
Ht 15 (Nominated) Stead, R.Lobb, Stephens, Neath (ret), 56.70	36	54

Tuesday 1 June, 1999
SIMPSON PLANT HIRE INDIVIDUAL CHALLENGE

Rider	Scores	Total
Wayne Barrett	3 0 3 3 - - -	9
Patrice Deloubes	0 1 1 0 - - -	2
Kevin Phillips	2 F F 1 - - -	3
Gary Phelps	1 3 X 2 - - -	6
Jason Prynne	2 1 2 3 - - -	8
Rob Hayward	R 2 M - - - -	2
Martin Williams	1 2 2 1 - - -	6
Adrian Newman	3 2 3 2 - - -	10
Seemond Stephens	3 3 3 3 - - -	12
Simon Phillips	2 3 2 X - - -	7
Ray Dickson	1 X R 1 - - -	2
Gavin Horsborough	0 1 1 2 - - -	4

PROGRAMME CHANGES:-
None!

Note: Rob Hayward was excluded from Heat-9 and wasn't replaced. The same rider also missed out on Heat-12, and again, wasn't replaced. Scheduled B and C Finals were not staged due to rain.

1st ADRIAN NEWMAN; 2nd WAYNE BARRETT
Note: There was no third place as only two riders finished

Ht 1	Barrett, K.Phillips, Phelps, Deloubes, 57.53
Ht 2	Newman, Prynne, Williams, Hayward (ret), 57.74
Ht 3	Stephens, S.Phillips, Dickson, Horsborough, 57.97
Ht 4	S.Phillips, Newman, Prynne, Barrett, 59.00
Ht 5	Stephens, Williams, Deloubes, K.Phillips (fell), 60.60
Ht 6	(Re-Run) Phelps, Hayward, Horsborough, Dickson (f,ex), 60.34
Ht 7	Barrett, Prynne, Deloubes, Dickson (ret), 59.57
Ht 8	Newman, Williams, Horsborough, K.Phillips (fell), 57.17
Ht 9	(Re-Run) Stephens, S.Phillips, Phelps (f,ex), Hayward (ex, 2 mins), 60.44 (3 Riders Only)
Ht 10	Stephens, Newman, Dickson, Deloubes, 60.69
Ht 11	(Re-Run) Prynne, Phelps, Williams, S.Phillips (f,ex), 61.75
Ht 12	Barrett, Horsborough, K.Phillips, 73.03 (3 Riders Only)
Ht 13	(A Final – Re-Run) Newman, Barrett, Stephens (f,ex), Prynne (ex, not under power), 63.78

Tuesday 8 June, 1999 – Conference League
ST.AUSTELL 'GULLS' 47 MILDENHALL 'FEN TIGERS' 43

ST.AUSTELL

Gary Lobb R/R	- - - - - -	-
Jason Prynne	R2 R0 - - -	2
Seemond Stephens	3 3 3 3 3 3 -	18
Martin Williams	2¹1 0 3 - -	6 1
Wayne Barrett	2 3 2 1 2¹2 -	12 1
Kevin Phillips	M0 n - - - -	0
Adrian Newman	3 0 1 1 2¹0 -	7 1
Richard Ford (No.8)	2 R - - - - -	2

MILDENHALL

Garry Sweet	3 2 3 2 1 - -	11
Gavin Hedge R/R	- - - - - -	-
Simon Phillips	1 2 3 2 1 - -	9
Peter Johnson	0 0 1 1¹X - - -	1 1
Dean Garrod	3 3 2 0 0 3 -	11
Mark Thompson	1 2 1 1¹X - -	5 1
Ricky Scarboro	1¹1 2¹1 1 - -	6 2
Chris Sweet (No.8)	- - - - - - -	-

PROGRAMME CHANGES:-
Ht 1: R/R Ford; R/R Thompson; Ht 5: R/R Johnson; Ht 6: R/R Ford; Ht 8: R/R G.Sweet; Ht 10: R/R Barrett; Scarboro replaced Johnson; Ht 11: T/S Stephens for K.Phillips; R/R Garrod; Ht 13: R/R Stephens; Ht 14: Newman replaced K.Phillips, who was unable to partake in the re-run

		Gulls	Mild
Ht 1	G.Sweet, Ford, Thompson, Prynne (ret), 58.56	2	4
Ht 2	Newman, Thompson, Scarboro, K.Phillips (ex, 2 mins), 60.00 (3 Riders Only)	5	7
Ht 3	Stephens, Williams, S.Phillips, Johnson, 56.87	10	8
Ht 4	Garrod, Barrett, Scarboro, Newman, 58.37	12	12
Ht 5	Stephens, G.Sweet, Williams, Johnson, 57.13	16	14
Ht 6	Garrod, Prynne, Thompson (f,rem), Ford (ret), 59.63	18	18
Ht 7	Barrett, S.Phillips, Johnson, K.Phillips, 57.60	21	21
Ht 8	G.Sweet, Scarboro, Newman, Prynne (ret), 59.19	22	26
Ht 9	Stephens, Garrod, Thompson, Williams, 58.82	25	29
Ht 10	S.Phillips, Barrett, Scarboro, Prynne, 58.00	27	33
Ht 11	Stephens, G.Sweet, Barrett, Garrod, 57.62	31	35
Ht 12	(Re-Run) Stephens, S.Phillips, Newman, Thompson (f,ex), 58.06	35	37
Ht 13	Stephens, Barrett, G.Sweet, Garrod, 60.38	40	38
Ht 14	(Re-Run) Williams, Newman, Scarboro, Johnson (f,ex), K.Phillips (f,ns), 60.12	45	39
Ht 15	(Nominated) Garrod, Barrett, S.Phillips, Newman, 59.87	47	43
	Bronze Helmet: Stephens, Garrod, 59.70		

Tuesday 15 June, 1999
FRED PAUL BEST PAIRS

Seemond Stephens	4 4 4 3 - - -	15
Ray Dickson	0 2 2 2¹ - - -	6 1
Jason Prynne	3 3 4 3 - - -	13
Richard Ford	2¹2¹2¹3¹2¹ - - -	9 4
Wayne Barrett R/R	4 4 3 4 - - -	15
Ian Leverington	F 2 0 0 - - -	2
Adrian Newman	3 F - - - - -	3
Jamie Holmes	2¹3 2 3 - - -	10 1
Martin Williams	3 4 4 4 - - -	15
Gavin Horsborough	0 0 0 2 - - -	2

PROGRAMME CHANGES:-
Ht 2: R/R Williams; Ht 3: R/R Prynne; Ht 4: R/R Newman; Ht 9: R/R Stephens; Ht 13: R/R Holmes

Notes: Rather confusingly, rider-replacement was operated for Wayne Barrett with members of other pairings taking rides in turn! Adrian Newman was a non-starter in Heats-8 & 10 and was not replaced in either. Seemond Stephens (in Heats-7 & 9) and Martin Williams (in Heat-10) were handicapped after touching the tapes. Stephens' first offence saw him penalised 25-yards, but the subsequent handicaps were only measured at 20-yards.

1st JASON PRYNNE & RICHARD FORD
2nd SEEMOND STEPHENS & RAY DICKSON
3rd MARTIN WILLIAMS & GAVIN HORSBOROUGH

Ht 1	Stephens, Prynne, Ford, Dickson, 58.4
Ht 2	Williams, Newman, Holmes, Leverington (fell), 59.9
Ht 3	Prynne, Williams, Leverington, Horsborough, 58.2
Ht 4	Stephens, Newman, Dickson, Leverington, 56.0
Ht 5	Williams, Prynne, Ford, Horsborough, 57.4
Ht 6	Stephens, Holmes, Dickson, Newman (fell), 58.2
Ht 7	(Re-Run) Williams, Stephens (25 yards), Dickson, Horsborough, 57.6
Ht 8	Prynne, Ford, Holmes, 61.2 (3 Riders Only)
Ht 9	(Re-Run) Stephens (20 yards), Prynne, Ford, Leverington, 58.8
Ht 10	(Re-Run) Williams (20 yards), Holmes, Horsborough, 61.2 (3 Riders Only)
Ht 11	(Semi-Final) Prynne, Williams, Ford, Horsborough (fell), 59.0
Ht 12	(Semi-Final) Dickson, Stephens, Holmes, Leverington, 60.8
Ht 13	(3rd Place Run-Off) Williams, Holmes, Horsborough, Leverington, 60.4
Ht 14	(Grand Final) Stephens, Prynne, Ford, Dickson, 59.3

Notes: Points were awarded thus:- 1st 4-points; 2nd 3-points; 3rd 2-points; 4th 0-points. Times were given to one decimal point only.

Tuesday 22 June, 1999 – Conference League
ST.AUSTELL 'GULLS' 67 RYE HOUSE 'ROCKETS' 23

ST.AUSTELL

Gary Lobb	2 3 2'2'- - -	9	2
Jason Prynne	1'2'2 3 - - -	8	2
Seemond Stephens	3 3 3 3 3 - -	15	
Martin Williams	2'2'2'2'3 2'- -	11	4
Wayne Barrett	2 3 3 3 - - -	11	
Richard Ford	2'2'0 2'1 - -	7	3
Adrian Newman	3 1'T 2'- - -	6	2

RYE HOUSE

Simon Wolstenholme	3 3 F 3 R 1 -	10	
Steven Eaves	0 1 1 - - - -	2	
Peter Collyer	1 X 1 R 0 - -	2	
Ian Clarke	0 0 R R - - -	0	
Jamie Barton R/R	- - - - - - -	-	
Simon Moon	1 1 1 1 1 0 1	6	
Simon Phillips	0 0 1 2 R - -	3	

PROGRAMME CHANGES:-
Ht 4: R/R Wolstenholme; Ht 6: R/R Collyer; Ht 7: Moon replaced Collyer; Ht 8: T/S Wolstenholme for Eaves; Ford replaced Newman in the re-run; Ht 9: R/R Clarke; Ht 13: T/S Collyer for R/R; Ht 14: Moon replaced Clarke

		Gulls	RH
Ht 1	Wolstenholme, Lobb, Prynne, Eaves, 57.46	3	3
Ht 2	Newman, Ford, Moon, Phillips, 56.72	8	4
Ht 3	Stephens, Williams, Collyer, Clarke, 56.81	13	5
Ht 4	Wolstenholme, Barrett, Newman, Phillips, 57.09	16	8
Ht 5	Stephens, Williams, Eaves, Wolstenholme (fell), 57.63	21	9
Ht 6	(Re-Run) Lobb, Prynne, Moon, Collyer (f,ex), 58.47	26	10
Ht 7	Barrett, Ford, Moon, Clarke, 57.34	31	11
Ht 8	(Re-Run) Wolstenholme, Prynne, Phillips, Ford, Newman (ex, tapes), 56.68	33	15
Ht 9	Stephens, Williams, Moon, Clarke (ret), 57.28	38	16
Ht 10	Prynne, Lobb, Collyer, Clarke (ret), 59.00	43	17
Ht 11	Barrett, Ford, Eaves, Wolstenholme (f,rem, ret), 58.37	48	18
Ht 12	Stephens, Newman, Moon, Collyer (ret), 57.69	53	19
Ht 13	Barrett, Lobb, Wolstenholme, Collyer, 58.12	58	20
Ht 14	Williams, Phillips, Ford, Moon, 58.59	62	22
Ht 15	(Nominated) Stephens, Williams, Moon, Phillips (ret), 58.84	67	23
	Bronze Helmet: Stephens, Wolstenholme, 58.21		

Tuesday 29 June, 1999 – Southern Challenge Shield
ST.AUSTELL 'GULLS' 44 BRISTOL 'BULLDOGS' 49

ST.AUSTELL

Seemond Stephens	2 3 2 3 2 1 -	13	
Martin Williams	1'1'0 1 - - -	3	2
Gary Lobb	1'1'F 2 - - - -	3	1
Jason Prynne	2 1 2 3 0 - -	8	
Wayne Barrett	2 3 R 0 - - -	5	
Richard Ford	2'1 1 2'- - -	6	2
Adrian Newman	3 1'1 1'- - -	6	2

BRISTOL

Steve Bishop	3 2 6 2'3 3 -	19	1
Patrice Deloubes R/R	- - - - - - -	-	
Frank Smart	3 R 2 2 3 - -	10	
Gordon Meakins	0 R R R 1 - -	1	
Roger Lobb	3 3 2'3 3 1 2'	17	2
Gary Fawdrey	1 0 1 0 X - -	2	
Rob Hayward	0 0 - - - - -	0	

PROGRAMME CHANGES:-
Ht 1: R/R Meakins; Ht 5: Stephens replaced G.Lobb; R/R Smart; Ht 8: Golden Double T/S Bishop for R/R; T/S R.Lobb for Hayward; Ht 11: R/R R.Lobb; Ht 14: Fawdrey replaced Hayward

Note: After a tapes infringement in Heat-15, Seemond Stephens partook in the re-run off a 15-yard handicap

		Gulls	Bris
Ht 1	Bishop, Stephens, Williams, Meakins, 55.66	3	3
Ht 2	Newman, Ford, Fawdrey, Hayward, 56.56	8	4
Ht 3	Smart, Prynne, G.Lobb, Meakins (ret), 55.12	11	7
Ht 4	R.Lobb, Barrett, Newman, Hayward, 56.69	14	10
Ht 5	Stephens, Bishop, Prynne, Smart (ret), 56.03	18	12
Ht 6	R.Lobb, Stephens, Williams, Fawdrey, 57.10	21	15
Ht 7	Barrett, Smart, Ford, Meakins (ret), 57.56	25	17
Ht 8	Bishop (GD), R.Lobb, Newman, Williams, 56.35	26	25
Ht 9	R.Lobb, Prynne, Fawdrey, G.Lobb (fell), 57.15	28	29
Ht 10	Stephens, Smart, Williams, Meakins (ret), 55.44	32	31
Ht 11	R.Lobb, Bishop, Ford, Barrett (ret), 55.97	33	36
Ht 12	Smart, G.Lobb, Newman, Fawdrey, 55.85	36	39
Ht 13	Bishop, Stephens, R.Lobb, Barrett, 56.06	38	43
Ht 14	(Awarded) Prynne, Ford, Meakins, Fawdrey (f,ex), No Time	43	44
Ht 15	(Nominated – Re-Run) Bishop, R.Lobb, Stephens (15-yards), Prynne, 56.00	44	49

Tuesday 6 July, 1999 – Conference League
ST.AUSTELL 'GULLS' 59 LINLITHGOW 'LIGHTNING' 31

ST.AUSTELL

Seemond Stephens	3 3 3 3 3 - -	15	
Martin Williams	2'1 0 2'- - -	5	2
Gary Lobb	3 3 3 2'2'- -	13	2
Jason Prynne	X 1 1 1'- - -	3	1
Wayne Barrett	2'3 3 1 - - -	9	1
Richard Ford	1 1 1 2 - - -	5	
Adrian Newman	0 3 3 3 - - -	9	

LINLITHGOW

Jonathan Swales	1 2 2 0 0 - -	5	
David McAllan R/R	- - - - - - -	-	
Scott Courtney	0 2 2 1 1 T -	6	
Robert McNeil	1'R X - - - -	1	1
Steven Jones	0 2 2 2 2 3 1	12	
Ryan Millburn	3 0 0 0 0 0 -	3	
Rob Grant	2'1 1'X - - -	4	2

PROGRAMME CHANGES:-
Ht 1: R/R Courtney; Ht 5: R/R Millburn; Ht 8: R/R Swales; Ht 11: R/R Jones; Ht 14: T/S Jones for McNeil; Ht 15: Millburn replaced Courtney in the re-run

		Gulls	Lin
Ht 1	Stephens, Williams, Swales, Courtney, 58.10	5	1
Ht 2	Millburn, Grant, Ford, Newman, 59.03	6	6
Ht 3	Lobb, Courtney, McNeil, Prynne (ex, crossed white line), 59.63	9	9
Ht 4	Newman, Barrett, Grant, Jones, 56.44	14	10
Ht 5	Lobb, Swales, Prynne, Millburn, 58.78	18	12
Ht 6	Stephens, Jones, Williams, Millburn, 57.53	22	14
Ht 7	Barrett, Courtney, Ford, McNeil (ret), 59.22	26	16
Ht 8	Newman, Swales, Grant, Williams, 57.96	29	19
Ht 9	Lobb, Jones, Prynne, Millburn, 59.62	33	21
Ht 10	(Re-Run) Stephens, Williams, Courtney, McNeil (f,ex), 59.44	38	22
Ht 11	Barrett, Jones, Ford, Swales (f,rem), 59.06	42	24
Ht 12	Newman, Lobb, Courtney, Millburn, 58.06	47	25
Ht 13	Stephens, Jones, Barrett, Swales, 57.97	51	27
Ht 14	(Awarded) Jones, Ford, Prynne, Grant (f,ex), No Time	54	30
Ht 15	(Nominated – Re-Run) Stephens, Lobb, Jones, Millburn, Courtney (ex, tapes), 58.59	59	31
	Bronze Helmet: Stephens, Jones, 57.69		

Tuesday 13 July, 1999 – West Country Cup
ST.AUSTELL 'GULLS' 50 SOMERSET 'REBELS' 40

ST.AUSTELL

Seemond Stephens	3 3 3 3 3 - -	15	
Martin Williams	0 1 R 1 - - -	2	
Gary Lobb	X 3 3 2 - - -	8	
Jason Prynne	1 1 0 2 - - -	4	
Wayne Barrett	3 1 3 - - - -	7	
Richard Ford	1 0 1 1'- - -	3	1
Adrian Newman	3 2 2'3 1'0 2'-	11	3

SOMERSET

Gary Phelps	2 2 2 1'- - -	7	1
Jay Stevens	1'0 1'0 - - -	2	2
Danny Bird	3 3 R 3 2 - -	11	
Glen Phillips	2'2'2 3 1 - -	10	2
Simon Phillips	0 2 2 0 - - -	4	
Chris Harris	R R 1'0 - - -	1	1
Mark Phillips	2 1 2 0 - - -	5	

PROGRAMME CHANGES:-
Ht 13: Newman replaced Barrett; T/S Bird for S.Phillips

		Gulls	Som
Ht 1	Stephens, Phelps, Stevens, Williams, 57.75	3	3
Ht 2	Newman, M.Phillips, Ford, Harris (ret), 56.71	7	5
Ht 3	Bird, G.Phillips, Prynne, Lobb (ex, foul riding), 58.35	8	10
Ht 4	Barrett, Newman, M.Phillips, S.Phillips, 58.81	13	11
Ht 5	Lobb, Phelps, Prynne, Stevens, 59.53	17	13
Ht 6	Stephens, S.Phillips, Williams, Harris (ret), 61.03	21	15
Ht 7	Bird, G.Phillips, Barrett, Ford, 58.25	22	20
Ht 8	Newman, M.Phillips, Stevens, Williams (ret), 57.75	25	23
Ht 9	Lobb, S.Phillips, Harris, Prynne, 58.65	28	26
Ht 10	Stephens, G.Phillips, Williams, Bird (f,rem, ret), 58.59	32	28
Ht 11	Barrett, Phelps, Ford, Stevens, 58.25	36	30
Ht 12	Bird, Lobb, Newman, Harris, 58.00	39	33
Ht 13	Stephens, Bird, Phelps, Newman, 57.86	42	36
Ht 14	G.Phillips, Prynne, Ford, M.Phillips, 58.66	45	39
Ht 15	(Nominated) Stephens, Newman, G.Phillips, S.Phillips, 57.81	50	40

Tuesday 20 July, 1999 – Conference League
ST.AUSTELL 'GULLS' 61 KING'S LYNN 'BRAVES' 29

ST.AUSTELL

Gary Lobb R/R	- - - - - -	-	
Jason Prynne	2'3 3 3 - - -	11	1
Seemond Stephens	3 3 3 3 3 - -	15	
Kevin Phillips	1 1 2'R X - -	4	1
Martin Williams	3 2'1'3 2 - -	11	2
Richard Ford	2'2 2'1 1 - -	8	2
Adrian Newman	3 3 X 2'2'2'-	12	3
Adrian Rowe (No.8)	- - - - - -	-	

KING'S LYNN

Freddie Stephenson	0 X 3 2 3 3 X	11	
David Nix	1 2 1 1 0 - -	5	
Peter Boast R/R	- - - - - -	-	
Darren Hatton	R 0 0 - - - -	0	
Les Rowlands	1 1'0 1 - - -	3	1
Luke Clifton	1 2 2 1 1 2'1	10	1
Mark Phillips	0 R R R - - -	0	
Oliver Hackett (No.8)	- - - - - -	-	

PROGRAMME CHANGES:-
Ht 1: R/R Williams; Ht 3: R/R Clifton; Ht 6: R/R Newman; Ht 7: R/R Stephenson; Ht 10: R/R Ford; R/R Nix; Ht 12: R/R M.Phillips; Ht 13: R/R K.Phillips; Ht 14: T/S Stephenson for Hatton; Clifton replaced M.Phillips

		Gulls	KL
Ht 1	Williams, Prynne, Nix, Stephenson (f,rem), 57.41	5	1
Ht 2	Newman, Ford, Clifton, M.Phillips, 57.28	10	2
Ht 3	Stephens, Clifton, K.Phillips, Hatton (ret), 59.75	14	4
Ht 4	Newman, Williams, Rowlands (f,rem), M.Phillips (ret), 57.60	19	5
Ht 5	(Re-Run) Stephens, Nix, K.Phillips, Stephenson (ex, foul riding), 57.81	23	7
Ht 6	(Awarded) Prynne, Clifton, Rowlands, Newman (f,ex), No Time	26	10
Ht 7	Stephenson, Ford, Williams, Hatton (f,rem), 60.07	29	13
Ht 8	Prynne, Newman, Nix, M.Phillips (ret), 60.34	34	14
Ht 9	Stephens, K.Phillips, Clifton, Rowlands, 58.16	39	15
Ht 10	Prynne, Ford, Nix, Hatton, 59.78	44	16
Ht 11	Williams, Stephenson, Ford, Nix, 58.91	48	18
Ht 12	Stephens, Newman, Clifton, M.Phillips (ret), 57.50	53	19
Ht 13	Stephenson, Williams, Rowlands, K.Phillips (ret), 59.35	55	23
Ht 14	(Awarded) Stephenson, Clifton, Ford, K.Phillips (f,ex), No Time	56	28
Ht 15	(Nominated - Re-Run) Stephens, Newman, Clifton, Stephenson (f,ex), 58.28	61	29
	Bronze Helmet: Stephens, Clifton, 59.78		

Sunday 25 July, 1999 – J & A Supporters' Trophy
ST.AUSTELL 'GULLS' 49 CLUB CRADLEY HEATH 41

ST.AUSTELL

Seemond Stephens	3 2 3 3 2'- -	13	1
Martin Williams	0 1'1'0 - - -	2	2
Gary Lobb	3 3 2 3 3 - -	14	
Jason Prynne	1 2'1'1'2 - -	6	2
Wayne Barrett	1'2 3 1 - - -	7	1
Richard Ford	1 R 2'0 - - -	3	1
Adrian Newman	X 2 2 R - - -	4	

CLUB CRADLEY HEATH

Dean Garrod	1'0 1 0 - - -	2	1
Phil Knowles	2 0 0 1 - - -	3	
Gary Phelps	2 1 1'1'1 - -	6	2
Steve Camden R/R	- - - - - -	-	
Chris Harris	3 3 3 3 2 3 1	18	
Gordon Meakins	2'0 0 0 - - -	2	1
Steve Camden	3 F 3 2 2 0 -	10	
Ashley Holloway (No.8)	- - - - - -	-	

PROGRAMME CHANGES:-
Ht 3: R/R Garrod; Ht 7: R/R Harris; Ht 10: R/R Camden; Ht 12: Camden replaced Meakins; Ht 13: Meakins replaced Garrod; Ht 14: R/R Phelps; T/S Harris for Camden

Club Cradley Heath originally had Simon Phillips programmed at no.7, but in the event, he was unavailable. Therefore, as it wasn't an official meeting, referee Barry Richardson allowed them to plug the gap in the side by operating rider-replacement for Steve Camden at no.4, while Camden himself rode at no.7!

		Gulls	Crad
Ht 1	Stephens, Knowles, Garrod, Williams, 57.69	3	3
Ht 2	(Re-Run) Camden, Meakins, Ford, Newman (f,ex), 59.82	4	8
Ht 3	Lobb, Phelps, Prynne, Garrod, 59.50	8	10
Ht 4	Harris, Newman, Barrett, Camden (fell), 56.69	11	13
Ht 5	Lobb, Prynne, Garrod, Knowles, 58.06	16	14
Ht 6	Harris, Stephens, Williams, Meakins, 56.84	19	17
Ht 7	Harris, Barrett, Phelps, Ford (ret), 59.03	21	21
Ht 8	Camden, Newman, Williams, Knowles, 59.56	24	24
Ht 9	Harris, Lobb, Prynne, Meakins, 58.12	27	27
Ht 10	Stephens, Camden, Phelps, Williams, 57.31	30	30
Ht 11	Barrett, Ford, Knowles, Garrod (f,rem), 60.06	35	31
Ht 12	Lobb, Camden, Phelps, Newman (ret), 59.53	38	34
Ht 13	Stephens, Harris, Barrett, Meakins, 58.00	42	36
Ht 14	Harris, Prynne, Phelps, Ford, 59.09	44	40
Ht 15	(Nominated) Lobb, Stephens, Harris, Camden, 57.85	49	41

Tuesday 27 July, 1999 – Knock-Out Cup Semi-Final, 1st Leg
ST.AUSTELL 'GULLS' 52 MILDENHALL 'FEN TIGERS' 38

```
ST.AUSTELL
Seemond Stephens      3 3 3 3 2'- -     14  1
Richard Ford          0 1 0 - - - -      1
Gary Lobb             3 3 3 3 2 3 - -    14
Martin Williams       1 2'0 1 - - -      4   1
Wayne Barrett         2 2 2 2'- - -      8   1
Jason Prynne          2 1'2'0 1'3 -      9   3
Adrian Newman         1'R 1 - - - -      2   1

MILDENHALL
Phil Knowles          1'0 X 0 - - -      1   1
Gavin Hedge           2 2 1 2'1 - -      8   1
Garry Sweet R/R       - - - - - - -
Simon Brown           0 R 0 - - - -      0
Dean Garrod           1 0 2 0 - - -      3
Barrie Evans          0 2 1'1 3 1 1      9   1
Steve Camden          3 3 3 3 3 2 X     17
Kevin Phillips (No.8) - - - - - - -      -
```

PROGRAMME CHANGES:-
Ht 3: R/R Hedge; Ht 7: R/R Camden; Ht 10: Prynne replaced Ford; R/R Garrod; Evans replaced Brown; Ht 11: Camden replaced Knowles; Ht 12: Prynne replaced Newman; R/R Knowles; Ht 13: Evans replaced Garrod

		Gulls	Mild
Note: The second leg was subsequently staged at Mildenhall on 22 August, when the Gulls forced a 45-45 draw to take an aggregate victory of 97-83.			
Ht 1	Stephens, Hedge, Knowles, Ford, 55.18	3	3
Ht 2	Camden, Prynne, Newman, Evans, 56.44	6	6
Ht 3	Lobb, Hedge, Williams, Brown, 58.00	10	8
Ht 4	Camden, Barrett, Garrod, Newman (ret), 57.09	12	12
Ht 5	Lobb, Williams, Hedge, Knowles, 57.03	17	13
Ht 6	Stephens, Evans, Ford, Garrod, 57.22	21	15
Ht 7	Camden, Barrett, Prynne, Brown (ret), 57.57	24	18
Ht 8	Camden, Hedge, Newman, Ford, 57.57	25	23
Ht 9	Lobb, Garrod, Evans, Williams, 59.54	28	26
Ht 10	Stephens, Prynne, Evans, Garrod, 58.03	33	27
Ht 11	Camden, Barrett, Hedge, Prynne, 58.19	35	31
Ht 12	(Re-Run) Evans, Lobb, Prynne, Knowles (f,ex), 57.16	38	34
Ht 13	Stephens, Barrett, Evans, Knowles, 57.22	43	35
Ht 14	Prynne, Camden, Williams, Brown, 58.00	47	37
Ht 15	(Nominated – Awarded) Lobb, Stephens, Evans, Camden (f,ex), No Time	52	38
	Bronze Helmet: Stephens, Evans, 57.97		

Tuesday 3 August, 1999 – Conference League
ST.AUSTELL 'GULLS' 43 NEWPORT 'MAVERICKS' 47

```
ST.AUSTELL
Seemond Stephens      3 2 2 2 3 - -     12
Richard Ford          1 1 1'R - - - -    2   1
Gary Lobb             R 3 2 3 1 - -      9
Martin Williams       2 X - - - - -      2
Wayne Barrett         R R R - - - -      0
Jason Prynne          3 2 1'1 0 R -      7   1
Adrian Newman         1 3 3 1'2'1 -     11   2

NEWPORT
Chris Neath           2 1'3 3 3 0 -     12   1
Steve Aston           0 2 1'- - - -      3   1
Andrew Appleton       3 3 0 0 3 - -      9
Rob Finlow R/R        - - - - - - -
Bobby Eldridge        1 1 1'3 3 1 2 -   11   1
Jamie Holmes          0 0 2 1 - - -      3
Graig Gough           2 2 1 F 2'2'-      9   2
Darren Hatton (No.8)  - - - - - -        -
```

PROGRAMME CHANGES:-
Ht 3: R/R Eldridge; Ht 7: R/R Gough; Ht 8: Holmes replaced Gough; Ht 9: Prynne replaced Williams; Gough replaced Holmes; Ht 10: Newman replaced Ford; R/R Neath; Ht 11: Gough replaced Aston; Ht 13: Prynne replaced Barrett; Ht 14: Newman replaced Williams; R/R Appleton

		Gulls	New
Ht 1	Stephens, Neath, Ford, Aston, 55.41	4	2
Ht 2	Prynne, Gough, Newman, Holmes, 58.41	8	4
Ht 3	Appleton, Williams, Eldridge, Lobb (ret), 56.48	10	8
Ht 4	Newman, Gough, Eldridge, Barrett (ret), 56.89	13	11
Ht 5	(Re-Run) Lobb, Aston, Neath, Williams (f,ex), 59.20	16	14
Ht 6	Eldridge, Stephens, Ford, Holmes, 56.10	19	17
Ht 7	Appleton, Prynne, Gough, Barrett (ret), 56.08	21	21
Ht 8	Newman, Holmes, Aston, Ford, 58.47	24	24
Ht 9	Eldridge, Lobb, Prynne, Gough (fell), 58.23	27	27
Ht 10	Neath, Stephens, Newman, Appleton, 56.84	30	30
Ht 11	Neath, Gough, Prynne, Barrett (ret), 58.89	31	35
Ht 12	Lobb, Newman, Holmes, Appleton (f,rem), 58.50	36	36
Ht 13	Neath, Stephens, Eldridge, Prynne, 55.89	38	40
Ht 14	Appleton, Gough, Newman, Prynne (ret), 57.17	39	45
Ht 15	(Nominated – Re-Run) Stephens, Eldridge, Lobb, Neath, 57.03	43	47
	Bronze Helmet: Stephens, Eldridge, 56.50		

Tuesday 10 August, 1999
CORNISH FORD KA3 ECLIPSE CLASSIC

James Birkinshaw	2 1 2 1 R - -	6
Martin Williams	1 0 1 3 0 - -	5
Adrian Rowe	0 0 0 0 0 - -	0
Wayne Barrett	3 2 3 1 3 - -	12
Adrian Newman	3 3 3 3 1 - -	13
Adam Allott	2 3 1 0 3 - -	9
Gary Phelps	1 2 R 2 2 - -	7
Mark Thompson	X 0 1 1 X - -	2
Jason Prynne	3 2 3 3 3 - -	14
Kevin Phillips	F 1 X 1 2 - -	4
Ian Clarke	2 1 0 0 0 - -	3
Jamie Holmes	1 1 0 0 1 - -	3
Richard Ford	0 0 2 2 2 - -	6
Shane Colvin	1 2 2 3 2 - -	10
Gary Lobb	2 3 2 2 3 - -	12
Chris Harris	3 3 3 2 1 - -	12
Gavin Horsborough (Res)	- - - - - - -	-

PROGRAMME CHANGES:-
None!

Note: Jamie Holmes went from a 15-yard handicap in the re-run of Heat-3, having touched the tapes at the first attempt.

1st CHRIS HARRIS;
2nd JASON PRYNNE; 3rd ADRAIN NEWMAN

Ht 1	Barrett, Birkinshaw, Williams, Rowe, 56.97
Ht 2	(Re-Run) Newman, Allott, Phelps, Thompson (f,ex), 55.46
Ht 3	(Re-Run) Prynne, Clarke, Holmes (15-yards), Phillips (fell), 58.38
Ht 4	Harris, Lobb, Colvin, Ford, 56.69
Ht 5	Newman, Prynne, Birkinshaw, Ford, 55.63
Ht 6	Allott, Colvin, Phillips, Williams, 56.40
Ht 7	Lobb, Phelps, Clarke, Rowe, 57.93
Ht 8	Harris, Barrett, Holmes, Thompson, 57.62
Ht 9	Harris, Birkinshaw, Allott, Clarke, 57.69
Ht 10	Newman, Lobb, Williams, Holmes, 56.23
Ht 11	Prynne, Colvin, Thompson, Rowe, 57.63
Ht 12	(Re-Run) Barrett, Ford, Phelps (ret), Phillips (f,ex), 57.94
Ht 13	Colvin, Phelps, Birkinshaw, Holmes, 57.00
Ht 14	Williams, Ford, Thompson, Clarke, 58.03
Ht 15	Newman, Harris, Phillips, Rowe, 56.78
Ht 16	Prynne, Lobb, Barrett, Allott, 57.93
Ht 17	(Re-Run) Lobb, Phillips, Birkinshaw (ret), Thompson (f,ex), 59.19
Ht 18	Prynne, Phelps, Harris, Williams, 58.82
Ht 19	Allott, Ford, Holmes, Rowe, 58.90
Ht 20	Barrett, Colvin, Newman, Clarke, 58.56
Final	(Re-Run) Harris, Prynne, Newman, Barrett (ret), 57.10

Tuesday 17 August, 1999 – Conference League
ST.AUSTELL 'GULLS' 49 BUXTON 'HITMEN' 41

ST.AUSTELL

Seemond Stephens	3 3 3 3 3 -	18
Richard Ford	0 0 1 0 - - -	1
Gary Lobb	1 3 3 X X - -	7
Martin Williams	0 2¹1 - - - -	3 1
Wayne Barrett R/R	- - - - - - -	-
Jason Prynne	1 0 2 X 1 - -	4
Adrian Newman	3 3 3 2 3 2¹-	16 1
Kevin Phillips (No.8)	0 - - - - - -	0

BUXTON

Neil Painter	2 X 2 1¹- - -	5 1
Mark Steel	1¹1 2 1¹- - -	5 2
Aidan Collins	3 3 2 3 1 - -	12
Paul Burnett	2¹1 1¹2 - - -	6 2
Adam Allott	2 2 2 2 0 - -	8
Lee Smethills	2 1¹1¹F 1 - -	5 2
Paul Macklin	R R X - - - -	0

PROGRAMME CHANGES:-
Ht 4: R/R Prynne; Smethills replaced Macklin; Ht 7: R/R Phillips; Ht 11: R/R Stephens; Ht 13: R/R Lobb; Ht 14: Newman replaced Williams

		Gulls	Bux
Ht 1	Stephens, Painter, Steel, Ford, 57.94	3	3
Ht 2	Newman, Smethills, Prynne, Macklin (ret), 56.34	7	5
Ht 3	Collins, Burnett, Lobb, Williams, 57.65	8	10
Ht 4	Newman, Allott, Smethills, Prynne, 57.50	11	13
Ht 5	(Awarded) Lobb, Williams, Steel, Painter (f,ex), No Time	16	14
Ht 6	Stephens, Allott, Smethills, Ford, 57.94	19	17
Ht 7	Collins, Prynne, Burnett, Phillips, 59.25	21	21
Ht 8	Newman, Steel, Ford, Macklin (ret), 58.22	25	23
Ht 9	Lobb, Allott, Williams, Smethills (fell), 58.17	29	25
Ht 10	Stephens, Collins, Burnett, Ford, 58.25	32	28
Ht 11	(Re-Run) Stephens, Painter, Steel, Prynne (f,ex), 58.15	35	31
Ht 12	(Re-Run) Collins, Newman, Smethills, Lobb (f,ex), 57.85	37	35
Ht 13	(Awarded) Stephens, Allott, Painter, Lobb (f,ex), No Time	40	38
Ht 14	(Awarded) Newman, Burnett, Prynne, Macklin (f,ex), No Time	44	40
Ht 15	(Nominated) Stephens, Newman, Collins, Allott, 59.16	49	41
	Bronze Helmet: Stephens, Collins, 57.08		

Tuesday 31 August, 1999 – Challenge Match
ST.AUSTELL 'GULLS' 58 SOUTHAMPTON 'SAINTS' 31

ST.AUSTELL

Seemond Stephens	2 3 3 3 2¹- -	13	1
Richard Ford	1¹1 1 2¹- -	5	2
Gary Lobb	2¹2 X 1¹- - -	5	2
Martin Williams	3 0 3 1 - - -	7	
Gary Phelps	2¹1¹0 2¹- - -	5	3
Jason Prynne	2¹2 2 3 - - -	9	1
Adrian Newman	3 3 3 3 2 3 - -	14	

SOUTHAMPTON

Chris Courage	3 3 2 3 0 0 -	11	
Geoff Batt	0 1 X 1 1 - -	3	
Colin Crook	1 F - - - - -	1	
Steve Targett	0 0 0 - - - -	0	
Chris Harris	1 2 3 R 1 1 -	8	
Jay Stevens	1 0 2 3 2 - -	8	
Nathan Irwin	0 0 0 - - - -	0	

PROGRAMME CHANGES:-
Ht 7: T/S Harris for Target; Ht 8: T/S Courage for Irwin; Ht 10: T/S Batt for Crook; Ht 12: Irwin replaced Crook; Ht 14: Stevens replaced Irwin

		Gulls	Sou
Ht 1	Courage, Stephens, Ford, Batt, 56.56	3	3
Ht 2	Newman, Prynne, Stevens, Irwin, 55.72	8	4
Ht 3	Williams, Lobb, Crook, Targett, 55.97	13	5
Ht 4	Newman, Phelps, Harris, Irwin, 56.12	18	6
Ht 5	Courage, Lobb, Batt, Williams, 57.72	20	10
Ht 6	Stephens, Harris, Ford, Stevens, 56.12	24	12
Ht 7	Harris, Prynne, Phelps, Crook (fell), 56.63	27	15
Ht 8	(Re-Run) Newman, Courage, Ford, Batt (f,ex), 57.53	31	17
Ht 9	(Re-Run) Williams, Stevens, Harris (f,rem, ret), Lobb (f,ex), 57.35	34	19
Ht 10	Stephens, Ford, Batt, Targett, 57.97	39	20
Ht 11	Courage, Prynne, Batt, Phelps, 58.63	41	24
Ht 12	Stevens, Newman, Lobb, Irwin, 57.62	44	27
Ht 13	Stephens, Phelps, Harris, Courage, 57.03	49	28
Ht 14	Prynne, Stevens, Williams, Targett, 58.71	53	30
Ht 15	(Nominated) Newman, Stephens, Harris, Courage, 57.75	58	31

Tuesday 7 September, 1999 – Challenge Match
ST.AUSTELL 'GULLS' 45 DEVON 'DEMONS' 45

ST.AUSTELL

Seemond Stephens	3 3 3 3 - - -	12	
Richard Ford	R R 3 1 2 - -	6	
Gary Lobb R/R	- - - - - - -	-	
Martin Williams	2 2 3 2¹0 - -	9	1
Adrian Newman	3 2 3 0 1 - -	9	
Jason Prynne	3 R 3 - - - -	6	
Adrian Rowe	0 1 F 0 1¹- -	2	1
Dominic Walsh-Newton (No.8)	1¹F 0 - - - -	1	1

DEVON

Wayne Barrett	2 3 2 2 3 - -	12	
Jamie Holmes	1¹1 2 1¹- - -	5	2
Chris Harris	3 3 2 3 2¹- -	13	1
Oliver Hackett	0 1 0 F - - -	1	
Gary Phelps	2 2 1¹1¹- - -	6	2
Kevin Phillips	2 1¹2 0 - - -	5	1
Gavin Horsborough	1¹0 1¹1 - - -	3	2

PROGRAMME CHANGES:-
Ht 3: R/R Walsh-Newton; Ht 5: R/R Walsh-Newton; Ht 9: R/R Walsh-Newton; Ht 11: Rowe replaced Prynne; Ht 12: R/R Ford

Note: Martin Williams went from a 15-yard handicap in the re-run of Heat-15, having fouled the tapes at the first attempt.

		Gulls	Dev
Ht 1	Stephens, Barrett, Holmes, Ford (ret), 56.19	3	3
Ht 2	Prynne, Phillips, Horsborough, Rowe, 59.22	6	6
Ht 3	Harris, Williams, Walsh-Newton, Hackett, 56.09	9	9
Ht 4	Newman, Phelps, Rowe, Horsborough, 57.44	13	11
Ht 5	Barrett, Williams, Holmes, Walsh-Newton (fell), 57.31	15	15
Ht 6	Stephens, Phelps, Phillips, Ford (ret), 57.10	18	18
Ht 7	Harris, Newman, Hackett, Prynne (ret), 59.25	20	22
Ht 8	Ford, Holmes, Horsborough, Rowe (fell), 59.59	23	25
Ht 9	Williams, Phillips, Phelps, Walsh-Newton, 57.82	26	28
Ht 10	Stephens, Harris, Ford, Hackett, 57.56	30	30
Ht 11	Newman, Barrett, Holmes, Rowe, 57.62	33	33
Ht 12	Harris, Ford, Rowe, Phillips (f,rem, f,rem), 57.28	36	36
Ht 13	Stephens, Barrett, Phelps, Newman, 56.72	39	39
Ht 14	Prynne, Williams, Horsborough, Hackett (fell), 60.32	44	40
Ht 15	(Nominated – Re-Run) Barrett, Harris, Newman, Williams (15 yards), 57.91	45	45
	West Country Bronze Helmet: Harris, Williams, 57.34		

Tuesday 14 September, 1999
CORNISH GRAND NATIONAL

Mark Simmonds	3 1 2 2 X - -	8
Richard Ford	2 0 R 0 2 - -	4
Roger Lobb	R 2 2 3 2 - -	9
Adrian Newman	R 1 1 1 0 - -	3
Gary Phelps	1 2 1 2 1 - -	7
Jason Prynne	0 2 2 0 1 - -	5
Michael Coles	3 3 3 3 3 - -	15
Seemond Stephens	2 3 F 3 3 - -	11
Wayne Barrett	3 1 3 1 1 - -	9
Jamie Holmes	1 0 0 0 0 - -	1
Chris Harris	X M 3 2 3 - -	8
Peter Jeffery	2 3 1 1 2 - -	9
Kevin Phillips (Res)	0 - - - - - -	0
Adrian Rowe (Res)	- - - - - - -	-

PROGRAMME CHANGES:-
Ht 6: Phillips replaced Harris

Notes: A three-man run-off was required to determine two of the finalists after a tie on points. Seemond Stephens went from a 15-yard handicap in the re-run of the final, having fouled the tapes at the first attempt.

1st MICHAEL COLES;
2nd ROGER LOBB; 3rd PETER JEFFERY

Ht 1	Simmonds, Ford, Lobb (ret), Newman (ret), 56.16
Ht 2	Coles, Stephens, Phelps, Prynne, 56.35
Ht 3	(Awarded) Barrett, Jeffery, Holmes, Harris (f,ex), No Time
Ht 4	Stephens, Phelps, Simmonds, Holmes, 56.16
Ht 5	Coles, Lobb, Barrett, Ford, 55.63
Ht 6	Jeffery, Prynne, Newman, Phillips, Harris (ex, 2 min), 56.85
Ht 7	Harris, Simmonds, Phelps, Ford (ret), 56.03
Ht 8	Coles, Lobb, Jeffery, Stephens (fell), 55.59
Ht 9	Barrett, Prynne, Newman, Holmes, 57.41
Ht 10	Stephens, Harris, Barrett, Ford, 56.66
Ht 11	Coles, Phelps, Newman, Holmes, 56.18
Ht 12	Lobb, Simmonds, Jeffery, Prynne, 55.90
Ht 13	Coles, Ford, Prynne, Holmes, 57.66
Ht 14	Harris, Lobb, Phelps, Newman, 56.07
Ht 15	(Re-Run) Stephens, Jeffery, Barrett, Simmonds (f,ex), 56.78
R/Off	Jeffery, Lobb, Barrett, 56.94
Final	(Re-Run) Coles, Lobb, Jeffery, Stephens (15 yards), 56.03

Tuesday 21 September, 1999
GOLDEN JUBILEE STARS OF TOMORROW

Adrian Rowe	2 F 2 2 - - -	6
Gavin Horsborough	0 2 0 1 - - -	3
Dominic Walsh-Newton	1 2 1 1 - - -	5
Darren Hatton	3 3 2 2 - - -	10
Jamie Holmes	3 3 3 3 - - -	12
Oliver Hackett	1 1 F 0 - - -	2
Ray Dickson	F 1 3 X - - -	4

PROGRAMME CHANGES:-
None!

1st JAMIE HOLMES;
2nd DARREN HATTON; 3rd DOMINIC WALSH-NEWTON

Ht 1	Hatton, Rowe, Hackett, Horsborough, 63.97
Ht 2	(Re-Run) Holmes, Horsborough, Walsh-Newton, Dickson (15 yards – fell), 68.41
Ht 3	Hatton, Walsh-Newton, Hackett, Rowe (fell), 63.28
Ht 4	Holmes, Hatton, Dickson, Horsborough, 59.80
Ht 5	Holmes, Rowe, Walsh-Newton, Hackett (fell), 59.19
Ht 6	Dickson, Hatton, Horsborough, Hackett, 61.31
Ht 7	(Re-Run) Holmes, Rowe, Walsh-Newton, Dickson (f,ex), 62.16
Final	(Top Four Riders) Holmes, Hatton, Walsh-Newton, Rowe, 60.25

Note: Ray Dickson went from a 15-yard handicap in the re-run of Heat-2, having fouled the tapes at the first attempt.

Sunday 26 September, 1999 – Challenge Match
ST.AUSTELL 'GULLS' 6 PLYMOUTH 'DEVILS' 12
Meeting abandoned after Heat-3

ST.AUSTELL

Jason Prynne	2 - - - - - -	2
Oliver Hackett	X - - - - - -	0
Richard Ford	3 - - - - - -	3
Dominic Walsh-Newton	0 - - - - - -	0
Gary Phelps	- - - - - - -	-
Brian Bedford	0 - - - - - -	0
Gavin Horsborough	1 - - - - - -	1

PLYMOUTH

Dean Garrod	3 - - - - - -	3	
Gary Fawdrey	1 - - - - - -	1	
Shane Colvin	2 - - - - - -	2	
Gordon Meakins	1' - - - - - -	1	1
Geoff Batt	- - - - - - -	-	
David Haddock	2' - - - - - -	2	1
Jamie Holmes	3 - - - - - -	3	

PROGRAMME CHANGES:-
None!

		Gulls	Ply
Ht 1	(Re-Run) Garrod, Prynne, Fawdrey, Hackett (f,ex), 61.73	2	4
Ht 2	Holmes, Haddock, Horsborough, Bedford, 62.88	3	9
Ht 3	Ford, Colvin, Meakins, Walsh-Newton, 60.91	6	12

Sunday 24 October, 1999 – Knock-Out Cup Final, 2nd Leg
ST.AUSTELL 'GULLS' 55 NEWPORT 'MAVERICKS' 35

ST.AUSTELL

Seemond Stephens	3 2 3 3 3 - -	14	
Richard Ford	2'1'0 - - - -	3	2
Gary Lobb	2 1 0 1'- - -	4	1
Gary Phelps	1'3 2 2'0 - -	8	2
Wayne Barrett	2'T 1'0 - - -	3	2
Jason Prynne	2'1 2 - - - -	5	1
Adrian Newman	3 3 3 2 2'2 3	18	1

NEWPORT

Chris Neath	1 2 3 3 2 2 -	13	
Graig Gough	0 0 1 0 - - -	1	
Andrew Appleton	3 3 2 0 3 1'-	12	1
Nick Simmons	0 0 1 - - - -	1	
Bobby Eldridge	X 0 3 1'0 - -	4	1
Chris Courage	1 1 0 - - - -	2	
Jamie Holmes	0 1 1 - - - -	2	

PROGRAMME CHANGES:-

Ht 6: T/S Appleton for Courage; Ht 7: Newman replaced Barrett in the re-run; Ht 8: T/S Neath for Holmes; Ht 10: Newman replaced Ford; Ht 14: Newman replaced Prynne; T/S Eldridge for Simmons

Note: The first leg of the KOC Final had already been staged at Newport on 16 October, when the 'Mavericks' won 52-38. However, St.Austell's 55-35 success in the second leg was sufficient for them to secure a 93-87 victory on aggregate.

		Gulls	New
Ht 1	Stephens, Ford, Neath, Gough, 56.31	5	1
Ht 2	Newman, Prynne, Courage, Holmes, 57.00	10	2
Ht 3	Appleton, Lobb, Phelps, Simmons, 61.94	13	5
Ht 4	(Awarded) Newman, Barrett, Holmes, Eldridge (f,ex), No Time	18	6
Ht 5	Phelps, Neath, Lobb, Gough, 57.25	22	8
Ht 6	Appleton, Stephens, Ford, Eldridge, 57.63	25	11
Ht 7	(Re-Run) Newman, Appleton, Prynne, Simmons, Barrett (ex, tapes), 57.09	29	13
Ht 8	Neath, Newman, Gough, Ford, 57.56	31	17
Ht 9	Eldridge, Phelps, Courage, Lobb, 57.03	33	21
Ht 10	Stephens, Newman, Simmons, Appleton, 56.84	38	22
Ht 11	Neath, Prynne, Barrett, Gough, 57.71	41	25
Ht 12	Appleton, Newman, Lobb, Courage, 55.75	44	28
Ht 13	Stephens, Neath, Eldridge, Barrett, 55.65	47	31
Ht 14	Newman, Phelps, Holmes, Eldridge (f,rem), 57.53	52	32
Ht 15	(Nominated) Stephens, Neath, Appleton, Phelps, 57.19	55	35

4

2000

All Gulls fans were eagerly awaiting the 2000 campaign as it seemed certain that the mega-popular Steve Bishop would be returning to the fold. However, as it transpired, 'Bish' was to link with a new track much closer to his Bristol home, namely the Somerset Rebels at their Oak Tree Arena home in Highbridge. This was a huge blow as the Gulls had already lost the services of both Seemond Stephens and Adrian Newman. It was a curious looking line-up that they therefore tracked for their opening fixture in the new Conference League Cup competition at picturesque Buxton on 30 April. Wayne Barrett occupied the no.1 slot, with Richard Ford, Gary Lobb, Martin Williams and Jason Prynne alongside. That accounted for five of the Gulls team berths, with rugby player Dominic Walsh-Newton having a go at another type of sporting discipline by lining up at no.4, while the rider replacement facility was operated at no.3 for Bobby Eldridge. This was something of a mystifying move, as Bobby was a full-time rider with Exeter in the Premier League and in the event, didn't make a single appearance for St Austell.

Anyway, the scores were always close in the match, but the Gulls moved into the ascendancy following a 4-2 from Barrett and Ford in heat eleven. The St Austell boys then managed to stay in front, eventually running out 47-43 victors. Wayne Barrett headed the scoring with a massive 16-point tally, while Jason Prynne (14+2) and Martin Williams

Dominic Walsh-Newton.

Charly Kirtland.

(10) lent excellent support. However, it was super no.2 Richard Ford, who was the real hero of the afternoon, chipping in with a match-winning 7+2 return from five starts. Meanwhile, in Dean Felton (15+1), Paul Burnett (13+1) and Neil Painter (10+2), the home side also possessed three men in double-figures, but they lacked the necessary back up to tip the match in their favour. The result might have been a good one, but the meeting was marred by a heat nine crash involving Gary Lobb. Poor Gary locked up in front of Lee Howard, who was left with nowhere to go, and the closely following Paul Burnett subsequently collided with both. Unfortunately, 'Lobby' hurt an arm and some ribs in the crash, which were to sideline him for a full month.

The roar of the machines returned to the Moto Parc on 2 May, as the tapes went up on the fourth season of racing at the super venue for the visit of Buxton Hitmen in the return Conference League Cup fixture. The Gulls were forced to bring in local youngster Kevin Hamley for this match, whilst also operating rider replacement for the injured Gary Lobb. Despite the problems with trying to raise a full team, the programme notes were upbeat and optimistic, due to an increased number of sides in the Conference League, with Peterborough and Sheffield, as well as Somerset joining the set-up. Maximum points from the reserve pairing of Martin Williams and Jason Prynne put St Austell ahead in heat two, and there was no looking back as they maintained their lead to claim a fairly comfortable 50-39 success. Wayne Barrett gave another sizzling display to rack up a full 18 point maximum, while Jason Prynne (15+1) and Martin Williams (11+1) again made telling contributions as they had at Buxton two days previously. The Hitmen were basically a two-man outfit, but in Dean Felton and Phil Pickering, they had a couple of gems, who never knew when to throw the towel in, both plundering 15+1 from seven rides apiece.

Off track, there was a new Supporters' Club committee in place, with the effervescent Albert Poulton in place as the Chairman. An enthusiastic team was selected to back Albert, with Jeanette Sims as treasurer, along with members Suzanne Knuckey, Christine Poulton, Keith Pilsbury and his daughter Aislin, who happily volunteered to help out in the track shop. A weekly raffle was organized and proved to be very popular with the fans. Albert's various money-raising schemes were to bear fruit, as throughout 2000 and 2001, several large presentations were made to various members of the home camp in times of need.

Following a week's break from racing, the Boston Barracuda-Braves (who rode their home matches at King's Lynn) were the next visitors as the Gulls kicked off their league campaign. The homesters' team problems were compounded prior to the start, when Richard Ford lost control on the warm-up lap and careered into the safety fence. That put 'Fordy' out of the meeting before it had started, with the Gulls having a blank space at no.2, while already operating rider replacement for Gary Lobb at no.3. Having started with only five riders, the Gulls were down to just four fit men after the third heat, which saw Dominic Walsh-Newton pull up in discomfort, having suffered a reaction to previously sustained wrist and collarbone injuries.

In spite of all their problems, a tight match ensued, but showing tremendous team spirit, the Gulls simply refused to buckle and eventually sealed a marvellous 46-44 win. Exciting racing was the order of the day, as ever at the china country circuit, and it was maximum points from Wayne Barrett and Gary Phelps in heat thirteen that virtually ensured a home success. The visitors did gain advantages in the last two races, but it was the tenacious Gulls who sneaked home by the narrowest of margins, courtesy of the fab four – Martin Williams (14+1), Wayne Barrett (14), Gary Phelps (10+2) and Jason Prynne (8+1). The battling Boston men had certainly played their part in a thrilling match, with Luke Clifton (12+2), Peter Boast (10) and veteran Robert Hollingworth (9+3) being the pick of the bunch.

Martin Williams.

By this time, Re-Run Videos had stopped filming the action at the Moto Parc, but thankfully, the racing was still being recorded for posterity. Dave Hawking, the normal man behind the camera, had decided to carry on and started up his own company known as D & L Videos. Big Dave, who hails from Plymouth, is quite a character and can still be found, along with his trusted camera at both Trelawny and Exeter throughout the speedway season.

With no fixtures to fulfil on the road, it was seven long days before the tapes again went up at the Clay Country Moto Parc for the annual Simpson Plant Hire Individual Challenge. History was made in this event, for appearing at no.9 was a young lady by the name of Charly Kirtland. The appearance of a female rider stirred up a considerable amount of interest and the popular Charly certainly wasn't disgraced, scoring five-points. The meeting featured a dozen riders, who raced over 12 heats, with grand prix style A, B and C finals to finish with. Jason Prynne continued his improvement to top the scoring on 11 points, with Martin Williams (10), Wayne Barrett (9) and Shane Colvin (9) joining him in the main final. Just to prove his performance in the heats had been no fluke, young Jason strode to a convincing victory to complete his finest night in the sport. The runner-up position went to Shane Colvin, while Wayne Barrett had to settle for third place. Further action in the second half featured six heats of sidecar speedway, which saw Ian McAuley emerge victorious from Ken Curnow. This represented something of a change for Ken, who was a former sidecar Champion on the grass-tracks and a road racer of some note.

The following week, it was back to Conference League business as the Gulls played host to Ashfield Giants. The visitors fomerly raced at Linlithgow, but had lost the use of their Heathersfield Stadium home; however, in an effort to hold their identity, their full title was actually Lightning Ashfield Giants. The weather wasn't so good leading up to start time, with rain swirling around and affecting the attendance. Conditions did improve though and those that did turn up witnessed another exciting meeting, with the homesters eventually securing a 52-36 success. The action was summed up succinctly by Paul Adams in Western Morning News thus 'Gulls survive chaos. The Clay Country Moto Parc served up yet another cracking night's racing as the St Austell BWOC Gulls survived yet more catastrophes to defeat the Lightning Ashfield Giants. This was grass roots speedway at its very best as the meeting contrived to serve up a venerable pot pourri of passing, crashes, near misses and the downright unexpected.'

With a dazzling 17 points from seven rides, the diminutive 'Millhouse' Williams headed the scoring, with Wayne Barrett (15+1) and Jason Prynne (11+2) backing him all the way. Meanwhile, for the gallant Giants, who contributed to a wholly wonderful evening, Scott Courtney topped the scorecard with 12 points. The performance of 'Prynner' was quite remarkable, for he fractured a scaphoid fracture in a heat four mêlée on the pits bend, yet still rode on to complete six rides in obvious discomfort. Gary Phelps suffered a broken wrist in the same crash, which was sufficient to rule him out, not only for the night, but also for a further six weeks.

The Gulls then went on the road, with away matches scheduled at Mildenhall and Rye House on successive nights. Although it was a sunny day at Mildenhall, sadly there was no speedway as a week of rainfall had left the track saturated, with no possibility of

2000 programme from the Gulls v. Somerset Conference League Cup clash.

preparing it for racing. Unfortunately, the meeting was never re-staged and this was to have a major bearing on the outcome of the Conference League Championship, but more about that later.

As mentioned during the review of 1999, the Rye House team had been running with a view to getting back into their former home at Hoddesdon. Many people felt this was merely a pipe dream, but the Rockets plugged away and turned dreams into reality in 2000. So, it was to Hoddesdon that the injury hit Cornish side journeyed on 29 May. The Gulls were already operating rider replacement for Gary Lobb, and although Jason Prynne bravely lined-up, they still had to draft in Mark Thompson, plus Rye House junior Steven Eaves. Thankfully, the weather was good, which had allowed Rye House promoter and track guru Len Silver to put a decent racing strip down, although in the event, the Gulls were no match for the powerful home side. David 'Magic Man' Mason romped to a paid maximum (14+1) as the Rockets stormed to a 57-32 success, with Nathan Morton (13+4) and Simon Wolstenholme (12+1) also weighing in with mighty contributions. That left the ever-reliable Wayne Barrett to do the major scoring for St Austell and a super effort saw him plunder 13+1 from a marathon seven ride stint. Following the match, Bronze Helmet holder David Mason retained the trophy after easily defeating Gulls representative Martin Williams.

The next match at the clay raceway was eagerly anticipated as it brought the first official visit of Somerset Rebels for a Conference League Cup engagement. The incident packed meeting resulted in a 48-40 win for the homesters, but the man who made a

The Gulls on parade with Somerset Rebels.

marvellous contribution for the visitors, was St Austell's pre-season target Steve Bishop. The former 'King of Cornwall' returned to his old stamping ground and rode as if he'd never been away, taking six straight victories, before suffering a seventh race exclusion, as he was not under power at the time team-mate Ray Dickson had been excluded for a fall. Ex-Gull Adrian Newman had also linked with the Highbridge outfit, but they were forced to operate rider replacement as 'Skippy' was appearing in a Premier Trophy match for the Isle of Wight against Swindon. The Rebels were further depleted after heat three, when comeback man Dave Roberts, who had previously represented Weymouth, Exeter and Poole in the mid-1980s, was unable to avoid the fallen Mark Thompson and somersaulted across the track, breaking an ankle.

Despite the rider shortage, Somerset battled on gamely, with 'Bish' superbly aided by brothers and former Gulls favourites Mark and Simon Phillips, who occupied the reserve berths. The over-worked duo provided plenty of entertainment on their way to paid 10 and 11 point tallies respectively. One of the quiet men in the home camp came up trumps in this match, with Richard Ford finding his best form to score 12+1 from six starts. The performance of 'Fordy' was matched by the gutsy Jason Prynne, who rode in spite of the visible pain from his wrist each time he took to the track. Gary Lobb is also worthy of mention, as he made a good return to the saddle, notching 9 points from his four programmed rides.

Turning to the off-track fraternity, ace photographer Bernard White was honoured in 2000, not for anything to do with speedway, but for giving 17 years' service as a volunteer coastguard at Newquay. The year also saw Denis Huddy step down as the Clerk of the Course at the Moto Parc, with Pat Whymer taking over the important duties.

Back on the road, St Austell had the distinction of being the very first team to visit the Oak Tree Arena as Somerset opened their gates to great acclaim on 2 June. The track had been due to open the previous week, when Buxton would have provided the opposition, but the meeting fell victim of inclement weather. The action was fast and furious on the wonderfully shaped 300-metre raceway, but with the Rebels tracking a full-strength side, it came as no surprise when the Gulls slipped to a 35-55 reverse. Gary Lobb missed this one, and with Gary Phelps still sidelined, St Austell brought in Darren Andrews as well as operating the rider replacement facility. Steve Bishop was in dominant mood for the Rebels, rocketing to a paid maximum (14+1), while the lanky Glen Phillips (13+1) and Mark Phillips (9+1) gave tremendous support. Mark Phillips was an instant hit with the 2,000 strong crowd, and was suitably attired in black cape and hat to play along with his 'Undertaker' nickname. The Gulls were proud to play their part in the opening of the new track, and it was Wayne Barrett who kept the Rebels on their toes, plundering 14 points from seven starts. Aside from the rider connections between the two sides, there was another one off-track, with ever-enthusiastic Dave Stallworthy in place at race control to do all the announcing.

Mildenhall were the next team to visit Cornwall, as the Gulls got back down to league racing on 6 June, but in a disastrous display, they went down to a crushing 35-55 defeat. Gary Lobb again returned to the side, while former Poole rider Will James was also in the team, having been tempted into making a comeback on the shale. Will didn't appear for Poole after 1987, and he hadn't actually ridden a speedway bike

Wayne Barrett edges ahead of Mildenhall's Steve Camden.

since appearing in some second half races at Exeter in 1988-89, although he had raced at the top level on the grass, prior to retiring in the 1990s. In the meantime, he had set up in business as an hotelier in Newquay, and this meant he wouldn't be available for all the away matches. Despite the return of 'Lobby' and Will James' reappearance, the Gulls still had team problems that certainly didn't help in their efforts to contain the formidable Fen Tigers. Unfortunately, Martin Williams was missing with a vertebra injury sustained while riding for Stoke at Workington two nights beforehand, while Gary Phelps was still on the sidelines with his wrist problem. Both Jason Prynne and Wayne Barrett rode manfully to keep the Gulls in the match, with paid 15 and paid 13 points respectively, but the rest of the side simply couldn't live with the all-powerful visiting trio of Steve Camden (16+1), Paul Lydes-Uings (15+1) and Barrie Evans (14+2).

It was not unnatural to expect sunny weather in midsummer, but a scheduled challenge match against Southampton had to be called off on 13 June, with the Moto Parc enveloped in heavy mist. The weather was far nicer five nights later, however, when the Gulls journeyed up to the beautiful Peak District for a league encounter with Buxton. This turned out to be another unenjoyable experience as the homesters ran riot to win by 60 points to 30. Young Lee Smethills revealed his undoubted ability to achieve a brilliant 15-point maximum, while team-mates James Mann (11+1), Daniel Hodgson (10+2) and Steve Mildoon (8+3) all scored heavily. For the beleaguered Gulls just two men stood out as Wayne Barrett (14) and Jason Prynne (10) combined to score

24 of the side's 30 point total. There was one hair-raising incident that livened up the proceedings though, when Richard Ford's machine actually caught fire, with the track staff reacting quickly to bring it under control with the aid of two extinguishers.

The Gulls were due to face Peterborough at the Longstone Pit on 20 June, but with the weather forecast looking dodgy, coupled with the opposition struggling to raise a full team, the meeting was called off at 8am. Therefore, it was more away action next, with a trip up to Newport for another Conference League meeting. Although the match resulted in a 40-50 reverse, it was a much better showing from the St Austell boys, for whom Wayne Barrett and Jason Prynne were the main source of points, with 12 and 11+1 respectively. Meanwhile, the victorious Mavericks included two maximum men in Scott Pegler (15) and Chris Courage (14+1).

After successive postponements, the Gulls at last returned to track action at the Moto Parc, entertaining Buxton Hitmen in a league encounter on 27 June. Thankfully, it was a return to winning ways too, with a super 15 points from Jason Prynne leading the way as the Gulls gleaned a 51-38 success. As ever, Wayne Barrett was there or thereabouts, notching paid 14, but he was eclipsed by a superb paid 15 point haul from Will James, who looked absolutely terrific on an old upright machine. The pick of the Hitmen was the classy James Mann, who stood head and shoulders above his team-mates to plunder 11 points from five impressive rides. Following the meeting, former Gull Seemond Stephens, who had linked with Exeter at the close of the 1999 season, took the opportunity of a few laps' practice, along with Australian Travis McGowan, who rode for the Elite League side King's Lynn.

The programme from the Buxton match included an interesting article from the pen of *Western Morning News* scribe Paul 'Grizzly' Adams. Among other things, the popular newshound welcomed new Clerk of the Course and Cambridge United FC supporter Pat Whymer, while also wondering whether anything could possibly be done about Dave Stallworthy's choice of music on race nights! Also mentioned were the Cornish pasties that incident recorder Beryl Sinclair specially made for referee Barry Richardson every time he came down to officiate. Poor Beryl took no end of stick for only ever supplying Barry, when of course, the bus was full of other undernourished officials! On one occasion, Graham Reeve, another top referee, joked about the pasties Barry received and the Annears actually produced a massive version of the Cornish delicacy and presented it to him by the starting gate later in the season. It has to be said that the meeting officials certainly enjoyed their trips down to Cornwall in the days of the Gulls, as the speedway was run in an informal and friendly manner, compared with the pressures attached to Elite and Premier League racing.

Moving into July, Rye House came visiting with league points up for grabs, but they were convincingly dispatched by 53 points to 37. Gary Lobb looked quite superb on his way to a super paid 16 point return, while Jason Prynne continued his rich vein of form to net paid 14. There was a certain amount of sympathy for the Rockets, however, as they arrived in town with only four fit riders. For the match, they borrowed local junior Gerry Sims and operated rider replacement for Phil Ambrose, with a blank space at no.2 in the side. Their situation meant they tracked just one

Referee Graham Reeve is presented with a large Cornish pasty by Andy Annear.

rider in three of the heats, which certainly affected their chances as well as diminishing the spectacle for the paying public. The diminutive David Mason lapped it up on the 230 metre raceway, fairly scorching to 16 points, whilst experienced Rockets skipper Simon Wolstenholme rode steadily to accumulate 10 points.

After his fabulous performance, Gary Lobb was due to challenge Mason for the Bronze Helmet, but he unluckily twisted his ankle when defeating the top Rocket in the nominated heat, with Jason Prynne being ultimately unsuccessful after taking his place. In the programme, it was revealed that the Supporters' Club had generously handed over two cheques, one for £280 to cover the fuel purchased for home and away matches thus far in 2000, while the other for £175 covered the purchase of seven tyres. Gulls captain Jason Prynne also went into print, thanking the Supporters' Club for their help and explaining just how expensive speedway was for the riders.

The following week, St Austell entertained Somerset in a Conference League fixture that will be talked about for many years to come. The meeting was more like the showdown at the OK Coral, with several falls and many spectacular incidents as things threatened to boil over. A lot of problems were caused by the track, which many people thought to be over-watered, but in fairness, it had been a boiling hot summer's day.

Perhaps the meeting was best summed up in the under the banner of 'Gritty Gulls get ugly', with Paul Adams reporting 'A mid-meeting boycott, a visiting official banned, five riders injured, crashes, controversy and incidents galore – the good, the bad and

Will James leads from team-mate Gary Lobb and the partially hidden Nathan Morton of Rye House.

129

the ugly sides of speedway were all on display last night. The good was the pure entertainment and drama the meeting provided; the bad came in the number of injuries, fortunately none too serious, and the dispute about the track; and the ugly came in the form of Rebels team manager Greg Daniels, whose outburst on the centre green microphone, together with the conduct of one or two of his team, left a lot to be desired. If it was not for the firm control exhibited by senior speedway referee Paul Ackroyd, the meeting may have descended into a downright disgrace. Both sides started the match with six riders, but as the meeting wore on Gulls Richard Ford and Will James, and Rebels Dean Garton and Mark Phillips had to withdraw through injury as the meeting turned into a war of attrition. Each side sprang last minute team changes on each other – Somerset brought in former Gull Garton, but more significantly, Gary Phelps declared himself fit and the St Austell side was only too delighted to have him back, as he was to prove the eventual match winner.'

Adams' report continued, '... the first five races were full of crashes and re-runs as both sides tried to cope with a heavy surface, the climax of which was a 5-0 to St Austell, when neither Rebel finished the heat. Controversy then reigned as Daniels withdrew his side from the meeting, claiming the track was far too dangerous to ride. There was a 20-minute delay, including a lengthy and animated meeting between Ackroyd, the Conference League co-ordinator Peter Morrish and both teams, during which Somerset left a bike and three of their riders on the track as a sign of their protest. Eventually, racing continued without Daniels, who was banned from the meeting after some outbursts on the microphone. He also collected a £250 fine and will be reported to the Speedway Control Board by the referee. Not that the crashes and excitement got any less as the match progressed and the meeting officials were inundated with crash reports, medical certificates and protests aplenty as feelings between the two sides threatened to boil over. Sandwiched in between the carnage was some superb entertainment as the dwindling number of riders from both sides fought tooth and nail for their respective causes, producing one of the best meetings ever staged at the Moto Parc. Roll on, the second league encounter between the two sides at Somerset in two weeks' time!'

Next on the agenda was the long trek up to Glasgow, as the Gulls faced Ashfield Giants in a Conference League fixture on 17 July. With Will James unavailable to travel, the short-handed St Austell side was patched up with local junior James Denholm, while the rider replacement facility was used for long-term injury victim Martin Williams. Although the scores remained close in the early stages, the Scottish side gradually built up a lead after heat six, before amassing a comfortable 55-35 success. Christian Henry was only beaten by Gary Phelps and scored a massive 17 point total for the Giants, while talented reserve Scott Courtney chipped in with 13+2. Meanwhile, 'Phelpsy' (11+1) and Jason Prynne (11) headed the Gulls scoring, with Wayne Barrett finishing on 9 points after a last race engine failure.

There was more action at the Moto Parc the evening after the match against Ashfield, but at least the Gulls could take it easy after their long journey, as the programme of events was somewhat different. Billed as the 'Cornwall Y2K Championship', a composite style meeting featured a 'Stars of Tomorrow' event, along with quad racing

Gary Lobb.

and a 1000cc sidecar speedway challenge match. Six youngsters partook in the mini speedway event, with Marty Matthews finishing on top, having gathered 10 points from four starts. In finishing order, the other participants in the contest were Oliver Hackett (8), Gavin Horsborough (8), Gerry Sims (4), Tom Brown (3) and Adrian Rowe (3).

The sidecar speedway was run as a team event between St Austell BWOC Gulls and Devon Demons, with the homesters going down to a 28-31 defeat in a highly entertaining ten-heat challenge. The points scorers were: Gulls – Ken Curnow 12 (maximum); Wayne Westaway 9+1; Matthew Tyrell 3; Justin Westaway 3; Steve Courtney 1+1; Demons – Andy Robson 8; Ricky McAuley 7+1; Ian McAuley 6+1; Paul Robson 5+2; Clive Stoneman 5. As they had done before, the sidecar boys certainly sprayed the shale around, with the girls in the track shop having to run for cover, while the video man's car windscreen was shattered!

Completing a busy night of activity, the quad racing tournament was held over five heats, with Nigel Hodge accumulating the most points to take victory from Peter Pollard and Simon Pickard. Incidentally, the 'From the Pit' article in the programme briefly referred back to the Somerset match of the previous week, stating 'just to put the record straight, the track was not over-watered or doctored as alleged by some people. We had put on extra shale as requested by some of our riders, but after watering, the sun disappeared quickly and the track took longer to dry than normal. If you look at the race times, they were as quick as any other meeting this year.'

Back on the road, the Gulls appeared at Peterborough on 23 July, with Mark Thompson filling Will James' shoes at no.4, while rider replacement again covered for

Martin Williams. First, St Austell took the lead and then the home side came back in a pulsating encounter. Maximum points from Wayne Barrett and Richard Ford again put the Gulls ahead in heat eleven, but in a grandstand finish, the Pumas grabbed successive 5-1's in the last two heats to snatch a 46-44 victory. Veteran Ian Barney starred in heats fourteen and fifteen, winning the first and following Jamie Smith home in the latter to finish with an outstanding 17+1 total from seven rides. The aforementioned Smith played a full part in Peterborough's success, weighing in with 13 points, while the Gulls were best served by Wayne Barrett and Gary Phelps who also each netted a baker's dozen.

Two nights later, the Peterborough boys made the return journey to Cornwall for a match that saw Will James resume in the Gulls side. It was amazing to see the difference a few years had made to the visitors, for they had been such a force in 1997, when they plundered a 39-38 victory at the Moto Parc. However, this time around, they were absolutely swamped by 63 points to 27, as the Gulls literally ran riot. An opening heat maximum from Wayne Barrett and Richard Ford set the ball rolling and a further seven 5-1's were walloped home before the Pumas could escape from the onslaught. Peterborough stalwart Ian Barney fought a lone battle, scoring 15 of his side's 27 points, while the Gulls boasted five riders who were paid for double figures, namely Gary Phelps 14+1 (paid maximum), Jason Prynne 12+3 (paid maximum), Gary Lobb 11, Wayne Barrett 10+1 and Richard Ford 8+3.

In the programme, the ever-jovial Albert Poulton closed his Supporters' Club column with the news that the weekly collection would go towards a new ribbon for his typewriter! Albert also mentioned the difficulties committee member Keith Pilsbury had found in selling raffle tickets the previous week. Having returned with as many tickets as he went with, his very attractive daughter, Bethan decided to have a go and had no trouble in shifting a bucket load!

On Friday 28 July, the Gulls and many of their supporters made the trip up to Highbridge for the eagerly awaited return league match with Somerset. Those that travelled certainly weren't disappointed either as the well-prepared Oak Tree Arena circuit served up a cracking meeting. The home side were spearheaded by former top Gull Steve Bishop, and in another link with the past, brothers Mark and Simon Phillips lined up at reserve. The popular Adrian Newman was also due to represent the Rebels, but in the event, 'Skippy' was called up to ride for Young Australia against Young England at Oxford, with Somerset opting to use rider replacement instead. The Gulls won the meeting 46-44, and the encounter was incident packed. Heat one had to be re-run following an unsatisfactory start, with 'Bish' subsequently going under the fast-starting Richard Ford on the second bend, before brilliantly driving under Wayne Barrett entering the third corner. However, with 'Bish' steaming to another race win, disaster struck on the back straight of lap three as a wire snapped on his ignition, leaving the Gulls to collect an unexpected 5-1. The second heat saw Gary Phelps away well, with Simon Phillips tucked in behind and Gary Lobb holding third. Mark Phillips went past 'Lobby' on the pits bend, only to slow on the following lap and let the Gull back into third place for another heat advantage to the visitors. Although Mark got his machine going again, he was unable to make any impression and after the race it was discovered that a wasp had got into his fuel line, causing him to slow in mid-race!

The Gulls pairing of Jason Prynne and Will James made the start in the third heat, with Malcolm 'Mad Wellie' Holloway and Glen Phillips trailing at the back. In a desperate move on the third lap, Holloway went hard under James on the first bend, causing the Gull to fall, with the referee having no choice but to exclude the Rebel for foul riding. Somewhat surprisingly a re-run was called, but it benefited the home side as Glen Phillips roared from the trap to win comfortably. Phelps again made the gate in the fourth race, with team-mate Lobb in second place. Gary buckled under pressure though, as both of the Phillips brothers managed to get underneath on the first turn of lap two for a share of the points. There was an alarming start to the next heat when Holloway reared as the tapes rose and lost control, before coming down in an untidy heap just 20 metres from the line. Unfortunately, 'Wellie' aggravated an old shoulder injury in the process, although he eventually got to his feet and gingerly walked back to the pits. With Holloway excluded, Barrett made the start and rode a steady four laps to keep Glen Phillips at bay, and with Ford collecting the odd-point, the Gulls took another heat advantage. This left the Rebels reeling, as they were behind by eight points at 11-19. Once again, Phelps shot away in the sixth heat, but Bishop surged inside the Gull on the pits bend, while Mark Phillips found a way through on the inside of Prynne to grab third place for a Rebels 4-2.

Jason Prynne made a rocket start to the seventh heat, but after a determined chase, Glen Phillips produced a tremendous outside burst to win the race coming off the final bend. However, with Simon Phillips unable to make any headway at the back, the points were shared, leaving the Rebels trailing at 18-24. Mark Phillips won a very hard battle for first bend supremacy in the next, which saw Lobb take up second place and Ray Dickson third. Despite the frantic efforts of Ford at the back, Dickson tenaciously held on for the duration to give the Rebels a 4-2, cutting their deficit back to just four-points in the process. The Gulls immediately hit back with a maximum from Phelps and Barrett in the ninth though, with Glen Phillips trailing home third. Malcolm Holloway bravely took his place in the race, but pulled up at the end of the second lap, obviously in some discomfort from his recurring shoulder injury. So again, the homesters found themselves 8 points down at 23-31.

Will James got the start in the tenth heat and moved Bishop over on the first turn, but on the next lap, the Rebels' no.1 produced his favourite manoeuvre to cut inside the St Austell man on the pits bend. There was no contact as 'Bish' went through, but James lifted and fell by the fence, although he sportingly re-mounted at the double to finish the race. Prynne was second, with Ray Dickson again collecting the odd-point to leave Somerset trailing 27-33. The St Austell pairing of Barrett and Ford were quickly away in heat eleven, but on the back straight Bishop and Simon Phillips went either side of Ford to take up the chase on the Gulls no.1. 'Bish' probed away for the rest of the race, but Barrett rode the perfect line and simply would not yield, holding on for a superb victory to share the heat. The Gulls were sharper away at the starts all through the meeting, and heat twelve was no exception as Phelps and Prynne stormed away from the unrelated Somerset duo of Glen Phillips and Mark Phillips. Some sensational riding followed as the two Rebels charged through the opposition and within a lap, they had gone from 1-5 down to 5-1 ahead. Phelps made daring efforts to get back into contention, but fell on the pits bend of the last lap. So a Rebels maximum cut their deficit to just 2-points with three heats to go.

Barrett got the jump in the thirteenth heat, with 'Bish' pressing close behind. Going into the second lap, Phelps cut inside Glen Phillips for third place, while on the pits bend Bishop went underneath Wayne to take the lead. The positions seemed set, until the last bend, when Phelps got a puncture and did well to keep his machine upright, however, this allowed Glen Phillips to nip through for third place to tie the scores up at 39-points apiece. There was more drama in Heat 14, as the meeting produced another twist in true Alfred Hitchcock manner. James made the start to lead from Mark Phillips, with Lobb third and Simon Phillips at the rear. Phillips junior went under Lobb on the third lap, while Phillips senior tried to go under James on the pits bend. Will and Mark Phillips ended up in a pile on the track, with Mark being excluded as being the primary cause of the stoppage, much to the disgust of the homester. After a long delay, a re-run was ordered and James made no mistake, while Simon Phillips again had to work hard, coming through to pass Lobb for second place and set up a last-heat decider with Somerset trailing 41-43.

Tension filled the air as Bishop and Glen Phillips lined up against 'Phelpsy' and Barrett. Sharp-gating Barrett got the drop, with 'Bish' in close attendance, but Phelps absolutely wound it on to storm around the outside of the second bend and up the

The sidecar boys in action at the Moto Parc.

back straight to join his team-mate at the front. Somehow Bishop managed to get the better of the two Gulls with superb track craft and took the lead, but with Glen Phillips suffering machine problems and pulling up, the Gulls were left to share the race and win the match by 2-points. Quickly running through the men of the meeting, Steve Bishop (14) and Glen Phillips (13) were Somerset's best, while Wayne Barrett (14+2) and Gary Phelps (13) led St Austell to their narrow and exciting success in a match witnessed by 1,650 spectators.

August began with Boston again appearing at the clay raceway, this time in the first leg of the Knock-Out Cup semi-final. Former road racer and American flat-tracker Peter Boast headed the Barracuda-Braves score-chart with 11 points, but he could do nothing to save his side from a 33-57 defeat. The exciting Will James led the way for the Gulls, scoring a fabulous paid maximum (15+3) from six rides, while Wayne Barrett (14) and Gary Lobb (11+2) also made big contributions. Following the meeting, the question on everyone's lips was whether a 24 point advantage would be sufficient to see the Gulls reach their third successive cup final?

On 8 August, the Moto Parc played host to another mixed meeting, with the main ingredient being the West of England Speedway Sidecar Championship. In the previous weeks programme, Chris Bridges had mentioned that the sidecar boys would be back, encouraging folk to turn up by commenting 'come and feel the earth move'. That remark was absolutely spot on and there was no better way of describing the action every time these monster machines were in town.

Nine heats of fast and furious action took place and saw Weston-Super-Mare's Joe Mogg take victory with a 12-point maximum. Veteran Ian McAuley, who actually began his racing career in the 1960s, was runner-up on 8 points, and in a real family affair, his son Ricky filled third spot, having mustered 7 points. One of the pre-meeting favourites was Ken Curnow, but an engine failure in his first race put paid to his chances and he was forced to miss the rest of his programmed races. It really was a fantastic night of entertainment, although there was an alarming moment in heat five, when Ian McAuley took off on the pits bend and turned a somersault before landing with a thud. Thankfully though, Ian and his passenger Mark Courtney were able to walk away from the accident unscathed. With both Wayne and Justin Westaway partaking in the meeting, it was certainly a busy night for dad Ken, who flitted between the two with knowledgeable help and advice. Referee Graham Flint, who made his first trip to St Austell, was worthy of praise for exhibiting an excellent sense of humour, while coping with the inevitable programme changes and alterations throughout.

As usual, a full programme of events was on the agenda for the spectators to enjoy, with the sidecar racing being interspersed with speedway and quad demonstrations. Gary Phelps came out on top in the three heats of speedway, outscoring Jason Prynne, Oliver Hackett and Adrian Rowe, while the quad event went to Nigel Hodge from Tim Jones, Peter Pollard and Nigel Polkinghorne.

On 13 August, the Gulls made a wasted journey up to Sheffield for a Conference League encounter. Heavy rain started to fall shortly before the scheduled 6pm start time, and with the track awash, the meeting was postponed a quarter of an hour later.

Newport Mavericks were the Gulls' next visitors as the cut and thrust of league

Martin Williams battles for supremacy with Newports Tom Brown.

business returned to the agenda. At the time, the Welsh side were sitting pretty at the head of the table, however, they were comfortably dispatched 55-33, with St Austell hitting six 5-1's during the course of the evening. Martin Williams made his return to the saddle and although understandably tentative, he rode steadily to notch a paid four-point total. The Gulls reserves were certainly potent for this one though, each taking seven rides, with Gary Lobb hitting 16+2 points, while Will James weighed in with 14+4. Gary Phelps also did well, scoring 12 points for the homesters, while a 10 point return from Chris Courage proved to be the Mavericks' best on the night. The Newport side also included a youngster appearing in his first season of British Speedway, namely Lee Herne, who rode impressively for eight-points and would later start the 2001 campaign representing Trelawny Tigers. The win and aggregate bonus point hoisted St Austell to the top of the league, but it was something of a false position as they had ridden more matches than anyone else and seemed certain to slide downwards.

Five nights later, St Austell made the journey across country for the second leg of the Knock-Out Cup semi-final with Boston. Unfortunately, Gary Lobb missed the trip and the Gulls plugged the gap at reserve with Darren Andrews. It looked like the Barracuda-Braves were up for the meeting right from the off as Luke Clifton and Freddie

Stephenson sped to maximum points, but the Gulls rallied and were only 9-15 down after four heats. However, the Boston boys went on the rampage thereafter and went on to complete a 65-25 rout, giving them an aggregate success by 98 points to 82. Carl Wilkinson set the track alight with his exciting style, romping to a paid 18 point maximum, while team-mate Luke Clifton was also paid for a full-house total of 15. For the beleaguered Gulls, it was a very disappointing evening indeed, with Will James' 8-point tally being sufficient to head the scoring.

The Gulls completed their home league programme on 22 August, when eventual champions Sheffield Prowlers provided powerful opposition. Despite operating rider replacement for James Birkinshaw, the visitors' team was still packed with exciting young talent and resembled the classic Peterborough unit of 1997. It came as no surprise therefore, when Sheffield ended the night as 52-38 victors after fifteen heats of super racing. Teenager Adam Allott roared to a magnificent 18-point maximum, and he had a tremendous pedigree, as his great uncle Tommy, grandfather Guy and father Nick had all previously enjoyed careers on the shale. Meanwhile, Andrew Moore, the son of former grass-track star Richard, zipped to a fine 14-point haul, and old-hand Jamie Young recorded a paid 10 total from the reserve berth as a full-strength Gulls team were well and truly swamped on their own patch. Briefly running through the rest of the Prowlers, future Exeter rider Matt Cambridge notched 8+1, Luke Priest scored 3 and David Speight netted a solitary point. Only Gary Phelps revealed anything like normal

The vintage boys at the Moto Parc in 2000. From left to right: Jim Gregory, Brian Bassett, Terry Stone, Peter Clarke and Tom Richardson.

form for the homesters, scoring 10 points, but everyone was left with nothing but admiration for the rampant Sheffield boys.

On another bumper programme of racing, the fans were treated to an exhibition of vintage and classic speedway racing after the break. Five man heats were the order of the day, with a different scoring system, and it was Peter Clarke who emerged triumphant in the vintage category, having gleaned a 17-point tally. Jim Gregory was second on 15 points, with the remaining competitors being Tom Richardson (14), Brian Bassett (8) and Terry Stone (5). In the classic section, it was Jock Davidson who cleaned up with a 19 point tally, with the other scorers being Ian Paskin (16), Mike Ross (11), Peter Clarke (4) and Terry Stone (2).

Unbeknownst to many of the Moto Parc regulars, time was running out for the Gulls, and what turned out to be their final home team match took place on 29 August, when the previously rained off challenge match against Southampton was restaged. The match turned out to be littered with falls, exclusions and re-runs, with St Austell racking up an easy 61-29 victory. Only Shane Colvin offered any resistance to the drubbing, scoring a dozen points, while the Gulls scoring included four men who were paid for double figures, namely Will James 15+3 (paid maximum), Wayne Barrett 11, Gary Phelps 10+1 and Jason Prynne 9+1. To complete the entertainment, three vintage sidecar speedway races took place in the second half, with Ken Westaway, Phil Williams and Wayne Westaway each gaining a victory apiece.

On 5 September, the GT Motorcycles Cornish Grand National took place and this proved to be the last ever meeting held under the auspices of the Annear family. Mark Simmonds had won the event in 1997 and 1998, with Michael Coles taking glory in 1999, however, a change to the rules meant Premier League riders were not eligible to participate. In spite of this, a good field was put together, including all the regular Gulls, together with Jamie Holmes, Shane Colvin, Lee Herne, the ever-popular Adrian Newman and Scott Pegler, who would go on and lift the Conference League Riders' Championship four days later. The meeting was run over 15 heats, with a grand final to decide the winner. This really was a smashing event, featuring plenty of close racing and passing, with the main protagonists proving to be Gary Phelps (12 points), Will James (11), Shane Colvin (11) and Martin Williams (10). When it came to the final, James lost control approaching the first turn, damaging Phelps' rear wheel as he fell. Referee Barry Richardson showed leniency and allowed all-four back in the re-start, with James having to borrow a machine from 'Skippy' Newman. With three Gulls in the race, a home victory was expected, but Shane Colvin turned out to be a real shock merchant, leaping ahead and pulling away to win from James and Prynne, with Phelps forced out by equipment problems.

It had been mooted that a 4-team tournament might have been held the following week, but this never took place and the Annears' reign at the Moto Parc, to all intents and purposes, was over. The Gulls might have completed their home fixtures, but the season was far from over, as there were still three away matches to be fitted in at Boston, Mildenhall and Sheffield. The match against Boston was scheduled for 7 October at King's Lynn, but with rain lashing across England, the meeting was inevitably called off. The following day, St Austell did complete one of their outstanding fixtures, however, when they travelled up to the well-appointed Owlerton Stadium to take on the formidable Sheffield outfit. The meeting formed the first half of a double-header and turned out to be a real cracker, despite Will James being unavailable and the fact that Wayne Barrett was appearing for Exeter in a Premier League match at Stoke. Covering the absentees, the Gulls operated rider replacement at no.1, while Darren Andrews was drafted in for another outing at no.4.

The scores remained level for the opening three heats, prior to the battling Cornish side taking the lead in heat four, courtesy of maximum points from Gary Lobb and Jason Prynne. Sheffield hit back and were leading by the seventh heat, but in a nip and tuck encounter, the Gulls came right back and regained the lead through a 5-1 from 'Lobby' and Richard Ford in heat eight. By the tenth race, things were all square again, with the Prowlers edging ahead in the following heat, thanks to a 4-2 from Andrew Moore and Matt Cambridge. After that, the homesters remained on top and went on to win 48-42, but the Gulls had played a full part in a wonderful match, which sadly, would turn out to be their last. Amazingly, 17-year-old Adam Allott repeated his performance at the Moto Parc, going through the card to notch an 18-point maximum for Sheffield, while team-mate Andrew Moore (16+1) lent marvellous support. Meanwhile, the Gulls' best performers on the day were Gary Lobb, who rode exceptionally well for 14 points, and Jason Prynne, who notched a paid 12-point total.

After the interval, Sheffield got down to the business of facing Rye House in another league match, which unfortunately had to be abandoned after heat thirteen. The Prowlers were leading 40-38 at the time and Adam Allott had just collected his eleventh straight victory of the day, when he collapsed by the pits. The medical team rushed to give the youngster assistance, before he was rushed to hospital for further attention, where he thankfully made a speedy recovery. However, with little chance of the ambulance returning before Sheffield's 10pm curfew, referee Dave Dowling had no option but to abandon the proceedings. A win was far from mathematically certain, but the fact that the meeting had gone beyond 12 heats meant the result had to stand, therefore giving Sheffield two more points on their charge to the Championship.

It had long since become apparent that the Gulls promotional team were tiring, but this was quite understandable as their geographical location made for almost twice as much travelling than most other tracks. Then, there was the fact that in the past, they only had to look after Annear's Garage and the speedway, however in 2000, there was also a petrol station and a scooter business to run. Dad Brian largely took a back seat on the speedway front throughout the year, leaving brothers Steve and Andy to do the bulk of the work, but with an increased work load and young families to cater for, it ineviatably became a strain. This was fully emphasized on 18 October, when the Gulls again tried to race their match against Boston at King's Lynn, but they had a 740-mile round trip in vain as the meeting again fell foul to inclement weather. Steve Annear took up the story in the Speedway Star track review, 'We got there and all the lights were out, no-one had called us. We don't blame Boston, but with King's Lynn having a big meeting the next day, we could see why they would not run in bad weather. It had been such a waste of time and money!'

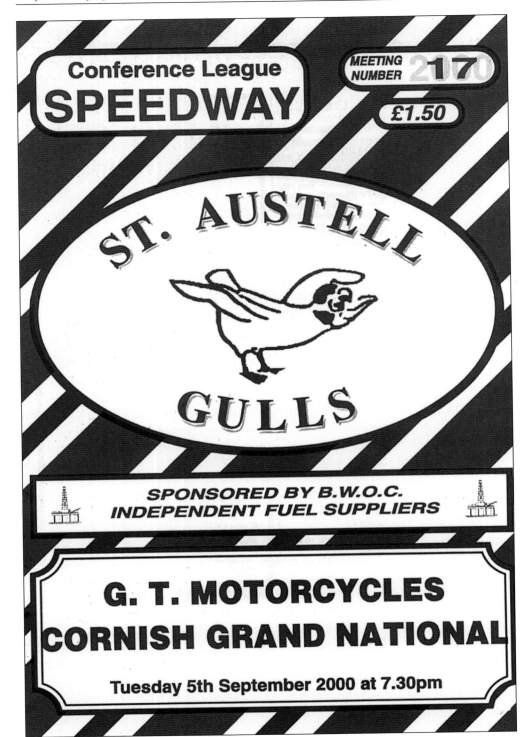

The programme from the Cornish Grand National, 2000.

Shane Colvin gets a kiss from girlfriend and mechanic Charly Kirtland after winning the Cornish Grand Prix.

In an effort to complete the outstanding fixtures, a double-header was scheduled at Mildenhall on 28 October, when the Gulls hoped to face both the Fen Tigers and Boston. Yet again, the weather won the day though, and it was so wet that the chance of trying again the following day was quickly ruled out. Not only did the Gulls want to get their fixtures completed, but also Mildenhall had a particular interest in winning what should have been their final match as it would have given them the league title. Both Boston and Mildenhall hoped that the authorities would allow them to extend the season and fulfil the fixtures as a double-header the following weekend. The SCB subsequently upheld the BSPA management committee decision to award Mildenhall the bonus point after their victory at the Moto Parc earlier in the season, but forbade the proposed double-header to go ahead. With the league table incomplete, Sheffield and Mildenhall sat on top with 31 points apiece, but it was the South Yorkshire side who lifted the Championship, thanks to a superior race points difference.

Looking at the Gulls, seventh place in the final table was a bit of a disappointing way to end the four-year journey, but they certainly weren't helped by the injury toll. The ever-reliable Wayne Barrett was top man as far as the averages were concerned, scoring 249 points from 21 official matches for an 8.64 figure. Meanwhile, Gary Phelps enjoyed a good season, albeit with two months on the sidelines while his wrist injury healed, recording an impressive 7.93 average. Spectacular returnee Will James was next in the figures on 7.92, and he proved to be a mighty popular addition to the squad with his on-track tenacity. The battle-scarred Jason Prynne was worthy of high praise for appearing in all 22 of the Gulls' official meetings to score 198 points and achieve a 7.52 average, despite riding for much of the time with a fractured scaphoid. Gary Lobb also missed matches through injury, but when he rode, he put in some mighty impressive performances; none more so than his 14 point tally at Sheffield in the Gulls' last match. 'Lobby' finished with an average of exactly seven, while the other representatives ended thus: Martin Williams (6.07); Richard Ford (5.55); Mark Thompson (2.71).

The usual end of season social get together was a low-key affair and was run as a 'Farewell to the Gulls' at Will and Andrea James' Glendeveor Hotel in Mount Wise, Newquay on Friday 8 December. Unlike previous years, the famous old trophies from the Rocky Park days were not used as they had been returned to Roger Kessell. Special one-off trophies were therefore handed out, with Gary Phelps receiving the rider of the year award, while Will James took the accolades as the most exciting racer in the Gulls camp. Track man supreme Nigel Prynne deservedly won a trophy for the super job he had done on the circuit, not only in 2000, but also right from the start in 1997. Wayne Barrett was also presented with a trophy for scoring the most points, with Richard Ford claiming a similar award for being the bonus point king. Special guests on the night included Exeter riders Chris Harris and Seemond Stephens, along with Ray Purvis, who would later play a big part in future racing at the brilliant Longstone Pit venue.

Richard Ford.

Will James.

David Collins.

Once the dust had settled down after the close of the season, the future of Cornish speedway initially seemed in serious doubt, however, there was a glint of light, when a new consortium came forward with plans to introduce Premier League racing at a new venue in Mitchell, with the team riding under the name of Trelawny Tigers. The story of how the new team ended up racing at the Moto Parc is taken up by press officer David Collins, 'Trelawny's presence at the Moto Parc in 2001 came as quite a surprise – especially to Trelawny! During the previous year, the whole concept of a new Cornish club was little more than an idea in the minds of two enthusiastic individuals. They had found a site that looked promising and the two had become a consortium of four. The intention was to plan for the 2002 season, but things were to change dramatically. On a cold, miserable morning towards the end of the 2000 campaign, I received a phone call from Brian Annear. After the pleasantries were exchanged, the conversation went something like this: "Right Dave, are you in with the Trelawny lot?" "Yes," I replied. "Would you like the Moto Parc for next season?" "Are you pulling my leg?" "No, I'm pulling out. It's there for the taking if you want it, but I'm not prepared to talk to them at this stage. I don't want four of them keep ringing me up and having to go through the same things over and over. Would you be the go-between until we've established enough common ground and then you can arrange to get us all together?" he asked.'

'I certainly would – and did. I immediately phoned Shirley Stephens and Ray Purvis (two members of the new consortium), who had set off with Seemond Stephens for Exeter's fixture at Hull. Shirley will never forget that call, "I know the exact spot on the A30 that we were on when we got the call and it took sometime to sink in." Twenty minutes later, they got another call to say the Hull match was off and returned home. For the next few weeks, it was all questions and answers as the

Moto Parc was rented, but the buildings, safety fence, lights etc., were all Brian's. There was also a little matter of two double-decker busses and an enormous amount of old tyres. Negotiations continued for several weeks until eventually, we all met on 28 December at the Moto Parc, where the deal was wrapped up and the keys handed over to the Trelawny management.'

David concluded by stating, 'I was the first person to be taken on to Brian's staff in November 1996 – six months before the St Austell Gulls rode their first match at the Moto Parc. I am grateful to him for asking me to be involved right up to the last day, and I'm equally thankful to Trelawny for bringing me in on day one.'

Having decided to give up, Brian Annear was left with the problem of disposing of the buses and he decided to advertise them in the local free-advertising newspapers. A number of amusing telephone calls followed as one person wanted a bus to keep a woman in, while another wished to have one of the vehicles as a wendy house in his garden, in order to wind the neighbours up! Just for good measure, the latter caller also proudly announced that he had an old-fashioned telephone box in his lounge! Both buses eventually found a new home at Callington, although rumours abounded, quite wrongly, that Brian had ditched them in the lake beside the track. Having sorted the buses out, the next issue was getting rid of the tyres that surrounded the track. A long-running debate took place over these tyres and whose responsibility they were, with Brian pointing out the fact that they had actually been there before the speedway track was ever thought of. Anyway, the situation was eventually resolved and the tyres were taken away by the lorry load.

The final words from Brian were a big thank you to the four riders he listed as his particular favourites from the Moto Parc era, namely Roger Lobb, Frank Smart, Paul Macklin and Chris Harris. These were singled out for the way they would always make an effort to race, even if they had to borrow equipment, or would simply turn up to help out and ride in return for a drink in a local bar afterwards.

Tuesday 2 May, 2000 – Conference League Cup
ST.AUSTELL 'GULLS' 50 BUXTON 'HITMEN' 39

ST.AUSTELL

Rider	Scores	Total	
Wayne Barrett	3 3 3 3 3 3 -	18	
Kevin Hamley	F M 1'0 - - -	1	1
Gary Lobb R/R	- - - - - - -	-	
Dominic Walsh-Newton	1 1'0 X F -	2	1
Richard Ford	2'1 - - - - -	3	1
Martin Williams	3 2 R 2'1 3 -	11	1
Jason Prynne	2'3 2 2 3 3 0	15	1
Gerry Sims (No.8)	- - - - - - -	-	

BUXTON

Rider	Scores	Total	
Dean Felton	2 3 3 3 1 2 1'	15	1
Daniel Hodgson	M R R R - - -	0	
James Mann R/R	- - - - - - -	-	
Phil Pickering	2 2'3 2 2 2 2	15	1
Lee Howard	1 R 0 - - - -	1	
Neil Painter	1 2 1 1'1'- -	6	2
Paul Burnett	1'0 F R 1'- -	2	2
Oliver Hackett (No.8)	- - - - - - -	-	

PROGRAMME CHANGES:-
Ht 1: Burnett replaced Hodgson; Ht 3: R/R Barrett; R/R Hodgson; Ht 5: R/R Williams; Ht 7: R/R Felton; Ht 8: T/S Felton for Hodgson; Ht 9: R/R Prynne; T/S Pickering for Howard; Ht 10: R/R Prynne; Prynne replaced Ford; Ht 11: R/R Burnett; Ht 12: R/R Walsh-Newton; R/R Pickering; Ht 13: Williams replaced Ford; Ht 14: Painter replaced Burnett

Note: Although Kevin Hamley was excluded from Heat-6 for exceeding the 2-minute allowance, he was not replaced.

Heat	Result	Gulls	Bux
Ht 1	Barrett, Felton, Burnett, Hamley (fell), Hodgson (ex, 2 mins), 57.71	3	3
Ht 2	Williams, Prynne, Painter, Burnett, 57.34	8	4
Ht 3	Barrett, Pickering, Walsh-Newton, Hodgson (ret), 57.97	12	6
Ht 4	Prynne, Ford, Howard, Burnett (fell), 59.00	17	7
Ht 5	Felton, Williams, Walsh-Newton, Hodgson (ret), 58.84	20	10
Ht 6	Barrett, Painter, Howard, Hamley (ex, 2 mins), 58.00 (3 Riders Only)	23	12
Ht 7	Felton, Pickering, Ford, Williams (ret), 58.62	24	17
Ht 8	Felton, Prynne, Hamley, Burnett (ret), 58.19	27	20
Ht 9	Pickering, Prynne, Painter, Walsh-Newton, 57.75	29	24
Ht 10	Barrett, Pickering, Burnett, Hamley, 58.31	32	27
Ht 11	Prynne, Williams, Felton, Hodgson (ret), 58.32	37	28
Ht 12	(Awarded) Prynne, Pickering, Painter, Walsh-Newton (f,ex), No Time	40	31
Ht 13	Barrett, Felton, Williams, Howard, 58.82	44	33
Ht 14	Williams, Pickering, Painter, Walsh-Newton (fell), 57.95	47	36
Ht 15	(Nominated) Barrett, Pickering, Felton, Prynne, 58.10	50	39

Tuesday 9 May, 2000 – Conference League
ST.AUSTELL 'GULLS' 46 BOSTON 'BARRACUDA-BRAVES' 44

ST.AUSTELL

Rider	Scores	Total	
Wayne Barrett	2 3 3 3 3 R-	14	
Richard Ford	- - - - - -	-	
Gary Lobb R/R	- - - - - -	-	
Dominic Walsh-Newton	R- - - - - -	-	
Gary Phelps	2 2'1 2 2'1	10	2
Martin Williams	1'3 2 3 R 3 2	14	1
Jason Prynne	R 1'1 3 3 M0	8	1
Kevin Hamley (No.8)	- - - - - -	-	

BOSTON

Rider	Scores	Total	
Peter Boast	3 0 3 1 3 - -	10	
Ricky Scarboro	0 2 2 1 - - -	5	
Carl Wilkinson	1 R 1'- - - -	2	1
David Chadburn	T 1 2 1 - - -	4	
Dean Garrod	0 2 0 M- - -	2	
Luke Clifton	2 3 1'2 2 0 2'	12	2
Robert Hollingworth	1'3 1'1'1'3 - -	9	3

PROGRAMME CHANGES:-
Ht 1: Williams replaced Ford; Ht 3: R/R Williams; Hollingworth replaced Chadburn in the re-run; Ht 4: Clifton replaced Hollingworth; Ht 5: R/R Barrett; Prynne replaced Walsh-Newton; Ht 9: R/R Phelps; Prynne replaced Walsh-Newton; Ht 12: R/R Williams; Hollingworth replaced Wilkinson; Ht 13: Clifton replaced Garrod; Ht 14: Prynne replaced Walsh-Newton

Note: After crashing into the safety fence during the warm-up lap, Richard Ford took no part in the match. He was replaced in his first ride (Heat-1), but St.Austell had no replacement for his other rides (Heats-6, 8 & 10). The 'Gulls' were further hampered in Heat-3, when Dominic Walsh-Newton pulled up and took no further part in the meeting, having aggravated old wrist and collarbone injuries.

Heat	Result	Gulls	Bos
Ht 1	Boast, Barrett, Williams, Scarboro, 57.84	3	3
Ht 2	Williams, Clifton, Hollingworth, Prynne (ret), 56.47	6	6
Ht 3	(Re-Run) Hollingworth, Williams, Wilkinson, Walsh-Newton (ret), Chadburn (ex, tapes), 58.40	8	10
Ht 4	Clifton, Phelps, Prynne, Garrod, 58.15	11	13
Ht 5	Barrett, Scarboro, Prynne, Boast, 57.27	15	15
Ht 6	Barrett, Garrod, Clifton, 58.41 (3 Riders Only)	18	18
Ht 7	Williams, Phelps, Chadburn (f,rem), Wilkinson (ret), 58.12	23	19
Ht 8	Prynne, Scarboro, Hollingworth, 58.10 (3 Riders Only)	26	22
Ht 9	Prynne, Clifton, Phelps, Garrod, 58.13	30	24
Ht 10	Barrett, Chadburn, Wilkinson, 58.12 (3 Riders Only)	33	27
Ht 11	Boast, Phelps, Scarboro, Williams (ret), 58.16	35	31
Ht 12	Williams, Clifton, Hollingworth, Prynne (ex, 2 mins), 57.34 (3 Riders Only)	38	34
Ht 13	Barrett, Phelps, Boast, Clifton, Garrod (ex, 2 mins), 58.00	43	35
Ht 14	Hollingworth, Williams, Chadburn, Prynne, 59.57	45	39
Ht 15	(Nominated) Boast, Clifton, Phelps, Barrett (ret), 58.74	46	44

145

Tuesday 16 May, 2000
SIMPSON PLANT HIRE INDIVIDUAL CHALLENGE

1st JASON PRYNNE;
2nd SHANE COLVIN; 3rd WAYNE BARRETT

Wayne Barrett	3 2 2 2 - - -	9
Simon Phillips	2 1 1 3 - - -	7
Shane Colvin	1 2 3 3 - - -	9
Oliver Hackett	M F R - - - -	0
Jason Prynne	2 3 3 3 - - -	11
Jamie Holmes	1 3 3 1 - - -	8
Martin Williams	3 3 2 2 - - -	10
Richard Ford	R 1 1 2 - - -	4
Charly Kirtland	2 0 2 1 - - -	5
Gavin Horsborough	1 R R R - - -	1
Gerry Sims	0 R 0 0 - - -	0
Chris Bennett	3 2 0 0 - - -	5

PROGRAMME CHANGES:-
None!

Note: Oliver Hackett was a non-starter in Heat-1, and was not replaced as there was no meeting reserve. Hackett later missed Heat-6 and the C Final following 2-minute exclusions, with the races featuring 3 riders only as a result.

Ht 1	Barrett, Phillips, Colvin, 58.65 (3 Riders Only)
Ht 2	Williams, Prynne, Holmes, Ford (ret), 57.94
Ht 3	Bennett, Kirtland, Horsborough, Sims, 62.28
Ht 4	Prynne, Barrett, Ford, Horsborough (ret), 58.41
Ht 5	Williams, Colvin, Phillips, Kirtland, 57.59
Ht 6	Holmes, Bennett, Sims (ret), Hackett (ex, 2 mins), 59.78 (3 Riders Only)
Ht 7	Prynne, Barrett, Phillips, Sims, 58.37
Ht 8	Colvin, Williams, Ford, Bennett, 59.32
Ht 9	Holmes, Kirtland, Hackett (fell), Horsborough (ret), 61.56
Ht 10	Phillips, Ford, Kirtland, Sims, 60.25
Ht 11	Prynne, Williams, Hackett (ret), Horsborough (ret), 58.72
Ht 12	Colvin, Barrett, Holmes, Bennett, 58.35
Ht 13	(C Final) Ford, Horsborough, Sims, Hackett (ex, 2 mins), 60.28 (3 Riders Only)
Ht 14	(B Final) Holmes, Phillips, Bennett, Kirtland, 59.87
Ht 15	(A Final) Prynne, Colvin, Barrett, Williams, 58.82

Tuesday 23 May, 2000 – Conference League
ST.AUSTELL 'GULLS' 52 ASHFIELD 'GIANTS' 36

ST.AUSTELL

Wayne Barrett	3 3 3 3 2'1-	15 1
Kevin Hamley	0 0 0 1 - - -	1
Gary Lobb R/R	- - - - - - -	-
Richard Ford	1 2 F 3 2'- -	8 1
Gary Phelps	n - - - - - -	0
Martin Williams	3 3 2 R 3 3 3	17
Jason Prynne	2'1 1 3 2 2'-	11 2
Gerry Sims (No.8)	R - - - - - -	0

ASHFIELD

Scott Courtney	2 3 2 3 F 2 -	12
Robert McNeil	1'1 3 2 1 - -	8 1
Christian Henry	2 3 2 - - - -	7
Iain MacAulay	0 1 0 - - - -	1
David McAllan R/R	- - - - - - -	-
Gary Flint	R 2 1'X X 0 -	3 1
Derek Sneddon	1 X 2'R 1 1 0	5 1

PROGRAMME CHANGES:-
Ht 3: R/R Barrett; Ht 4: R/R Flint; Williams replaced Phelps, who was unable to partake in the re-run; Ht 5: R/R Sims; Ht 6: R/R Courtney; Ht 9: R/R Prynne; R/R McNeil; Ht 11: Prynne replaced Phelps; Ht 12: R/R Ford; Sneddon replaced Henry; Ht 13: Williams replaced Phelps; R/R Sneddon; Ht 14: Flint replaced MacAulay

Note: Gary Phelps was unable to partake in Heat-7, and was not replaced.

Note: To give them their full title, the 'Gulls' opposition for this match were actually called Lightning Ashfield 'Giants'.

		Gulls	Ash
Ht 1	Barrett, Courtney, McNeil, Hamley, 56.72	3	3
Ht 2	Williams, Prynne, Sneddon, Flint (f,rem, ret), 58.80	8	4
Ht 3	Barrett, Henry, Ford, MacAulay, 60.34	12	6
Ht 4	(Re-Run) Williams, Flint, Prynne, Sneddon (f,ex), Phelps (f,ns), 60.37	16	8
Ht 5	Courtney, Ford, McNeil, Sims (ret), 57.94	18	12
Ht 6	Barrett, Courtney, Flint, Hamley, 58.44	21	15
Ht 7	Henry, Williams, MacAulay, 56.85 (3 Riders Only)	23	19
Ht 8	McNeil, Sneddon, Prynne, Hamley, 62.15	24	24
Ht 9	(Re-Run) Prynne, McNeil, Ford (fell), Flint (f,ex), 61.87	27	26
Ht 10	Barrett, Henry, Hamley, MacAulay, 58.72	31	28
Ht 11	Courtney, Prynne, McNeil, Williams (ret), 59.06	33	32
Ht 12	Ford, Prynne, Sneddon (ret), Flint (f,rem, ex, lapped), 62.22	38	32
Ht 13	Williams, Barrett, Sneddon, Courtney (fell), 58.84	43	33
Ht 14	Williams, Ford, Sneddon, Flint, 58.03	48	34
Ht 15	(Nominated) Williams, Courtney, Barrett, Sneddon, 58.19	52	36

146

Tuesday 30 May, 2000 – Conference League Cup
ST.AUSTELL 'GULLS' 48 SOMERSET 'REBELS' 40

ST.AUSTELL

Rider	Scores	Pts	
Wayne Barrett	2 2'X 2 2 - -	8	1
Richard Ford	1'3 2 1 2 3 -	12	1
Gary Lobb	3 2 3 1 - - -	9	
Mark Thompson	X 1 0 0 - - -	1	
Gary Phelps	- - - - - - -	-	
Martin Williams	3 0 1'1'1'1 - -	6	2
Jason Prynne	1 3 3 3 R 2'-	12	1
Gerry Sims (No.8)	- - - - - - -	-	

SOMERSET

Rider	Scores	Pts	
Steve Bishop	3 3 3 3 3 3 X	18	
Jason Newitt	0 1'- - - - -	1	1
Adrian Newman R/R	- - - - - - -	-	
Dave Roberts	n - - - - - -	0	
Ray Dickson	F 0 1'X 0 X -	1	1
Simon Phillips	2 1 1 M 2 2 3	11	
Mark Phillips	0 2 2 1 2 X 2'	9	1

PROGRAMME CHANGES:-
Ht 3: R/R Newitt; M.Phillips replaced Roberts, who was unable to partake in the re-run; Ht 4: R/R Thompson; Ht 5: S.Phillips replaced Newitt; Ht 7: R/R Ford; T/S Bishop for Newman; M.Phillips replaced Roberts; Ht 8: S.Phillips replaced Newitt; Ht 10: R/R Bishop; M.Phillips replaced Roberts; Ht 11: R/R Barrett; Ht 12: R/R Dickson; Ht 13: R/R Williams; Ht 14: Prynne replaced Thompson; S.Phillips replaced Roberts

Note: Simon Phillips replaced Jason Newitt in Heat-8, but was excluded for exceeding the time allowance, with the race featuring three riders only as a result. Newitt was a non-starter in Heat-11 and was not replaced, leaving just three riders to contest the race.

		Gulls	Som
Ht 1	Bishop, Barrett, Ford, Newitt, 55.38	3	3
Ht 2	Williams, S.Phillips, Prynne, M.Phillips, 56.22	7	5
Ht 3	(Re-Run) Lobb, M.Phillips, Newitt, Thompson (f,ex), Roberts (f,ns), 58.38	10	8
Ht 4	Prynne, M.Phillips, Thompson, Dickson (fell), 57.78	14	10
Ht 5	Bishop, Lobb, S.Phillips, Thompson, 55.37	16	14
Ht 6	Ford, Barrett, S.Phillips, Dickson, 58.00	21	15
Ht 7	Bishop, Ford, M.Phillips, Williams, 56.12	23	19
Ht 8	Prynne, M.Phillips, Ford, S.Phillips (ex, 2 mins), 57.47 (3 Riders Only)	27	21
Ht 9	Lobb, S.Phillips, Dickson, Thompson, 61.37	30	24
Ht 10	(Re-Run – Awarded) Bishop, Ford, Barrett (f,ex), M.Phillips (f,ex), No Time	32	27
Ht 11	Bishop, Barrett, S.Phillips, 56.21 (3 Riders Only)	35	30
Ht 12	(Awarded) Prynne, S.Phillips, Lobb, Dickson (f,ex), No Time	39	32
Ht 13	Bishop, Barrett, Williams, Dickson, 56.40	42	35
Ht 14	S.Phillips, M.Phillips, Williams, Prynne (ret), 58.03	43	40
Ht 15	(Nominated – Re-Run) Ford, Prynne, Dickson (f,ex), Bishop (ex, not under power), 70.15	48	40

Tuesday 6 June, 2000 – Conference League
ST.AUSTELL 'GULLS' 35 MILDENHALL 'FEN TIGERS' 55

ST.AUSTELL

Rider	Scores	Pts	
Wayne Barrett	2 3 1 2'2 1 1	12	1
Mark Thompson	0 0 2 - - - -	2	
Gary Phelps R/R	- - - - - - -	-	
Will James	1 0 1 R - - -	2	
Gary Lobb	2 2'0 0 0 X -	4	1
Jason Prynne	2 1'2 3 3 1 2	14	1
Richard Ford	R M 1'0 - - -	1	1

MILDENHALL

Rider	Scores	Pts	
Steve Camden	3 2 3 3 3 2'-	16	1
Phil Knowles	1 1 3 2'1 - -	8	1
Shane Colvin R/R	- - - - - - -	-	
Ian Leverington	0 0 0 - - - -	0	
Barrie Evans	3 3 2'1 2'3 -	14	2
Paul Lydes-Uings	3 2'1 3 3 3 -	15	1
Jitendra Duffill	1 0 0 1 - - -	2	

PROGRAMME CHANGES:-
Ht 3: R/R Barrett; R/R Camden; Ht 4: Prynne replaced Ford; Ht 5: R/R Prynne; Ht 7: R/R Lydes-Uings; Ht 9: R/R Lobb; Ht 10: Prynne replaced Thompson; R/R Evans; Ht 12: T/S Barrett for R/R; R/R Knowles; Ht 14: Lydes-Uings replaced Leverington

		Gulls	Mild
Ht 1	Camden, Barrett, Knowles, Thompson, 58.03	2	4
Ht 2	Lydes-Uings, Prynne, Duffill, Ford (ret), 57.44	4	8
Ht 3	(Re-Run) Barrett, Camden, James, Leverington, 57.47	8	10
Ht 4	Evans, Lobb, Prynne, Duffill, Ford (ex, 2 mins), 57.88	11	13
Ht 5	Camden, Prynne, Knowles, James, 57.81	13	17
Ht 6	Evans, Lydes-Uings, Barrett, Thompson, 57.13	14	22
Ht 7	Prynne, Lobb, Lydes-Uings, Leverington, 57.34	19	23
Ht 8	Knowles, Thompson, Ford, Duffill (f,rem), 57.62	22	26
Ht 9	Lydes-Uings, Evans, James, Lobb, 56.62	23	31
Ht 10	Prynne, Barrett, Evans, Leverington, 57.25	28	32
Ht 11	Camden, Knowles, Prynne, Lobb, 56.62	29	37
Ht 12	Lydes-Uings, Barrett, Knowles, Ford, 57.03	31	41
Ht 13	Camden, Evans, Barrett, Lobb, 57.00	32	46
Ht 14	Lydes-Uings, Prynne, Duffill, James (ret), 57.07	34	50
Ht 15	(Nominated – Re-Run) Evans, Camden, Barrett, Lobb (f,ex), 57.50	35	55

147

Tuesday 27 June, 2000 – Conference League
ST.AUSTELL 'GULLS' 51 BUXTON 'HITMEN' 38

```
ST.AUSTELL
Wayne Barrett      3 2 3 1 2'2 -    13  1
Oliver Hackett     R X F - - - -     0
Will James         3 2 2'3 2 1'-    13  2
Richard Ford       2'X R 2'- - -     4  2
Gary Phelps R/R    - - - - - - -     -
Jason Prynne       3 F 3 3 3 -      15
Gary Lobb          2'2 0 2 0 - -     6  1

BUXTON
James Mann         2 3 2 1 3 - -    11
Daniel Hodgson     1'1 R - - - -     2  1
Neil Painter       1 1 2 1 - - -     5
Lee Howard         R 1'1 - - - -     2  1
Paul Burnett       3 1 1'R - - -     5  1
Phil Pickering     1 3 0 2 3 F -     9
Steve Mildoon      T 1 3 0 X - -     4
```

PROGRAMME CHANGES:-
Ht 4: R/R Prynne; Ht 6: Lobb replaced Hackett;
Ht 7: R/R James; Pickering replaced Howard;
Ht 11: R/R Barrett; Mildoon replaced Hodgson;
Ht 13: R/R Prynne

		Gulls	Bux
Ht 1	Barrett, Mann, Hodgson, Hackett (ret), 57.47	3	3
Ht 2	(Re-Run) Prynne, Lobb, Pickering, Mildoon (ex, tapes), 57.60 (3 Riders Only)	8	4
Ht 3	James, Ford, Painter, Howard (ret), 58.25	13	5
Ht 4	Burnett, Lobb, Mildoon, Prynne (fell), 58.78	15	9
Ht 5	(Re-Run) Mann, James, Hodgson, Ford (f,ex), 57.69	17	13
Ht 6	Pickering, Barrett, Burnett, Lobb, 57.50	19	17
Ht 7	Prynne, James, Painter, Pickering, 57.66	24	18
Ht 8	Mildoon, Lobb, Hodgson (ret), Hackett (ex, crossed white line), 58.13	26	21
Ht 9	James, Pickering, Burnett, Ford (ret), 58.57	29	24
Ht 10	Barrett, Painter, Howard, Hackett (fell), 58.00	32	27
Ht 11	Prynne, Mann, Barrett, Mildoon, 57.25	36	29
Ht 12	Pickering, James, Painter, Lobb, 57.90	38	33
Ht 13	Prynne, Barrett, Mann, Burnett (ret), 58.06	43	34
Ht 14	(Re-Run) Prynne, Ford, Howard, Mildoon (f,ex), 58.10	48	35
Ht 15	(Nominated) Mann, Barrett, James, Pickering (fell), 57.16	51	38

Tuesday 4 July, 2000 – Conference League
ST.AUSTELL 'GULLS' 53 RYE HOUSE 'ROCKETS' 37

```
ST.AUSTELL
Wayne Barrett      3 1 2 3 - - -     9
Oliver Hackett     1 0 0 1'- - -     2  1
Jason Prynne       2 3 3 3 1'1 -    13  1
Richard Ford       1'1 1 2 2'- -     7  2
Gary Phelps R/R    - - - - - - -     -
Will James         3 0 1 1'3 - -     8  1
Gary Lobb          2'2 3 2 2'3 -    14  2

RYE HOUSE
Simon Wolstenholme 2 2 2 3 1 0 -    10
No Rider           - - - - - - -     -
David Mason        3 3 2 3 3 2 -    16
Gerry Sims         0 0 0 - - - -     0
Phil Ambrose R/R   - - - - - - -     -
Simon Moon         0 2'2 0 0 0 -     4  1
Nathan Morton      1 1 3 1'0 1 -     7  1
```

PROGRAMME CHANGES:-
Ht 4: R/R James; R/R Mason; Ht 6: R/R Morton;
Ht 7: R/R Prynne; Ht 8: Moon filled the absent
rider slot; Ht 9: R/R Wolstenholme; Ht 11: R/R
Ford; Ht 13: R/R Lobb; R/R Morton; Ht 14:
Moon replaced Sims

Note: Gary Lobb was due to challenge David
Mason for the Bronze Helmet, however, he
sustained an ankle injury while winning Heat-
15, and was subsequently replaced by Jason
Prynne.

Note: Having arrived with just four riders, Rye House had to operate rider-replacement for Phil Ambrose, as well as borrowing St.Austell junior Gerry Sims. However, that still left them with a gap at No.2, and aside from Heat-8, this meant they could only track one rider in Heats-1, 5 & 11.

		Gulls	RH
Ht 1	Barrett, Wolstenholme, Hackett, 56.75 (3 Riders Only)	4	2
Ht 2	James, Lobb, Morton, Moon, 58.25	9	3
Ht 3	Mason, Prynne, Ford, Sims, 56.19	12	6
Ht 4	Mason, Lobb, Morton, James, 57.53	14	10
Ht 5	Prynne, Wolstenholme, Ford, 57.65 (3 Riders Only)	18	12
Ht 6	Morton, Moon, Barrett, Hackett, 60.62	19	17
Ht 7	Prynne, Mason, James, Sims, 57.65	23	19
Ht 8	Lobb, Moon, Morton, Hackett, 59.65	26	22
Ht 9	Prynne, Wolstenholme, Ford, Moon, 57.43	30	24
Ht 10	Mason, Barrett, Hackett, Sims, 56.19	33	27
Ht 11	Wolstenholme, Ford, James, 57.69 (3 Riders Only)	36	30
Ht 12	Mason, Lobb, Prynne, Moon, 57.06	39	33
Ht 13	Barrett, Lobb, Wolstenholme, Morton, 57.34	44	34
Ht 14	James, Ford, Morton, Moon, 58.38	49	35
Ht 15	(Nominated) Lobb, Mason, Prynne, Wolstenholme, 57.81	53	37
	Bronze Helmet: Mason, Prynne, 57.60		

Tuesday 11 July, 2000 – Conference League
ST.AUSTELL 'GULLS' 49 SOMERSET 'REBELS' 39

ST.AUSTELL
Wayne Barrett	2 3 3 2 0 2 -	12
Richard Ford	1¹1 1¹1'M- -	4 3
Jason Prynne	1 2¹1¹1'2 - -	7 3
Gary Phelps	3 3 2 3 R- -	11
Martin Williams R/R	- - - - - - -	-
Will James	X 2 2 - - - -	4
Gary Lobb	3 1¹2 1 1¹2 1	11 2
Oliver Hackett (No.8)	- - - - - - -	-

SOMERSET
Steve Bishop	3 X 3 2 3 1 1	13
Dean Garton	R M- - - - -	0
Glen Phillips R/R	- - - - - - -	-
Ray Dickson	F 0 F 0 - - -	0
Adrian Newman	2 3 2 3 3 3 3	19
Mark Phillips	X - - - - - -	0
Simon Phillips	2 F X 0 3 0 2	7
Charly Kirtland (No.8)	- - - - - - -	-

PROGRAMME CHANGES:-
Ht 3: R/R Newman; Ht 4: R/R James; Ht 5: S.Phillips replaced Garton; Ht 6: S.Phillips replaced M.Phillips; Ht 7: R/R Ford; T/S Bishop for G.Phillips; Ht 8: T/S Dickson for Garton; Ht 10: R/R Bishop; Lobb replaced Ford; Ht 11: R/R Barrett; Lobb replaced James; Ht 12: R/R S.Phillips; T/S Newman for M.Phillips; Ht 13: R/R Prynne; Ht 14: Lobb replaced James

Note: Mark Phillips, Dean Garton and Ray Dickson were non-starters in Heats-9, 11 & 14 respectively, and were not replaced, with Somerset only tracking one rider in each race.

		Gulls	Som
Ht 1	Bishop, Barrett, Ford, Garton (ret), 57.28	3	3
Ht 2	(Re-Run) Lobb, S.Phillips, James (ex, not under power), M.Phillips (f,ex), 57.59	6	5
Ht 3	Phelps, Newman, Prynne, Dickson (fell), 58.06	10	7
Ht 4	Newman, James, Lobb, S.Phillips (fell), 57.06	13	10
Ht 5	(Re-Run) Phelps, Prynne, S.Phillips (f,ex), Bishop (ex, not under power), Garton (ex, 2 mins), 59.75	18	10
Ht 6	Barrett, Newman, Ford, S.Phillips, 58.38	22	12
Ht 7	Bishop, James, Ford, Dickson, 57.56	25	15
Ht 8	S.Phillips, Lobb, Ford, Dickson (fell), 59.34	28	18
Ht 9	Newman, Phelps, Prynne, 56.62 (3 Riders Only)	31	21
Ht 10	Barrett, Bishop, Lobb, Dickson, Ford (ex, 2 mins), 57.35	35	23
Ht 11	Bishop, Barrett, Lobb, 57.45 (3 Riders Only)	38	26
Ht 12	Newman, Lobb, Prynne, S.Phillips, 57.50	41	29
Ht 13	Newman, Prynne, Bishop, Barrett, 56.72	43	33
Ht 14	Phelps, S.Phillips, Lobb, 58.32 (3 Riders Only)	47	35
Ht 15	(Nominated) Newman, Barrett, Bishop, Phelps (ret), 57.25	49	39

Tuesday 18 July, 2000
CORNWALL Y2K CHAMPIONSHIP - STARS OF TOMORROW

Adrian Rowe	1 1 1 0 - - -	3
Gavin Horsborough	2 2 3 1 - - -	8
Gerry Sims	R 1 2 1 - - -	4
Marty Matthews	3 3 2 2 - - -	10
Oliver Hackett	F 3 2 3 - - -	8
Tom Brown	3 R X - - - -	3

PROGRAMME CHANGES:-
None!

Note: Tom Brown was a non-starter in Heat-6, and was not replaced.

1st MARTY MATTHEWS 10-pts;
=2nd GAVIN HORSBOROUGH & OLIVER HACKETT 8-pts

Ht 1	Matthews, Horsborough, Rowe, Sims (ret), 64.27
Ht 2	Brown, Horsborough, Sims, Hackett (fell), 63.81
Ht 3	Matthews, Sims, Rowe, Brown (ret), 64.13
Ht 4	(Awarded) Hackett, Matthews, Rowe, Brown (f,ex), No Time
Ht 5	Horsborough, Hackett, Sims, Rowe, 65.50
Ht 6	Hackett, Matthews, Horsborough, 63.91 (3 Riders Only)

Tuesday 25 July, 2000 – Conference League
ST.AUSTELL 'GULLS' 63 PETERBOROUGH 'PUMAS' 27

ST.AUSTELL
Wayne Barrett	3 2¹3 2 - - -	10 1
Richard Ford	2¹3 1¹1 1¹- -	8 3
Jason Prynne	3 3 2¹2¹2¹- -	12 3
Will James	R 2¹3 2¹- - -	7 2
Martin Williams R/R	- - - - - - -	-
Gary Phelps	3 3 2¹3 3 - -	14 1
Gary Lobb	1 2 2 3 3 - -	11
Oliver Hackett (No.8)	R 1 M- - - -	1

PETERBOROUGH
Tom Brown	1 0 R- - - -	1
James Horton	0 1 0 1 0 - -	2
Chris Schramm R/R	- - - - - - -	-
Gerry Sims	1¹0 0 - - - -	1 1
Gordon Meakins	1 0 2 1 1 0 0	5
Jason King	0 2 1 0 0 - -	3
Ian Barney	2 3 3 2 3 1 1	15

PROGRAMME CHANGES:-
Ht 3: R/R King; Ht 4: R/R Hackett; Ht 7: R/R Hackett; R/R Meakins; Ht 10: R/R Barney; Ht 11: R/R Hackett, who was subsequently replaced by Lobb; Ht 12: T/S Meakins for Schramm; Ht 13: R/R Ford; Barney replaced Brown; Ht 14: T/S Horton for Sims

		Gulls	Pet
Ht 1	Barrett, Ford, Brown, Horton, 56.90	5	1
Ht 2	Phelps, Barney, Lobb, King, 55.88	9	3
Ht 3	Prynne, King, Sims, James, 58.78	12	6
Ht 4	Barney, Lobb, Meakins, Hackett (ret), 56.66	14	10
Ht 5	Prynne, James, Horton, Brown, 57.04	19	11
Ht 6	Ford, Barrett, King, Meakins, 58.40	24	12
Ht 7	Phelps, Meakins, Hackett, Sims, 57.13	28	14
Ht 8	Barney, Lobb, Ford, Horton, 57.53	31	17
Ht 9	James, Prynne, Meakins, King, 56.56	36	18
Ht 10	Barrett, Barney, Ford, Sims, 57.91	40	20
Ht 11	Lobb, Phelps, Horton, Brown (ret), Hackett (ex, 2 mins), 59.53	45	21
Ht 12	Lobb, Prynne, Meakins, King, 59.91	50	22
Ht 13	Barney, Barrett, Ford, Meakins, 56.90	53	25
Ht 14	Phelps, James, Barney, Horton, 57.53	58	26
Ht 15	(Nominated) Phelps, Prynne, Barney, Meakins, 57.54	63	27

Tuesday 1 August, 2000 – Knock-Out Cup Semi-Final, 1st Leg
ST.AUSTELL 'GULLS' 57 BOSTON 'BARRACUDA-BRAVES' 33

ST.AUSTELL

Wayne Barrett	3 3 2 3 3 - -	14
Oliver Hackett	M 0 1 R - - -	1
Jason Prynne	0 2 R - - - -	2
Richard Ford	2 0 2 2' - - -	6 1
Gary Phelps	3 3 2'0 - - -	8 1
Will James	3 2'3 2'3 2' -	15 3
Gary Lobb	1 2'2'3 3 - -	11 2

BOSTON

Peter Boast	2 3 2 1 2 1 -	11
Gerry Sims	0 0 X - - - -	0
Robert Hollingworth	3 1 1 3 T - -	8
Dean Garrod	1 0 1 - - - -	2
Luke Clifton	1 2 3 1 1'0 -	8 1
David Chadburn	0 1'1 1 - - -	3 1
Ricky Scarboro	1 0 0 R - - -	1

PROGRAMME CHANGES:-
Ht 1: Lobb replaced Hackett; Ht 5: T/S Hollingworth for Sims; Ht 8: T/S Boast for Scarboro; Ht 12: James replaced Prynne; T/S Clifton for Chadburn; Scarboro replaced Hollingworth in the re-run; Ht 14: Chadburn replaced Garrod

Note: The Gulls subsequently travelled to Boston for the second leg on 20 August, but a 25-65 reverse saw them lose 82-98 on aggregate.

		Gulls	Bos
Ht 1	Barrett, Boast, Lobb, Sims, 56.65	4	2
Ht 2	James, Lobb, Scarboro, Chadburn, 57.13	9	3
Ht 3	Hollingworth, Ford, Garrod, Prynne, 56.75	11	7
Ht 4	Phelps, Lobb, Clifton, Scarboro, 57.13	16	8
Ht 5	Boast, Prynne, Hollingworth, Ford, 58.06	18	12
Ht 6	Barrett, Clifton, Chadburn, Hackett, 57.90	21	15
Ht 7	Phelps, James, Hollingworth, Garrod, 57.60	26	16
Ht 8	Lobb, Boast, Hackett, Sims, 57.60	30	18
Ht 9	Clifton, Ford, Chadburn, Prynne (ret), 57.25	32	22
Ht 10	Hollingworth, Barrett, Garrod, Hackett (ret), 58.25	34	26
Ht 11	(Awarded) James, Phelps, Boast, Sims (f,ex), No Time	39	27
Ht 12	(Re-Run) Lobb, James, Clifton, Scarboro, Hollingworth (ex, tapes), 57.81	44	28
Ht 13	Barrett, Boast, Clifton, Phelps, 57.10	47	31
Ht 14	James, Ford, Chadburn, Scarboro (ret), 57.65	52	32
Ht 15	(Nominated) Barrett, James, Boast, Clifton, 58.12	57	33

Tuesday 8 August, 2000
SPEEDWAY DEMONSTRATION

Gary Phelps	2 3 3 - - - -	8
Jason Prynne	3 2 2 - - - -	7
Adrian Rowe	0 0 0 - - - -	0
Oliver Hackett	1 1 1 - - - -	3

Note: This was scheduled to be run over six heats, featuring six riders, however, with only four riders present, it was changed to just a three race event. The demonstration formed an in-between attraction to the West of England Speedway Sidecar Championship.

1st GARY PHELPS 8-pts;
2nd JASON PRYNNE 7-pts; 3rd OLIVER HACKETT 3-pts

Ht 1	Prynne, Phelps, Hackett, Rowe, 57.41
Ht 2	Phelps, Prynne, Hackett, Rowe, 56.38
Ht 3	Phelps, Prynne, Hackett, Rowe, 56.88

Tuesday 15 August, 2000 – Conference League
ST.AUSTELL 'GULLS' 55 NEWPORT 'MAVERICKS' 33

ST.AUSTELL

Wayne Barrett	2 3 2 X - - -	7
Richard Ford	F 1 2'M - - -	3 1
Jason Prynne	X - - - - - -	0
Martin Williams	2 R 1'T - - -	3 1
Gary Phelps	0 3 3 3 3 - -	12
Will James	3 3 2'X 2'2'2'	14 4
Gary Lobb	2'2 3 2 1'3 3	16 2

NEWPORT

Chris Courage	3 2 3 X 2 - -	10
Rob Finlow	1 1'0 - - - -	2 1
Lee Herne	3 1 3 1 X 0 -	8
Tom Brown	1 0 0 M - - -	1
Scott Pegler	3 2 X 2 X - -	7
Jamie Holmes	F 0 0 1 - - -	1
Graig Gough	1 1 1 1 - - -	4

PROGRAMME CHANGES:-
Ht 5: James replaced Prynne; Ht 9: Lobb replaced Prynne; T/S Courage for Holmes; Ht 10: Lobb replaced Ford; Ht 11: T/S Pegler for Finlow; Ht 12: James replaced Prynne; Ht 14: T/S Herne for Brown; Lobb replaced Williams in the re-run; Ht 15: Holmes replaced Brown

		Gulls	New
Ht 1	Courage, Barrett, Finlow, Ford (fell), 59.40	2	4
Ht 2	James, Lobb, Gough, Holmes (fell), 61.01	7	5
Ht 3	(Re-Run) Herne, Williams, Brown, Prynne (f,ex), 59.50	9	9
Ht 4	Pegler, Lobb, Gough, Phelps, 58.81	11	13
Ht 5	James, Courage, Finlow, Williams (ret), 59.72	14	16
Ht 6	Barrett, Pegler, Ford, Holmes, 59.49	18	18
Ht 7	Phelps, James, Herne, Brown, 61.00	23	19
Ht 8	Lobb, Ford, Gough, Finlow, 60.28	28	20
Ht 9	(Re-Run) Courage, Lobb, Williams, Pegler (f,ex), 58.50	31	23
Ht 10	Herne, Barrett, Lobb, Brown, Ford (ex, 2 mins), 57.31	34	26
Ht 11	(Re-Run Twice) Phelps, Pegler, James (f,ex), Courage (f,ex), 56.53	37	28
Ht 12	Lobb, James, Herne, Holmes, 57.63	42	29
Ht 13	(Re-Run) Phelps, Courage, Barrett (f,ex), Pegler (f,ex), 57.06	45	31
Ht 14	(Re-Run – Awarded) Lobb, James, Gough (f,rem), Herne (f,ex), Williams (ex, tapes), No Time	50	32
Ht 15	(Nominated – Re-Run) Phelps, James, Holmes, Herne, Brown (ex, 2 mins), 57.41	55	33

Tuesday 22 August, 2000 – Conference League
ST.AUSTELL 'GULLS' 38 SHEFFIELD 'PROWLERS' 52

ST.AUSTELL

Wayne Barrett	2 2 1 2 - - -	7
Richard Ford	0 1'0 - - - -	1 1
Jason Prynne	2 2 3 1 0 - -	8
Martin Williams	1'0 M0 - - -	1 1
Gary Phelps	3 3 2 X 2 - -	10
Will James	1'1 1 1'1 - -	5 2
Gary Lobb	2 2'2 0 0 - -	6 1

SHEFFIELD

Adam Allott	3 3 3 3 3 3	18
Luke Priest	1 1 1 0 - - -	3
Andrew Moore	3 2 2 3 3 1	14
David Speight	0 0 1 - - - -	1
James Birkinshaw R/R	- - - - - - -	-
Matt Cambridge	3 0 F 0 2'3 -	8 1
Jamie Young	0 1 3 2'2'- -	8 2

PROGRAMME CHANGES:-
Ht 4: R/R Cambridge; Ht 6: R/R Allott; Ht 9: R/R Moore; James replaced Williams; Ht 10: Lobb replaced Ford; Young replaced Speight; Ht 13: R/R Speight; Ht 14: Cambridge replaced Speight

		Gulls	Shef
Ht 1	Allott, Barrett, Priest, Ford, 56.00	2	4
Ht 2	Cambridge, Lobb, James, Young, 55.80	5	7
Ht 3	Moore, Prynne, Williams, Speight (f,rem), 56.35	8	10
Ht 4	Phelps, Lobb, Young, Cambridge, 55.56	13	11
Ht 5	Allott, Prynne, Priest, Williams, 55.31	15	15
Ht 6	Allott, Barrett, Ford, Cambridge (fell), 55.43	18	18
Ht 7	Phelps, Moore, James, Speight (f,rem), 55.72	22	20
Ht 8	Young, Lobb, Priest, Ford, 57.00	24	24
Ht 9	Prynne, Moore, James, Cambridge, Williams (ex, 2 mins), 56.72	28	26
Ht 10	Moore, Young, Barrett, Lobb, 56.80	29	31
Ht 11	Allott, Phelps, James, Priest, 55.90	32	34
Ht 12	Moore, Cambridge, Prynne, Lobb, 56.71	33	39
Ht 13	(Re-Run) Allott, Barrett, Speight, Phelps (f,ex), 55.78	35	43
Ht 14	Cambridge, Young, James, Williams, 56.88	36	48
Ht 15	(Nominated) Allott, Phelps, Moore, Prynne, 56.02	38	52

Tuesday 29 August, 2000 – Challenge Match
ST.AUSTELL 'GULLS' 61 SOUTHAMPTON 'SAINTS' 29

ST.AUSTELL

Wayne Barrett	3 3 3 2 X - -	11
Richard Ford	0 2'0 2'- - -	4 2
Jason Prynne	2'2 2 3 - - -	9 1
Martin Williams	3 0 1'2'- - -	6 2
Gary Phelps	3 3 3 1'- - -	10 1
Will James	3 2'2'2'3 3 -	15 3
Gary Lobb	2'2'2 T - - -	6 2

SOUTHAMPTON

Shane Colvin	2 1 1 3 0 3 2	12
Jamie Holmes	1'3 3 1 X - -	8 1
Chris Hunt	1 1 0 1 1'- -	4 1
Terry Day	T T 1 R 1 - -	2
Adrian Newman R/R	- - - - - - -	-
Geoff Batt	1 1 M F 0 F -	2
Tom Brown	X 0 0 X - - -	0
Gareth Silk (No.8)	1 - - - - - -	1

PROGRAMME CHANGES:-
Ht 3: Brown replaced Day in the re-run; Ht 4: R/R Batt; Ht 6: R/R Silk; Brown replaced Batt; Ht 7: Batt replaced Day in the re-run; Ht 8: T/S Colvin; Ht 9: R/R Colvin; Ht 12: James replaced Lobb in the re-run; Ht 13: R/R Day; Ht 14: T/S Holmes for Brown

		Gulls	Sout
Ht 1	Barrett, Colvin, Holmes, Ford, 56.41	3	3
Ht 2	(Re-Run) James, Lobb, Batt, Brown (f,ex), 57.37	8	4
Ht 3	(Re-Run) Williams, Prynne, Hunt, Brown, Day (ex, tapes), 56.03	13	5
Ht 4	Phelps, Lobb, Batt, Brown, 55.56	18	6
Ht 5	Holmes, Prynne, Colvin, Williams, 57.09	20	10
Ht 6	Barrett, Ford, Silk, Brown (f,ex), Batt (ex, 2 mins), 57.44	25	11
Ht 7	(Re-Run) Phelps, James, Hunt, Batt (fell), Day (ex, tapes), 56.31	30	12
Ht 8	Holmes, Lobb, Colvin, Ford, 57.29	32	16
Ht 9	Colvin, Prynne, Williams, Batt, 56.79	35	19
Ht 10	Barrett, Ford, Day, Hunt, 57.60	40	20
Ht 11	Phelps, James, Holmes, Colvin, 57.09	45	21
Ht 12	(Re-Run) Prynne, James, Hunt, Batt (fell), Lobb (ex, tapes), 58.78	50	22
Ht 13	Colvin, Barrett, Phelps, Day (ret), 57.68	53	25
Ht 14	(Awarded) James, Williams, Day, Holmes (f,ex) No Time	58	26
Ht 15	(Nominated – Awarded) James, Colvin, Hunt, Barrett (f,ex), No Time	61	29

151

Tuesday 5 September, 2000
G.T. MOTORCYCLES CORNISH GRAND NATIONAL

1st SHANE COLVIN;
2nd WILL JAMES; 3rd JASON PRYNNE

Rider	Scores	Total
Wayne Barrett	3 1 2 R 3 - -	9
Richard Ford	1 0 1 1 1 - -	4
Jason Prynne	2 2 3 2 1 - -	10
Martin Williams	M - - - - - -	0
Gary Phelps	T 3 3 3 3 - -	12
Will James	3 X 3 3 2 - -	11
Gary Lobb	2 3 R R F - -	5
Jamie Holmes	1 2 1 0 1 - -	5
Shane Colvin	3 1 2 3 2 - -	11
Lee Herne	2 0 1 2 3 - -	8
Scott Pegler	1 2 X 2 2 - -	7
Adrian Newman	0 3 2 R R - -	5
Oliver Hackett (Res)	0 X - - - - -	0
Gerry Sims (Res)	0 0 1 F - - -	1

PROGRAMME CHANGES:-
Ht 1: Hackett replaced Williams; Ht 2: Sims replaced Phelps in the re-run; Ht 6: Hackett replaced Williams; Ht 9: Sims replaced Williams; Ht 11: Sims replaced Williams; Ht 14: Sims replaced Williams

Ht 1	Barrett, Prynne, Ford, Hackett, Williams (ex, 2 mins), 57.41
Ht 2	(Re-Run) James, Lobb, Holmes, Sims, Phelps (ex, tapes), 57.75
Ht 3	(Re-Run) Colvin, Herne, Pegler, Newman, 57.41
Ht 4	Phelps, Holmes, Barrett, Herne, 56.41
Ht 5	Lobb, Prynne, Colvin, Ford, 57.71
Ht 6	(Re-Run Twice) Newman, Pegler, Hackett (f,ex), James (f,ex), 57.06
Ht 7	(Awarded) Phelps, Barrett, Ford, Pegler (f,ex), No Time
Ht 8	Prynne, Newman, Holmes, Lobb (ret), 57.12
Ht 9	James, Colvin, Herne, Sims, 57.31
Ht 10	Colvin, Pegler, Ford, Holmes, 56.47
Ht 11	Phelps, Herne, Sims, Lobb (ret), 55.72
Ht 12	James, Prynne, Newman (ret), Barrett (ret), 57.75
Ht 13	Herne, James, Ford, Lobb (fell), 57.21
Ht 14	Phelps, Pegler, Prynne, Sims (fell), 55.93
Ht 15	Barrett, Colvin, Holmes, Newman (ret), 57.72
Ht 16	(Grand Final – Re-Run) Colvin, James, Prynne, Phelps (ret), 57.54

5

2001

The new team behind the Trelawny venture consisted of Peter Dearing, Godfrey Spargo, Ray Purvis and Shirley Stephens. Godfrey Spargo's background was with the BBC, while in his leisure time, he had been heavily involved in taking the 'wall-of-death' to various locations throughout the country for a number of years. Peter Dearing used to be a top grass-track rider in the Gloucester area in the 1970s, prior to a stint in South Africa, where he helped former speedway ace Buddy Fuller to promote meetings. Ray Purvis hailed from the outskirts of London and had always been involved in motorcycle sport, including partaking in the pre-75 class of grass-track racing in the Cornwall area. Last, but not least, Shirley Stephens was the fourth member of the new management team, and of course she is the mother of ten times Cornish Motocross Champion and fast-starting speedway ace Seemond.

Announcer Dave Stallworthy was under the impression that he would no longer be involved and was not given any contrary indication, even when he bumped into Godfrey Spargo at the annual indoor ice speedway meeting at Telford in February. However, about three weeks before the tapes were due to go up on the new season, Dave received a telephone call out of the blue from Ray Purvis, requesting that he carry on with the microphone duties throughout the Tigers' first campaign. The first engagement took the intrepid announcer through atrocious weather on his way down for the unveiling of the new side on press and practice day. Changes to the arena saw every-

The new-look Moto Park.

thing painted in the yellow team colours, while a completely new safety fence had been erected, along with an officials box and track shop. New track lighting was also in place and even the centre of the circuit, which had always been stony, had been covered with spray-on grass, which eventually turned it into a lovely shade of green. On top of all that, the pits looked more spacious than ever and new changing rooms were in place for the riders. The whole set-up was absolutely splendid, but it was entirely fitting as the public were going to be seeing international speedway stars for the first time at the venue. The club had also attracted much-needed sponsorship from a locally based communications company, and as such, would be known as the JAG Tigers throughout the season.

So, to the team, which saw Australian and former Peterborough rider Brett Woodifield brought in as the new no.1. Popular long-time Gull Wayne Barrett kept his love affair going with the Moto Parc in the no.2 slot, while a man who was destined to become 'Mr Popular' lined up at no.3, namely Czech Republic ace Pavel Ondrasik. Long-time Exeter Falcon Graeme Gordon felt a change of track would do him good and he not only took the no.4 race-jacket in the Tigers line-up, but was also named as team skipper. Another Exeter rider also changed track, with Chris Harris slotting in at no.5 and returning to the circuit where it all began for him as 'Baby Gull'. At reserve, the first position was filled by another former Gull in the shape of Gary Phelps, while Lee Herne arrived via Newport to fill the final place in the side. Not only was Gary Phelps a link with the previous set-up, but in the pits, he had ex-St Austell team manager Andy Annear helping out as his mechanic.

Unfortunately, there was a major off-track problem prior to the season, as foot and mouth had swept across the country. Local restrictions had been imposed and it looked like Trelawny would have to withdraw from the season-opening Premier Trophy tournament. Thankfully, the restrictions were lifted and the Tigers hoped to start a week later than they had originally planned, on 3 April. The Isle of Wight were to be the visitors that night, but heavy afternoon rain left the track awash and the big opening had to be delayed for a week. Prior to that, the new Tigers had taken to the track for the first time at Newport on 1 April, when they went down to a 38-52 defeat in a Premier Trophy encounter. Both Brett Woodifield and Pavel Ondrasik had looked particularly impressive, notching 13 points apiece, whilst the homesters were best served by Glenn Cunningham and Steve Masters, who each scored 11+1.

With Ray Purvis in place as team manager, the JAG Tigers made their home bow on 10 April, when Reading Racers were the visitors on Premier Trophy business. The meeting caused a conflict of interests for announcer Dave Stallworthy as his other speedway job was at the Berkshire track, but in spite of this, he somehow managed to remain impartial. Those in attendance had been used to great racing in the Conference League days, but for this match it was simply awesome. The visiting Racers were going through a purple patch at the time and they were led to a superb 51-39 victory by Danish star Charlie Gjedde, who weighed in with a fabulous paid maximum (14+1). Italian charger Armando Castagna (13) and 'Welsh Wizard' Phil Morris (11) lent support on a night that was littered with wheel-to-wheel racing and breathtaking passing. Castagna was involved in several thrilling scraps and ended the night as the track record

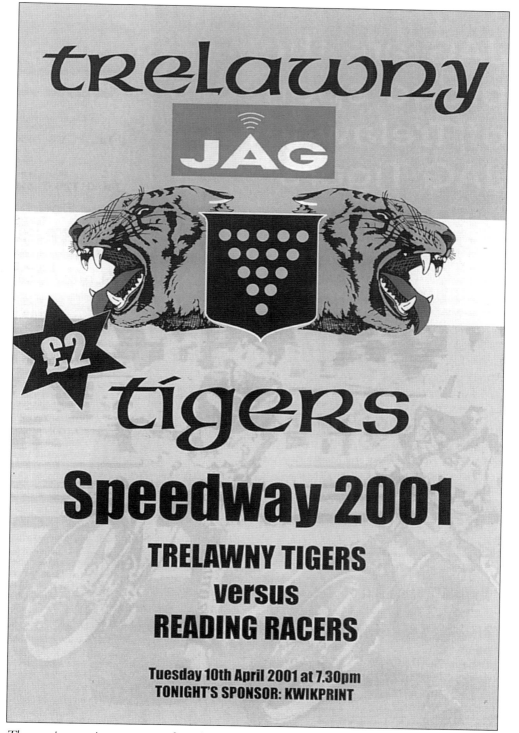

The opening meeting programme from the Trelawny Tigers era at the Moto Parc, 2001.

Gary Phelps heads the Reading duo of Shane Colvin (7) and Marc Norris (6) with Lee Herne at the rear.

holder, having clocked a new best time of 54.18 seconds in the third heat. Although they lost, the Tigers were by no means disgraced, with Pavel Ondrasik looking the pick of the side as he collected a fine paid 11-point tally.

Swindon were the visitors a week later and if the action had been outstanding the previous week, then the match against the Robins was literally out of this world. A blinding inside burst took Alan Mogridge to victory on the line from Brett Woodifield in the first heat and that kind of outstanding action was to become par for the course, not only throughout the evening, but for the entire season. The fifth heat saw an alarming smash, when Martin Dixon lost a chain on the last bend and his bike inadvertently sent Pavel Ondrasik straight into the safety fence at full pelt. Despite a bad gash to the leg, Pavel determinedly took his remaining rides and his gutsy performance saw the Tigers come back from a 19-29 deficit to snatch a marvellous 46-44 win. Chris 'Bomber' Harris topped the score-chart with a magnificent 15+1 total, while the battle-scarred Ondrasik finished on 10+1, and Graeme Gordon impressively totalled 7+3. Meanwhile, top men in a solid-scoring Swindon outfit that had played a full part in the evening's entertainment, were Alan Mogridge (10) and Paul Fry (9+1).

The Premier Trophy action continued on the Sunday afternoon of 22 April, when the previously rained off match against the Isle of Wight was rescheduled at the quarry raceway. Morning rain had left the track in a heavy condition and the wet conditions underfoot obviously affected the attendance, with only a smattering of people on the usually full back straight. Track guru Nigel Prynne did a great job to get the circuit suitable for racing though, and another cracker ensued for those fortunate enough to be present. The scores were close throughout, but it was the Tigers who had the edge in the latter stages and ended with a narrow 46-43 success. Brett Woodifield was in dynamic form, jetting to a super paid maximum (14+1), while team-mates Chris Harris (11) and Pavel Ondrasik (9+1) chipped in with splendid backing. The visiting Islanders lacked an out and out heat leader on the day, but in Ray Morton (9+1), Danny Bird (9) and Glen Phillips (8+3), they possessed three men who certainly kept the Tigers on their toes for the duration.

The following evening, Trelawny journeyed up country to face Reading, but they found the Racers in rampant mood at their Smallmead home and left on the back end of a 22-68 pasting. No less than six men were paid for double-figures in the home camp, namely Paul Clews (12+3), Charlie Gjedde (12), Phil Morris (11+1), Shane Colvin (10+3), Armando Castagna (10) and David Mullett (9+1), with the first three remaining unbeaten by an opponent. The Tigers' cause wasn't help by the fact that Chris Harris was riding in the Under-21 Championship at Wolverhampton, and Pavel Ondrasik was absent, having suffered a reaction to the leg injury he sustained against Swindon. Rider replacement was operated in place of the 'Bomber', while Newport's Australian import Scott Smith deputized for Pavel. On a disappointing night when the Tigers failed to win a single race, only Brett Woodifield offered any real resistance to the onslaught, scoring 8 points from six starts.

Riding their third match in as many days, the Tigers then faced Newport at the Moto Parc and sped to a morale-boosting 53-37 victory. Co-author Robert Bamford particularly enjoyed this meeting as it proved to be the first of several occasions during the season when he acted as substitute timekeeper in place of David Collins. With Pavel Ondrasik still out of action, Trelawny took advantage of a new rule that allowed them to use Elite League rider Brent Werner as a guest, and the American did a great job, top scoring with a dozen points. Little Chris Harris was back in his

Pavel Ondrasik.

rightful pace at no.5, plundering 11+1, while Gary Phelps was worthy of praise for gathering a well-taken 7+2 from four rides at reserve. For Newport, it was an evening best forgotten as new averages necessitated a wholesale change to their programmed line-up, and matters were further complicated by the non-appearance of Emil Lindqvist and the fact that Scott Smith couldn't ride, having picked up an injury whilst guesting for the Tigers at Reading the previous evening! The patched-up Wasps included Seemond Stephens, who guested in place of Steve Masters, but they amounted to little more than a two-man outfit, with Glenn Cunningham scoring 18 points, and Krister Marsh netting 9+1, each from marathon seven-ride stints.

May was due to begin with a trip to the Isle of Wight, but with wet stuff falling from the sky by the bucket load, the Islanders' management had little option but to postpone the fixture. The Tigers got back to track action two nights later at Swindon, but in a repeat of what had happened at Reading, they went down to a 22-68 mauling. The Robins seemed to be flying around their own strip, with Alan Mogridge (12+3), Paul Fry (12) and Claus Kristensen (11+1) going through the card unbeaten by a Trelawny man. On top of that, Oliver Allen zipped to 13 points, while veteran racer Martin Dixon bagged 8+2. On another desperate night for the Tigers, Chris Harris did his best to keep the Cornish flag flying with a 9-point return from six rides.

With little time to rest, Trelawny were back in action at Arena-Essex the following evening, when a spirited performance saw them go down to a 39-51 loss. Considering the tightness of the circuit and the thrashing they had suffered the night before, this was an exceptional effort. Chris Harris again led the way, netting a 13-point tally, while Pavel Ondrasik chipped in with a stylish 11-point contribution. For the homesters, the spectacular Leigh Lanham lost out to Pavel in his opening ride, before reeling off four straight wins to score 14, with team-mate Troy Pratt notching 11+1.

The Tigers then rode their third away match in a busy five day period on 7 May, when they took on local rivals Exeter in front of a bumper Bank Holiday crowd. Spurred on by a paid 14-point tally from Michael Coles and 11 points from Seemond Stephens, the Falcons eased to a 53-37 success. Meanwhile, Chris Harris returned to his former base and showed a liking of the track to again head the Tigers scoring with 12 points. After a gruelling spell on the road, Trelawny were glad to get back to the Moto Parc the following evening, with the return Premier Trophy clash against Exeter on the menu for an increased attendance to enjoy. The racing was as action-packed as ever, but with it being a derby match, there was an added edge that made for some spicy incidents, none more so than the opening heat, which twice saw Brett Woodifield hit the dirt in bruising first bend encounters. The Tigers were determined to win this one and grittily managed to eke out a 50-39 success. The tenacious Chris Harris topped the scoring with a paid 12 total, with Pavel Ondrasik close behind on 11, but the real heroes were Graeme Gordon and Gary Phelps, with telling contributions of paid 10 and paid 9 respectively. Exeter linchpin Michael Coles headed his team's scoring with 13+1 points, but it was a nightmare for former Gulls favourite Seemond Stephens, who finished the meeting with just three-points to his name.

After the hectic activity of the previous week, the Tigers had a complete break for seven days, with Arena-Essex providing the next opposition at the Moto Parc on 15 May.

Graeme Gordon.

The match saw the first of several team changes that would occur during the campaign, as the Tigers management attempted to find a winning combination. Lee Herne had only scored 27 points from the first ten Premier Trophy matches and in a team shake-up, he made way for German Steffen Mell, who came in at no.1 as he was saddled with a massive assessed average of 9.00. Both sets of riders put on another cracker of a meeting, with the scores close throughout, and although the Tigers battled away, they unfortunately slipped to a narrow 44-46 defeat. The match hinged on a last heat decider, which saw Chris Harris speed to victory, but with Troy Pratt and Shaun Tacey packing the middle order positions ahead of Pavel Ondrasik, it was sufficient to see the Hammers home. Once again, Chris Harris headed the Tigers score-chart with 12 points, while Arena-Essex were led superbly by the afore-mentioned duo of Pratt (12) and Tacey (11+3). New signing Steffen Mell certainly had an interesting riding style and his paid nine-point return included an encouraging win over Colin White in heat six.

In a break from Premier Trophy fixtures, the following day saw the Tigers make the long trek up to Hull on Knock-Out Cup business. The long and narrow 346-metre circuit was a stark contrast to the clay raceway that the Tigers were used to and it came as no surprise when the star-studded homesters cantered to a 54-36 victory. David Walsh (14+1) and Paul Thorp (12+3) skated to paid maximums for the Vikings, while the amazingly consistent Chris Harris plundered 12+1 to again lead the Trelawny scoring. The Tigers match formed the first part of a busy night at the Craven Park Stadium, for Hull then defeated Stoke 48-30 in a Premier Trophy match, which had to be curtailed due to the track's 10pm curfew.

The rearranged Premier Trophy match at the Isle of Wight took place on 21 May, but after conceding successive maximums in the opening two heats, the Tigers were on the rack. Although they rallied in mid-match, the Cornish side ended up on the end of a 35-55 reverse, with Pavel Ondrasik's 13-point tally being the Tigers best individual performance. The workmanlike Islanders side boasted three men who were paid for double-figures, with Scott Swain (14), Ray Morton (10+4) and Adam Shields (9+1) leading their charge to victory. That completed a disappointing Premier Trophy campaign, which saw the Tigers finish sixth in the seven-team southern group, having won just four matches from 12.

The following day, it was back on home territory and the Tigers faced the daunting prospect of trying to contain Hull in the second leg of the Knock-Out Cup tie. It was generally accepted that Trelawny had no chance of an aggregate success, but it was hoped they could win on the night. Time and again, the Vikings were sharper from the gate, but the Tigers plugged away and kept the scores close, before finally losing 43-47. At last, there was a change at the top of the points chart, with Brett Woodifield netting 12+1, and Pavel Ondrasik weighing in with 10+2. So, Hull moved sweetly through to the next round of the cup, courtesy of a 101-79 overall victory, with their leading lights being Paul Thorp (12+1) and Paul Bentley (10).

Next on the agenda was a trip up north as the Tigers began their Premier League fixtures, firstly stopping at Sheffield's pacy Owlerton circuit and then travelling on to the much tighter Armadale home of Edinburgh. This was to prove a disastrous foray, with the Tigers taking a 26-63 walloping at Sheffield and losing Wayne Barrett in an alarming heat six track spill. Unfortunately, Wayne went head first into the safety fence on the third bend, suffering a broken wrist, which would keep him out of the saddle for a considerable period of time. The Sheffield boys blasted to victory in all but one of the fifteen heats, with Simon Stead scorching to a fabulous paid 15-point maximum and Sean Wilson zipping to a four-ride full-house. Backing them up, Andrew Moore impressed greatly with a 10+2 return, while German flyer Robbie Kessler notched 9+2. For the beleaguered Cornish side, Pavel Ondrasik fought a one-man crusade, collecting their solitary race win on his way to a 12-point tally.

At Edinburgh the following night, the Tigers were forced to operate a rider replacement for Chris Harris, who was on his way to Pfaffenhofen, Germany for a qualifying round of the World Under-21 Championship. On top of this Wayne Barrett was nursing his wrist injury, although the Monarchs allowed them to plug the gap at reserve with local junior James Denholm. Needless to say, the match was a rout, with the Tigers suffering a 25-65 hammering. The mighty Monarchs main men were Robert Eriksson (14+1), Jan 'The Hammer' Andersen (13+1), Peter Carr (11+1) and Dalle Andersson (9+2), while Brett Woodifield stood alone for Trelawny, scoring 12 points from a strength-sapping seven starts. Despite the disappointments of the mini-tour, there was some cheer a couple of days later, when news filtered through that Chris Harris had scored 10 points in Germany, thereby progressing to the semi-finals of the Under-21 Championship.

May was brought to a close with a challenge match against the GT Motorcycle Turbos at the Moto Parc, when Jamie Holmes was drafted into the Tigers line-up, replacing the injured Wayne Barrett. This match was a tantalising prospect, as the Turbos side included former Gulls Seemond Stephens and Simon Phillips, as well as several riders who had previously done well at the track, in Brent Werner, Krister Marsh, Mark Simmonds and Shane Colvin. The visiting combination turned out to be a solid outfit and despite losing Malcolm Holloway in a heat seven crash, they eased to a 49-41 success. As expected, the Turbos' star turns were Werner (12), Simmonds (10) and Colvin (9+2), with the Tigers' top men being Brett Woodifield (14) and Pavel Ondrasik (12). Following the match, Ray Purvis stood down as team manager by mutual consent, with ex-St Austell rider Mark Phillips taking over the role. Including the meeting against the GT Motorcycle Turbos, Trelawny had lost seven matches on the trot, and it was felt that a change of boss could help to improve the motivation and performance of the side.

Mark's first match in charge was scheduled to occur the following Tuesday, when Exeter were in town for the first leg of the Tamar Trophy, but unfortunately, heavy showers left the track in a waterlogged state and the meeting was called off two hours before the start time.

The Tigers got back into action six nights later, with their second appearance of the year at Reading, this time on league business. After an impressive paid 8 return for the GT Motorcycle Turbos in the Moto Parc challenge match a fortnight previously, Simon Phillips was happy to accept the no.7 race-jacket, whilst also continuing to double-up with Somerset at Conference League level. However, it wasn't a good night for Simon, who failed to trouble the scorers, whilst brother Mark had a baptism of fire as team manager, as Reading ran riot to send the Tigers scuttling on the end of a 27-63 defeat. The homesters were led by a fabulous 15 point maximum from 'Italian Stallion' Armando Castagna, while home captain Phil Morris carded a paid 15 full-house. That

Mark Phillips.

wasn't the end of the high scoring in the home camp, for both Paul Clews and stylish American guest Brent Werner lent the top two solid support, each netting paid 11 from four starts. In stark contrast, Trelawny only managed three race winners all night, with a paid 9 point tally from Brett Woodifield being enough to head the scoring.

Back at home base the following evening, Mark Phillips injected some magic into his troops and they came out with a much improved performance, recovering from an early deficit to defeat Berwick 52-38. The meeting had a real international flavour, with no less than four riders from the Czech Republic on show in Tigers' favourite Pavel Ondrasik and the visiting Bandits trio of Adrian Rymel, Michal Makovsky and Josef Franc. On top of that, Australian Brett Woodifield and German Steffen Mell lined up on the Trelawny side of the pits, whilst Berwick included South African Bevan Compton at reserve. Knowing there was a keen and friendly rivalry between the four Czech Republic boys, Ken Westaway put up an extra cash prize for whichever of them scored the most points on the night. After a slight dip in form over the previous three weeks or so, Chris Harris came roaring back with a thunderous 15 point maximum, while Pavel Ondrasik's 12+2 return was to end up being his season's best. In what was a much more solid team showing, club skipper Graeme Gordon showed flashes of brilliance on his way to a paid 10 total, with the crowd greatly appreciating his wholehearted efforts. Although comfortably beaten in the end, Berwick had played a full part in another clay country classic, with Scott Robson and the aforementioned Makovsky always in the thick of things to net paid 10 points apiece.

As the season wore on, Trelawny must have become one of the best publicized tracks in British Speedway. Not only was the circuit's reputation for serving up fantastic racing talked about up and down the country, but in and around St Austell itself, posters had been put up all over the place and there was also a huge advertising hoarding on the main A30 roundabout.

The Moto Parc regulars didn't have long to wait for their next speedway fix, with Edinburgh being the visitors for a Sunday afternoon encounter on 17 June. This was always going to be an uphill struggle for the Tigers as they went into the meeting without the services of Pavel Ondrasik, Brett Woodifield and Steffen Mell, all of whom were competing in World Championship rounds. Troy Pratt was called up as a guest at no.1, with his Arena-Essex team-mate Shaun Tacey booked in to ride at no.5. Sadly, Tacey broke down en route, leaving Trelawny with little time to find a suitable replacement. Eventually, Shane Colvin was contacted and agreed to ride, despite not getting home until the wee small hours, having appeared in the Golden Jubilee meeting at Ipswich the night before. Shane had no chance of getting to the track on time and although he missed his first two rides and subsequently failed to score, he deserved credit for going to such great lengths to help out. The Trelawny management minimized their team shortages by operating rider replacement for Ondrasik and giving extra outings to reserves Gary Phelps and Simon Phillips. In view of all the problems, the fact that they only went down to a 41-49 loss, had to be seen as something of a moral victory. The dynamic 'Bomber' Harris gave a scintillating display on his way to 14 points for the homesters, with the Monarchs being led to victory by the big scoring threesome of Robert Eriksson (16), Dalle Andersson (12+3) and Peter Carr (11+1).

Mark Courtney.

Swindon beckoned next as the Tigers made the three hour journey up to Wiltshire with some trepidation, having suffered a 22-68 defeat on their previous visit on 3 May. The Robins had been hitting some big home scores, however, the formbook almost went out of the window for this match. The Tigers rode with great resilience and after twelve heats, Swindon only held a six-point advantage, but a snapped chain saw third placed Pavel Ondrasik tumble down in heat thirteen, thereby ending any hopes of a possible upset. The match finally ended in a 39-51 defeat for the Tigers, but it had been a gallant showing led superbly by a paid dozen from Chris Harris and paid 10 from the unlucky Ondrasik. There was more than a little relief in the Swindon camp, with gritty performances from Paul Fry (11+1), Alan Mogridge (11+1) and Mark Steel (9+2) being enough to get them home.

June ended with high-flying Newcastle paying their first-ever visit to the classy clay raceway and it was another exciting spectacle for the fans to enthuse over. The Tigers pulled away in the early stages and went 10 points clear by heat ten, however, in a grandstand finish, the Diamonds came back to snatch a 45-45 draw, with Andre Compton and Danish superstar Bjarne Pedersen securing maximum points in the final race. Pedersen gave an outstanding performance to score an unbeaten paid 18, whilst also equalling Armando Castagna's track record of 54.18 seconds in heat thirteen. The Dane received great backing from Compton, who finished with 14+1 from six starts and thoroughly entertained the crowd with his amazing exhibition of full lap wheelies. Meanwhile, for the Tigers, whose scoring was compact all the way down the line, Brett Woodifield finished on top with paid 11 points.

Reading journeyed down to Cornwall on 3 July and with the Berkshire side having previously won so convincingly in the season's opener at the Moto Parc, the Tigers expected a difficult match. Those expectations were well founded as the homesters slid to a 42-48 defeat, but it was another night of pulsating track action and incident. Prior to the match, Trelawny unveiled new signing Mark Courtney, who had been snapped up after being released from Glasgow. Mark's inclusion meant someone had to be left out and the man to make way was Steffen Mell. The German could consider himself a tad unfortunate as he had only ridden in ten official matches, scoring 36 points for an average of 4.20. However, with the sport being governed by averages, the Tigers management had to act quickly before Mell's assessed 9.00 average dropped dramatically. Courtney had a 6.67 figure and the opportunity to add some consistent scoring and stability to the side was simply too good to miss.

The Tigers new recruit duly got his debut off to the best possible start, impressively hugging the white line to take victory in the opening heat. Three heats later, bustling Italian Armando Castagna gave the fans plenty to talk about as he under-lined his liking for the circuit, when clocking a new track record time of 53.94 seconds. The crowd gasped even more after the very next heat though, when little Chris Harris set the track alight on his way to an even lower best time of 53.64 seconds. The racing was fast and furious as the Tigers held sway in the early heats, only for Reading to come on strongly in the latter stages and force a heat fifteen decider. That final heat proved to be dramatic as Pavel Ondrasik led, while Harris tussled with Reading veteran David Mullett for the all-important second position. Going up the back straight, there appeared to be some contact and Harris spectacularly tumbled. Referee Frank Ebdon made the decision to exclude the Trelawny man and this was not well received by the home supporters, some of whom vented their anger towards the officials box. Brendan Joyce then interviewed Tigers team manager Mark Phillips on the roving microphone and their comments regarding the incident did not go down well with the referee, who subsequently summoned them to the box, before issuing both with fines. In the meantime, the re-run of heat fifteen saw Ondrasik fall on the first turn and although he was permitted to partake in a second re-start, the popular Tiger could only trail home behind Castagna and Mullett. A look at the completed programme showed Harris on top of the home side's scoring with 10 points, whilst the triumphant Racers were headed by Mullett (12+2) and Castagna (12). Unfortunately, this defeat and Newport's subsequent home success over the Isle of Wight was to leave Trelawny languishing at the foot of the Premier League table.

Rain had started to fall in the latter stages of the match, and it is doubtful that the meeting would have actually been completed if Frank Ebdon had not been the man in charge. Frank was his usual efficient self and had his finger quickly on the two-minutes button in between heats, thus making sure the riders didn't have time to dawdle around. Almost as soon as the riders had completed the final heat, the rain really lashed it down and the skies cracked open with thunder and lightning.

Trekking up north, the Tigers faced Workington at the well-appointed Derwent Park Stadium on 7 July, but it proved a one-sided affair as they slumped to a 29-61 thrashing. Trelawny used the match to blood another new rider, with 24-year-old Swede Kenny Olsson joining the side at the expense of Gary Phelps. It had been hard for 'Phelpsy' to make the transition from Gull to Tiger, although he had put in several exceptionally good performances at the Moto Parc and netted a total of 67 points to average exactly 4.00. It was another Swede who caught the eye in the match though, as Peter Karlsson romped to a 15 point maximum for the Comets, while Grand Prix star Carl Stonehewer bagged a paid full-house (12+3). The home side also had big contributions from Neil Collins (10+1) and Rusty Harrison (9+2), while a paid 9 tally was sufficient for Chris Harris to head Trelawny's scoring once more. Meanwhile, Kenny Olsson enjoyed something of an inauspicious debut, scoring just two points from four starts.

Having been rained off early in June, the re-arranged first leg of the Tamar Trophy was next on the agenda at the super quarry raceway. The Trelawny boys looked to be really fired-up for the match against their closest rivals, Exeter, and cantered to a 54-36 success. A home rider took the chequered flag on no fewer than 13 occasions as the Tigers produced a powerhouse display. 'Bomber' Harris zipped to an imperious 15-point maximum, while Brett Woodifield gave an inspired performance to record an unbeaten 11+1 from four rides. Meanwhile, new signing Kenny Olsson gave a good account of himself on his home debut, netting a paid 13 point tally despite a somewhat ungainly style. On a disappointing night for the large contingent of Exeter supporters, only Michael Coles produced anything like the expected form, finishing with 11 points to his name.

Back on the road again, the next stop was Shielfield Park in Berwick and the Tigers went into the match operating rider replacement for Chris Harris, who was chasing fame and fortune in the semi-final of the World Under-21 Championship in Rybnik, Poland. The long 368-metre circuit certainly didn't suit the Cornish side and they conceded five maximums in succession, before Pavel Ondrasik stopped the rot with a win in heat six. By heat eight, the Tigers were trailing 11-37, when the heaven's opened and referee Will Hunter was forced to curtail the proceedings.

Again using rider replacement to cover for Chris Harris, the Tigers were in action at Newcastle the following night, when the weather thankfully remained dry for the duration. The tight Brough Park track proved a little more to the liking of the Trelawny side and it was no disgrace to go down 31-59 to the team that would go on and lift the Premier League Championship. Brilliant Dane Bjarne Pedersen simply oozed class on his way to a 15-point maximum, while team-mates Andre Compton (11+1), Kevin Little (10+2), Jesper Olsen (10+1) and Richard Juul (8+2) gave a full indication of what a powerful unit the Diamonds were. For the Tigers, Kenny Olsson and Graeme Gordon won a solitary race apiece, with the Swede netting a paid 11 to top the scoring, albeit from seven starts.

The Under-21 result from Poland came through on the old speedway grapevine, with Oxford's Lukas Dryml taking victory after amassing a 14 point total. As ever, Chris Harris had given his all, taking victory in his last ride to finish with eight-points to his name. Unfortunately, it wasn't quite enough for the 'Bomber' to reach the final, but it had been another important part of his learning curve and he had certainly come a long way since starting out with the Gulls in 1998.

Swindon were due to visit the Moto Parc on 17 July, but heavy morning rain had left the track awash and with more of the wet stuff expected in the afternoon, an early decision was made to postpone the fixture. That meant a wait of a week before Trelawny again set foot on track, when Sheffield provided the opposition. Good, close racing was again served up in a match that started brilliantly, with Brett Woodifield and Kenny Olsson taking a 5-1 over Sheffield legend Sean Wilson. That seemed to inspire the home side and they dug deep thereafter, maintaining their lead throughout to win 48-42. This was an exceptional performance, considering the visitors boasted three men in double-figures, namely Robbie Kessler (14+1), Sean Wilson (12) and Simon Stead (11). The home camp could be well satisfied, with scoring all the way down the line, headed by heat one heroes Woodifield and Olsson, who both ended the night with paid 12 point tallies.

Exeter was the destination on 30 July, as the Tigers made the relatively short journey for an away match. However, the eagerly awaited derby quickly turned into a disaster, with the Falcons piling on the agony from the start and inflicting a mammoth 32-60 drubbing. Both Seemond Stephens (14+1) and Mark Simmonds (13+2) wrapped up paid maximums for Exeter, while team-mates Michael Coles (14) and Jason Prynne (8+2) weighed in with heavyweight contributions. For the under-fire Tigers, Chris Harris battled away for 12 points, his total including a second place finish in heat eight, when brought in as a golden double tactical substitute.

The return match against Exeter took place the following evening, when a huge crowd packed into the clay country arena. The Tigers were looking for revenge, but it soon became apparent that they were no match for the Falcons from the gate. Time and again, the Exeter boys zipped ahead from the gate and it made for painful viewing as they succumbed to a 37-53 loss. Chris Harris did his utmost to keep the flag flying with 10 points, but he was the only man in the home side to hit double-figures, whereas the visitors included four big pointsmen in Michael Coles (12+1), Krister Marsh (11), Mark Simmonds (10+2) and Seemond Stephens (10+2).

With no activity for a week, the Tigers had the chance to recover from the huge setback against their local rivals, before Glasgow made the long trip down. However, if the Trelawny boys were hoping for a morale-boosting victory, they were in for a nasty shock. The meeting served up another tremendous slice of racing, but unfortunately

for the home supporters, it was the visiting Tigers from Glasgow who took a shine to the track and put on an exhibition of how to win races from the back. Despite this, the Trelawny boys managed to keep the scores tight and after heat twelve, the sides were locked together at 36 points apiece. After the interval, the announcement of the riders for heat thirteen was made, with referee Graham Flint promptly putting them on the two-minute time allowance. There was drama, when Glasgow's Les Collins just failed to make it from the pit gate in time and was excluded. Collins was incensed at the decision as he had spent the interval being interviewed on the centre green and claimed there had been no light or bell from

Chris Harris.

Brett Woodifield with Hull's Ross Brady.

the pits to signal racing was about to resume.

Collins' exclusion seemed to galvanize Glasgow, however, and James Grieves swept to victory when the race was eventually run, with Argentine team-mate Emiliano Sanchez subsequently taking the penultimate heat. That set up a last-heat decider with the teams locked together on 42 points each, and it came as no surprise when Glasgow gave Collins the nod to partake along with Grieves. There was a feeling that the veteran racer would make up for his disappointment at the events prior to heat thirteen, and he made a point of being the first rider to line up at the gate! Trelawny's hopes of pulling off victory were dashed when Chris Harris locked up on the first bend and fell, suffering the inevitable exclusion from the re-start. Collins and Grieves made no mistake at the second attempt, storming ahead of Pavel Ondrasik and giving a marvellous four-lap demonstration of classic team riding to record maximum points and condemn Trelawny to a 43-47 defeat. Harris was the top man in the home camp with a paid 11 return, but time and again, it was a visitor who took the chequered flag, with Grieves (12+1), Collins (11), Sanchez (9+2) and Henning Bager (9+1) forming a potent spearhead to Glasgow's attack.

Trelawny's next stop was at the tight Arena-Essex circuit on 10 August, but quickfire maximums from the homesters in the opening two heats effectively snuffed out the Tigers challenge from the start. The match finally resulted in a 33-57 loss, but the score was immaterial after a high-speed heat fifteen smash, which had seen Kenny Olsson pick up drive on the first turn and take home rider Colin White thundering into the fence with him. Thankfully, the Arena-Essex man was able to walk away and battle on in the meeting, but the Tigers' Swede was left trapped under the safety fence for a considerable amount of time. Knee and ankle injuries were later diagnosed and Olsson's season was at an end, necessitating yet another alteration to the Tigers line-up in a difficult baptismal year of Premier League competition. The timing of the injury was all the more galling as Olsson's assessed 9.00 average had dropped to 4.89, which meant he was due to move into a reserve berth when the next set of green sheet averages became operational. Back to the match and with a 10 point tally, Chris Harris again sat on top of the Tigers' scoring, while the brave White (13) was joined by Shaun Tacey (12+1) at the head of the Hammers scorecard.

One night later, the Tigers returned to Berwick for the re-run of the match that had been curtailed on 15 July. Acting quickly to cover Kenny Olsson's absence, the Trelawny management drafted in former Berwick rider and Shielfield Park track specialist Paul Bentley as a guest. The move worked a treat as Bentley followed Brett Woodifield home to give the Tigers a 5-1 in a dream start, and they held on to the lead until heat eight. That was when David Meldrum and Scott Lamb linked up to record maximum points as the Bandits nosed in front at 25-23. Gradually, the home side then pulled away to triumph 49-41, but it was hats off to the Tigers as this was the first time they had topped forty points in an away fixture and collected the aggregate league bonus point to boot. Chris Harris carded 12 points to again finish as the Tigers' highest pointsman, whilst guest 'Banger' Bentley also performed admirably, knocking up a fine paid 11 total. Meanwhile, the aforementioned duo of Meldrum and Lamb were the undoubted heroes in the home camp, netting scores of 16 and paid 14 respectively.

Having previously won at the Moto Parc in the Knock-Out Cup, high-flying Hull must have been confident of further success when they returned for a league match on 14 August. Wayne Barrett found himself recalled to the Trelawny side at reserve, as the men from Hull started the match well and moved into an early lead. The highlight of the opening stages was Paul Thorp's thrilling effort in heat five, when he equalled Chris Harris' track record time of 53.64 seconds. Garry Stead then provided the sandwich filling as Pavel Ondrasik and Graeme Gordon recorded a 4-2 in the sixth heat, restoring parity to the proceedings at 18 points apiece. The scores were close for the remainder of the match, although it looked like the meeting would not go the distance, when the dreaded fog descended over the track and greatly reduced the visibility.

Referee Craig Ackroyd handled the situation well though, keeping the meeting going at a frantic pace, only for the mist to disappear in the latter stages as if it hadn't arrived in the first place! By heat ten, Trelawny had opened up a 32-28 lead, but the Vikings quickly moved in front once more, courtesy of 4-2 and 5-1 advantages in heats eleven and twelve respectively. The visitors proved just too strong in the end, but it had been a gallant effort from the Tigers who went down by the narrowest of margins at 44-46. The amazing Chris Harris, as he had for much of the campaign, headed the homesters scoring with a paid 13 points, while Brett Woodifield notched a solid paid 10. Super-fast Hull skipper Paul Thorp ended a great personal night with 14 points to his name, but the match winner for the Vikings was surely reserve Mike Smith, who rode superbly to net 8+2 from his five rides. Aside from the usual high quality standard of racing the Moto Parc regulars had become accustomed to, some superb entertainment was provided by Andy Hobbs and his 'Over the Top' stunt motorcycle team. The show included various jumps and wheelies, but the highlight was the sight of former Swindon rider Barry Duke riding through a wall of fire for the first time in his life. Having performed prior to the meeting, the stunt team put on another show during the interval, but unfortunately, the crowd didn't get to see a lot of it as visibility outside the track had been obliterated by thick fog.

A quiet week followed for the Tigers, before Arena-Essex returned to Cornwall for the second time in 2001. Trelawny lined up as they had done the previous week, with Wayne Barrett holding on to his no.6 berth. The Tigers went into the match with optimism as the visitors were without no.1 Troy Pratt, who was nursing a shoulder injury, although they did track Edinburgh's Christian Henry as a guest replacement. The Tigers began the meeting in confident mood, scorching to successive 5-1's in the opening two heats, and although the Arena-Essex boys rallied in the latter stages, Trelawny's solid scoring septet held on to win 47-43. In spite of swirling mist and poor visibility, the racing was top drawer, highlighted by the penultimate heat ding-dong duel between Shaun Tacey and Brett Woodifield, which was eventually won by the Arena man. Pavel Ondrasik (10+1) and Chris Harris (9+1) led the Tigers to victory, while Simon Phillips produced his best form since joining the camp to record 7+2 points. The visiting Hammers might not have possessed Trelawny's strength in depth, but they did include a tremendous top trio in Colin White (15+1), Leigh Lanham (12+1) and the previously mentioned Tacey (9+1).

There was more action at the Moto Parc just two nights later, when Graham Reeve brought the Great Britain Under-16 side down to face their counterparts from Germany. At just 13 years of age, Jamie Westacott was the youngest member of the British side and yet he amazingly clocked a winning time of 60.01 seconds in heat ten. Incredibly, that was the slowest time of the match, with the youngsters regularly circumnavigating the track in times of around 57 seconds – just one second outside the times averaged by the Premier League stars. The meeting had a bizarre start, when 14-year-old Nicholas Mallett touched the tapes and was put back 15 metres. Unluckily, the enthusiastic youngster was then excluded, when referee Fred Parkin adjudged him to have moved

Shaun Tacey of Arena-Essex holds a slight advantage from Pavel Ondrasik and Graeme Gordon.

A happy bunch of British and German lads after their Under-16 international at the Moto Parc.

before the gate had been released for the re-run! The Germans moved ahead in the third attempt to run the opening race and stayed in front for the majority of the match. However, with defeat staring them in the face, Graham Reeve's lads produced a storming finish, taking successive 5-1's in the last two heats to clinch an unlikely 42-36 victory. Danny Norton and James Brundle were the last-gasp heroes and it was only fitting that they topped the score chart, with totals of paid 16 and paid 15 respectively. For the German side, Michael Hertrich was the undoubted star with a paid 14 tally, and although Sonke Petersen and Maxi Hacker didn't get the points their efforts deserved, they certainly looked to be exceptionally good prospects.

It was Bank Holiday action for the Tigers on 27 August, when they paid a visit to the Loomer Road home of Stoke. Sadly, the meeting was to turn into a disaster, as not only were Trelawny defeated 36-54, but they also lost top man Chris Harris for the remainder of the season after an alarming heat thirteen smash. In an unfortunate racing accident, Chris appeared to make contact with Paul Pickering as he tried to squeeze by on the back straight and was sent crashing into the safety boards, with his machine leaping into orbit and clearing the fence. It was later diagnosed that Chris had broken the main bone in his left wrist and it was of little consolation that he had headed the Trelawny scoring with 11 points. Stoke meanwhile boasted three men in double-figures, namely Jan Staechmann (14), the aforementioned Pickering (11+2) and Tony Atkin (11).

Back at home base the following night, the Moto Parc played host to its third meeting in a week, with the Tigers facing Newport in a real bottom of the table clash. Seemond Stephens was drafted in as a guest replacement for Chris Harris and another clay country classic was dished up for the loyal and faithful fans. Wasps reserve Carl Wilkinson took a real purler on the back straight in heat two, suffering facial injuries and taking no further part in the meeting. Indeed, when his helmet arrived in the box for referee Graham Reeve to inspect, it was full of blood, with the front crushed inwards. Fortunately, the injury looked worse than it actually was, but there is no doubt the helmet saved the rider from far more serious harm. The Tigers held the lead throughout the match, although Newport team manager Neil Street worked overtime to keep his side in the chase, making no fewer than four tactical substitutions. It was all to no avail, however, as the Tigers secured a hard-fought 47-43 success, led admirably by a paid 11 haul from the slick-starting Stephens and 10 points from popular Pavel Ondrasik. The win saw Trelawny leapfrog above the Welsh side at the foot of the Premier League table, but the visitors could be thankful for the spirited efforts of Scott Smith and Chris Neath, who did their utmost to keep them in contention, scoring 13 and 11 points respectively.

The Tigers went from one end of the league to the other the following night, with a visit to table-toppers Hull. As if the task wasn't hard enough without Chris Harris, the Cornish outfit were further hampered when skipper Graeme Gordon broke down en-route. It was, therefore, a strange-looking Trelawny side, with guest David Meldrum taking Harris' place, while Phil Pickering replaced Gordon and Mark Courtney's son

Brett Woodifield bravely dives in front of Newport's Chris Neath (2) and Anders Henriksson (1), while Pavel Ondrasik brings up the rear.

Scott took over from Wayne Barrett at reserve. Hull set out their stall right from the off and at the end of 15 heats, the Tigers were left reeling from a 27-62 pounding. Somewhat surprisingly, not one of the home riders recorded maximum points, with Mark Courtney proving to be a real spoiler on his way to an 11-point tally. The Vikings did possess five riders who were paid for double-figures though, with Paul Bentley (12+2), Ross Brady (12+2), Paul Thorp (10+1), David Walsh (9+2) and Jamie Smith (8+2) leading a powerhouse performance.

Off track, the Trelawny promotion had submitted a planning application to construct a new circuit at Hendra Farm, Mitchell, situated just off the Carland Cross roundabout on the A30, near Truro. The site had actually been home to motocross for some 20 years and supporters had been asked to write letters of support, which had been presented to Carrick District Council.

One final team change saw the Tigers sign a second man from the Czech Republic in the shape of 25-year-old Richard Wolff, who was a good friend and team-mate of Pavel Ondrasik at PSK Olymp Praha, back in their homeland. The Trelawny averages were such, that Wolff was able to join in place of Wayne Barrett, despite the burden of an assessed 9.00 figure. Having arrived in the country on 1 September, the new recruit was quickly in action the following afternoon, when the Trelawny boys made the long journey up to Glasgow.

The 302-metre Scottish venue had long since gained a reputation for serving up the type of racing that was so familiar at the Clay Country Moto Parc and this meeting was certainly no exception. Trelawny operated rider replacement for Chris Harris, while young Aussie Rory Schlein filled in at reserve for Simon Phillips, who didn't make the trip. After falling in the opening heat, Pavel Ondrasik again took a tumble in heat five, sustaining a hand injury and concussion, which was to rule him out action for the remainder of the meeting. In between Pavel's crashes, Richard Wolff had followed Mark Courtney home for maximum points in a dream debut ride, over the home pairing of Henning Bager and Aidan Collins.

Wrist injury victim Chris Harris is interviewed by Dave Stallworthy.

Tuesday 31 July, 2001 – Premier League
TRELAWNY 'TIGERS' 37 EXETER 'FALCONS' 53

TRELAWNY

Kenny Olsson	2 1'0 - - - -	3	1
Brett Woodifield	1'2 3 1 0 - -	7	1
Chris Harris	1 3 1 2 T 3 -	10	
Mark Courtney	0 1 1'1 - - -	3	1
Pavel Ondrasik	1 0 1'3 - - -	5	1
Graeme Gordon	2 2 2 3 X 0 -	9	
Simon Phillips	0 0 0 - - - -	0	

EXETER

Mark Simmonds	3 2 3 1'1'- -	10	2
Bobby Eldridge R/R	- - - - - - -	-	
Lawrence Hare	2'1 3 2 - - -	8	1
Seemond Stephens	3 3 0 2'2'- -	10	2
Michael Coles	2'3 3 2 2 - -	12	1
Jason Prynne	0 1 X 0 1'- -	2	1
Krister Marsh	3 3 0 2 0 3 -	11	

PROGRAMME CHANGES:-
Ht 1: R/R Prynne; Ht 5: R/R Marsh; Ht 8: T/S Harris for Phillips; Ht 11: R/R Marsh; Ht 12: Gordon replaced Harris in the re-run; Ht 13: T/S Woodifield for Olsson

Ht		Tigers	Exet
Ht 1	Simmonds, Olsson, Woodifield, Prynne, 54.24	3	3
Ht 2	Marsh, Gordon, Prynne, Phillips, 54.18	5	7
Ht 3	Stephens, Hare, Harris, Courtney, 54.70	6	12
Ht 4	Marsh, Coles, Ondrasik, Phillips, 55.12	7	17
Ht 5	Harris, Simmonds, Courtney, Marsh, 54.13	11	19
Ht 6	(Re-Run) Coles, Woodifield, Olsson, Prynne (f,ex), 55.25	14	22
Ht 7	Stephens, Gordon, Hare, Ondrasik, 55.19	16	26
Ht 8	(Re-Run) Woodifield, Marsh, Harris, Stephens, 55.28	20	28
Ht 9	Coles, Harris, Courtney, Prynne, 55.40	23	31
Ht 10	Hare, Stephens, Woodifield, Olsson, 55.65	24	36
Ht 11	Simmonds, Gordon, Ondrasik, Marsh, 55.64	27	39
Ht 12	(Re-Run) Gordon, Hare, Prynne, Phillips, Harris (ex, tapes), 55.87	30	42
Ht 13	Ondrasik, Coles, Simmonds, Woodifield, 55.90	33	45
Ht 14	(Awarded) Marsh, Stephens, Courtney, Gordon (f,ex), No Time	34	50
Ht 15	(Nominated) Harris, Coles, Simmonds, Gordon, 55.65	37	53

Tuesday 7 August, 2001 – Premier League
TRELAWNY 'TIGERS' 43 GLASGOW 'TIGERS' 47

TRELAWNY

Kenny Olsson	1'0 0 1'- - -	2	2
Brett Woodifield	2 2 3 1 - - -	8	
Chris Harris	3 3 1'3 X - -	10	1
Mark Courtney	0 2'2 2 - - -	6	1
Pavel Ondrasik	3 1 2 2 1 - -	9	
Graeme Gordon	3 0 1'1'- - -	5	2
Simon Phillips	1 1 0 1 - - -	3	

GLASGOW

James Grieves	3 1 3 3 2'- -	12	1
Aidan Collins	0 0 1'- - - -	1	1
Henning Bager	2 3 2'2 - - -	9	1
Emiliano Sanchez	1'2'3 3 - - -	9	2
Les Collins	2 3 3 M3 - -	11	
Simon Cartwright	2 1 2 0 0 0 R	5	
Robert McNeil	0 0 0 - - - -	0	

PROGRAMME CHANGES:-
Ht 8: Cartwright replaced McNeil; Ht 9: McNeil replaced Cartwright; Ht 11: Cartwright replaced A.Collins; Ht 13: Cartwright replaced L.Collins; Ht 14: Cartwright replaced McNeil

Note: Following a tapes infringement, Kenny Olsson went from a 15 metre handicap in the re-run of Heat-1.

Ht		Tigers	Glas
Ht 1	(Re-Run) Grieves, Woodifield, Olsson (15 met), A.Collins, 54.87	3	3
Ht 2	Gordon, Cartwright, Phillips, McNeil, 55.21	7	5
Ht 3	Harris, Bager, Sanchez, Courtney, 54.14	10	8
Ht 4	Ondrasik, L.Collins, Phillips, McNeil, 54.54	14	10
Ht 5	Harris, Courtney, Grieves, A.Collins, 54.60	19	11
Ht 6	L.Collins, Woodifield, Cartwright, Olsson, 55.56	21	15
Ht 7	Bager, Sanchez, Ondrasik, Gordon, 54.94	22	20
Ht 8	Woodifield, Cartwright, A.Collins, Phillips, 55.28	25	23
Ht 9	L.Collins, Courtney, Harris, McNeil, 54.17	28	26
Ht 10	Sanchez, Bager, Woodifield, Olsson, 55.07	29	31
Ht 11	Grieves, Ondrasik, Gordon, Cartwright, 55.36	32	34
Ht 12	Harris, Bager, Phillips, Cartwright, 55.90	36	36
Ht 13	Grieves, Ondrasik, Olsson, Cartwright, L.Collins (ex, 2 mins), 54.70	39	39
Ht 14	Sanchez, Courtney, Gordon, Cartwright (ret), 54.87	42	42
Ht 15	(Nominated – Re-Run) L.Collins, Grieves, Ondrasik, Harris (f,ex), 55.38	43	47

Tuesday 14 August, 2001 – Premier League
TRELAWNY 'TIGERS' 44 HULL 'VIKINGS' 46

TRELAWNY

Pavel Ondrasik	0 3 1 2 1 - -	7	
Graeme Gordon	1 1 2 3 - - -	7	
Mark Courtney	3 2 3 1 - - -	9	
Brett Woodifield	2'1'2'2 - - -	7	3
Chris Harris	3 3 2 1'3 - -	12	1
Wayne Barrett	2 0 0 R - - -	2	
Simon Phillips	0 0 0 0 - - -	0	

HULL

Paul Thorp	3 3 3 3 2 - -	14	
Ross Brady	2'0 3 1 - - -	6	1
Paul Bentley	1 1'2 3 0 - -	7	1
David Walsh	0 2 0 3 - - -	5	
Garry Stead	2 2 1 0 - - -	5	
Jamie Smith	1 R 0 - - - -	1	
Mike Smith	3 1'1 2'1 - -	8	2

PROGRAMME CHANGES:-
Ht 12: M.Smith replaced J.Smith

Note: Following a tapes infringement, Chris Harris went from a 15 metre handicap in the re-run of Heat-11.

		Tigers	Hull
Ht 1	Thorp, Brady, Gordon, Ondrasik, 54.64	1	5
Ht 2	M.Smith, Barrett, J.Smith, Phillips, 54.72	3	9
Ht 3	Courtney, Woodifield, Bentley, Walsh, 55.07	8	10
Ht 4	Harris, Stead, M.Smith, Phillips, 54.84	11	13
Ht 5	Thorp, Courtney, Woodifield, Brady, 53.64 (Equalled Track Record)	14	16
Ht 6	Ondrasik, Stead, Gordon, J.Smith (f,rem, ret), 54.78	18	18
Ht 7	Harris, Walsh, Bentley, Barrett, 54.74	21	21
Ht 8	Brady, Gordon, M.Smith, Phillips, 54.88	23	25
Ht 9	(Re-Run) Courtney, Woodifield, Stead, J.Smith, 55.08	28	26
Ht 10	Gordon, Bentley, Ondrasik, Walsh, 54.96	32	28
Ht 11	(Re-Run) Thorp, Harris (15 met), Brady, Barrett, 55.27	34	32
Ht 12	Bentley, M.Smith, Courtney, Phillips, 55.35	35	37
Ht 13	Thorp, Ondrasik, Harris, Stead, 55.11	38	40
Ht 14	Walsh, Woodifield, M.Smith, Barrett (ret), 55.54	40	44
Ht 15	(Nominated) Harris, Thorp, Ondrasik, Bentley, 55.55	44	46

Tuesday 21 August, 2001 – Premier League
TRELAWNY 'TIGERS' 47 ARENA-ESSEX 'HAMMERS' 43

TRELAWNY

Pavel Ondrasik	2'1 3 3 1 - -	10	1
Graeme Gordon	3 3 0 0 - - -	6	
Mark Courtney	1'3 0 2 - - -	6	1
Brett Woodifield	2 0 3 2 - - -	7	
Chris Harris	3 2 2 2'0 - -	9	1
Wayne Barrett	2'0 0 - - - -	2	1
Simon Phillips	3 1 1 1'1'- -	7	2

ARENA-ESSEX

Christian Henry	0 1'3 0 - - -	4	1
Shaun Tacey	1 2 2'1 3 - -	9	1
Colin White	3 3 2 2 3 2'-	15	1
Lee Dicken	0 1 1'- - - -	2	1
Leigh Lanham	2 2 3 1'1 3 -	12	1
Lee Herne	X 0 0 - - - -	0	
Luke Clifton	1 F X - - - -	1	

PROGRAMME CHANGES:-
Ht 8: T/S Lanham for Clifton; Ht 9: T/S White for Herne; Ht 14: Phillips replaced Barrett; T/S Tacey for Dicken

		Tigers	Arena
Ht 1	Gordon, Ondrasik, Tacey, Henry, 55.60	5	1
Ht 2	(Re-Run – Awarded) Phillips, Barrett, Clifton, Herne (f,ex), No Time	10	2
Ht 3	White, Woodifield, Courtney, Dicken, 56.00	13	5
Ht 4	Harris, Lanham, Phillips, Clifton (fell), 55.66	17	7
Ht 5	Courtney, Tacey, Henry, Woodifield, 56.02	20	10
Ht 6	Gordon, Lanham, Ondrasik, Herne, 57.07	24	12
Ht 7	White, Harris, Dicken, Barrett, 57.05	26	16
Ht 8	Lanham, Tacey, Phillips, Gordon, 57.40	27	21
Ht 9	Woodifield, White, Lanham, Courtney, 56.33	30	24
Ht 10	Ondrasik, White, Dicken, Gordon, 56.11	33	27
Ht 11	Henry, Harris, Tacey, Barrett, 55.64	35	31
Ht 12	White, Courtney, Phillips, Herne, 56.14	38	34
Ht 13	Ondrasik, Harris, Lanham, Henry, 56.26	43	35
Ht 14	(Re-Run) Tacey, Woodifield, Phillips, Clifton (f,ex), 57.14	46	38
Ht 15	(Nominated) Lanham, White, Ondrasik, Harris, 57.64	47	43

Thursday 23 August, 2001 – Under-16 International
GREAT BRITAIN 42 GERMANY 36

GREAT BRITAIN

Jamie Westacott	2 2 2 3 - - -	9	
Nicholas Mallett	T 0 0 - - - -	0	
William Lawson	1 2 2 1 - - -	6	
Andrew Tully	0 0 R R - - -	0	
James Brundle	2'3 3 3 2'- -	13	2
Danny Norton	3 1 2'3 2'3 -	14	2

GERMANY

Michael Hertrich	3 2'2 3 2 1 -	13	1
Stefan Kurz	1 1 0 1 2 0 -	5	
Sonke Petersen	3 3 1 0 - - -	7	
Tobias Genz R/R	- - - - - - -	-	
Maxi Hacker	1 1 3 1'0 - -	6	1
Christoph Demmel	0 3 1 0 1 - -	5	

PROGRAMME CHANGES:-
Ht 2: R/R Hertrich; Ht 4: R/R Kurz; Ht 9: R/R Demmel; Ht 11: R/R Hacker; Ht 12: Norton replaced Mallett

Note: Following a tapes infringement, Nicholas Mallett went from a 15 metre handicap in the re-run of Heat-1. However, the 14-year-old then moved before the start and referee Fred Parkin had no option but to exclude him.

		GB	Ger
Ht 1	(Re-Run Twice) Hertrich, Westacott, Kurz, Mallett (15 met, ex, tapes), 57.70	2	4
Ht 2	Petersen, Hertrich, Lawson, Tully, 57.51	3	9
Ht 3	Norton, Brundle, Hacker, Demmel, 56.74	8	10
Ht 4	Petersen, Westacott, Kurz, Mallett, 57.57	10	14
Ht 5	Demmel, Lawson, Hacker, Tully, 59.34	12	18
Ht 6	Brundle, Hertrich, Norton, Kurz, 58.26	16	20
Ht 7	Hacker, Westacott, Demmel, Mallett, 59.79	18	24
Ht 8	Hertrich, Lawson, Kurz, Tully (ret), 57.95	20	28
Ht 9	Brundle, Norton, Petersen, Demmel, 57.16	25	29
Ht 10	Westacott, Kurz, Hacker, Tully (ret), 57.95	28	32
Ht 11	Norton, Hertrich, Lawson, Hacker, 56.89	32	34
Ht 12	Brundle, Norton, Demmel, Petersen, 56.98	37	35
Ht 13	(Nominated – Re-Run) Norton, Brundle, Hertrich, Kurz, 57.46	42	36

Tuesday 28 August, 2001 – Premier League
TRELAWNY 'TIGERS' 47 NEWPORT 'WASPS' 43

TRELAWNY

Pavel Ondrasik	3 3 0 2 2 - -	10	
Brett Woodifield	1 1 2 3 - - -	7	
Mark Courtney	1 2 1 2 - - -	6	
Graeme Gordon	3 0 3 2 - - -	8	
Seemond Stephens	3 3 3 1'0 - -	10	1
Wayne Barrett	3 0 F 0 - - -	3	
Simon Phillips	2'0 0 1'- - -	3	2

NEWPORT

Anders Henriksson	0 3 1 1'3 - -	8	1
Chris Neath	2 1 3 2 2 1 -	11	
Glenn Cunningham	2 1'1'0 1 - -	5	2
Scott Smith	0 2 2 3 3 3 -	13	
Steve Masters	1'2 0 0 - - -	3	1
Rob Finlow	1 2 0 - - - -	3	
Carl Wilkinson	X - - - - - -	0	

PROGRAMME CHANGES:-
Ht 4: Finlow replaced Wilkinson; Ht 8: T/S Henriksson for Wilkinson; Ht 9: T/S Neath for Finlow; Ht 12: T/S Smith for Finlow; Ht 14: T/S Cunningham for Wilkinson

		Tigers	Newp
Ht 1	(Re-Run) Ondrasik, Neath, Woodifield, Henriksson, 55.47	4	2
Ht 2	(Re-Run) Barrett, Phillips, Finlow, Wilkinson (f,ex), 57.09	9	3
Ht 3	Gordon, Cunningham, Courtney, Smith, 55.48	13	5
Ht 4	(Re-Run) Stephens, Finlow, Masters, Phillips, 56.40	16	8
Ht 5	Henriksson, Courtney, Neath, Gordon, 56.37	18	12
Ht 6	Ondrasik, Masters, Woodifield, Finlow, 55.87	22	14
Ht 7	Stephens, Smith, Cunningham, Barrett, 56.98	25	17
Ht 8	Neath, Woodifield, Henriksson, Phillips, 56.08	27	21
Ht 9	Gordon, Neath, Courtney, Masters, 55.54	31	23
Ht 10	Woodifield, Smith, Cunningham, Ondrasik, 56.25	34	26
Ht 11	Stephens, Neath, Henriksson, Barrett (fell), 56.38	37	29
Ht 12	Smith, Courtney, Phillips, Cunningham, 56.17	40	32
Ht 13	Henriksson, Ondrasik, Stephens, Masters, 56.86	43	35
Ht 14	Smith, Gordon, Cunningham, Barrett, 56.29	45	39
Ht 15	(Nominated) Smith, Ondrasik, Neath, Stephens, 56.04	47	43

Tuesday 4 September, 2001 – Premier League
TRELAWNY 'TIGERS' 44 WORKINGTON 'COMETS' 46

TRELAWNY

Pavel Ondrasik R/R	- - - - - -	-	
Brett Woodifield	1'0 3 1 2 3 -	10	1
Richard Wolff	0 1'1'2 - - -	4	2
Mark Courtney	2 1 2 2 3 1 -	11	
Mark Simmonds	3 2 1 1 1'- -	8	1
Graeme Gordon	3 2'3 0 1'R -	9	2
Simon Phillips	0 2'0 - - - -	2	1

WORKINGTON

Carl Stonehewer	3 3 3 3 2 - -	14	
Lee Smethills	0 0 2'- - - -	2	1
Neil Collins	2'2 3 3 0 - -	10	1
Rusty Harrison	3 0 2'2 - - -	7	1
Peter Karlsson	1 3 3 0 - - -	7	
David McAllan	1'1 1 0 0 - -	3	1
James Mann	2 0 0 1'- - -	3	1

PROGRAMME CHANGES:-
Ht 1: R/R Courtney; Ht 4: Gordon replaced Phillips; Ht 6: R/R Simmonds; Ht 8: McAllan replaced Smethills; Ht 10: R/R Gordon; Ht 11: Phillips replaced Gordon; Ht 12: Gordon replaced Phillips; Ht 13: R/R Woodifield

		Tigers	Work
Ht 1	Stonehewer, Courtney, Woodifield, Smethills, 54.99	3	3
Ht 2	Gordon, Mann, McAllan, Phillips, 55.56	6	6
Ht 3	Harrison, Collins, Courtney, Wolff, 55.10	7	11
Ht 4	Simmonds, Gordon, Karlsson, Mann, 55.78	12	12
Ht 5	Stonehewer, Courtney, Wolff, Smethills, 54.36	15	15
Ht 6	Karlsson, Simmonds, McAllan, Woodifield, 55.35	17	19
Ht 7	Gordon, Collins, Simmonds, Harrison, 54.95	21	21
Ht 8	Woodifield, Phillips, McAllan, Mann, 56.66	26	22
Ht 9	Karlsson, Courtney, Wolff, McAllan, 55.08	29	25
Ht 10	Collins, Harrison, Woodifield, Gordon, 55.77	30	30
Ht 11	Stonehewer, Smethills, Simmonds, Phillips, 55.81	31	35
Ht 12	Collins, Wolff, Gordon, McAllan, 55.68	34	38
Ht 13	Stonehewer, Woodifield, Simmonds, Karlsson, 55.11	37	41
Ht 14	Courtney, Harrison, Mann, Gordon (ret), 55.55	40	44
Ht 15	(Nominated) Woodifield, Stonehewer, Courtney, Collins, 55.25	44	46

Tuesday 11 September, 2001 – Premier League
TRELAWNY 'TIGERS' 62 STOKE 'POTTERS' 28

TRELAWNY

Pavel Ondrasik	2 3 3 2'- - -	10	1
Brett Woodifield	1'2'3 2'- - -	8	3
Richard Wolff	2'2'1 2 1 - -	8	2
Mark Courtney	3 3 3 3 3 - -	15	
Seemond Stephens	2 3 1'3 - - -	9	1
Graeme Gordon	3 1 2 1 - - -	7	
Simon Phillips	2'1'1 1'- - -	5	3

STOKE

Paul Pickering	3 R 2 3 1 0 -	9	
Jon Armstrong	0 R 1 1 0 - -	2	
Tony Atkin	1 2 R 0 2 - -	5	
Buzz Burrows R/R	- - - - - - -	-	
Jan Staechmann	3 R 2 3 0 2 -	10	
Wayne Broadhurst	1 1 0 0 - - -	2	
Will Beveridge	0 0 0 0 - - -	0	

PROGRAMME CHANGES:-
Ht 3: R/R Armstrong; Ht 7: R/R Beveridge; Ht 8: T/S Pickering for Armstrong; Broadhurst replaced Beveridge; Ht 9: Beveridge replaced Broadhurst; Ht 10: T/S Armstrong for Burrows; Ht 12: T/S Staechmann for Broadhurst; Ht 14: R/R Atkin; Broadhurst replaced Beveridge

		Tigers	Stoke
Ht 1	Pickering, Ondrasik, Woodifield, Armstrong, 55.05	3	3
Ht 2	(Re-Run) Gordon, Phillips, Broadhurst, Beveridge, 56.07	8	4
Ht 3	Courtney, Wolff, Atkin, Armstrong (ret), 54.90	13	5
Ht 4	Staechmann, Stephens, Phillips, Beveridge, 54.54	16	8
Ht 5	Courtney, Wolff, Armstrong, Pickering (ret), 55.80	21	9
Ht 6	Ondrasik, Woodifield, Broadhurst, Staechmann (ret), 55.57	26	10
Ht 7	Stephens, Atkin, Gordon, Beveridge, 55.12	30	12
Ht 8	Woodifield, Pickering, Phillips, Broadhurst, 55.74	34	14
Ht 9	Courtney, Staechmann, Wolff, Beveridge, 55.04	38	16
Ht 10	Ondrasik, Woodifield, Armstrong, Atkin (ret), 56.14	43	17
Ht 11	Pickering, Gordon, Stephens, Armstrong, 55.49	46	20
Ht 12	Staechmann, Wolff, Phillips, Atkin, 55.86	49	23
Ht 13	(Re-Run) Stephens, Ondrasik, Pickering, Staechmann, 55.67	54	24
Ht 14	Courtney, Atkin, Gordon, Broadhurst, 56.25	58	26
Ht 15	(Nominated) Courtney, Staechmann, Wolff, Pickering, 55.24	62	28

Sunday 23 September, 2001 – Premier League
TRELAWNY 'TIGERS' 34 ISLE OF WIGHT 'ISLANDERS' 58

TRELAWNY			
Pavel Ondrasik	3 0 4 1'2'1 -	11	2
Brett Woodifield	X 1 0 2 3 - -	6	
Richard Wolff	0 0 1 1 - - -	2	
Mark Courtney	2 1 0 1 - - -	4	
Mark Simmonds	1 0 1'- - - -	2	1
Graeme Gordon	3 1 2 3 0 - -	9	
Simon Phillips	0 0 0 - - - -	0	

ISLE OF WIGHT			
Ray Morton	1'3 R R 2'- -	6	2
Davey Watt	2 1 2'3 3 - -	11	1
Danny Bird	3 3 3 3 2 - -	14	
Scott Swain R/R	- - - - - - -	-	
Adam Shields	3 3 2'1 3 - -	12	1
Sebastian Tresarrieu	2 2'2'3 2'- -	11	3
Glen Phillips	1'2'1 0 0 - -	4	2

PROGRAMME CHANGES:-
Ht 3: R/R Watt; Ht 7: R/R Tresarrieu; Ht 8: GD T/S Ondrasik for S.Phillips; Ht 10: R/R G.Phillips; Ht 13: T/S Woodifield for Simmonds; Ht 14: R/R Bird

Note: Following a tapes infringement, Ray Morton went from a 15 metre handicap in the re-run of Heat-1.

		Tigers	IOW
Ht 1	(Re-Run Twice) Ondrasik, Watt, Morton (15 met), Woodifield (f,ex), 54.90	3	3
Ht 2	Gordon, Tresarrieu, G.Phillips, S.Phillips, 55.07	6	6
Ht 3	Bird, Courtney, Watt, Wolff, 54.18	8	10
Ht 4	Shields, G.Phillips, Simmonds, S.Phillips, 55.24	9	15
Ht 5	Morton, Watt, Courtney, Wolff, 55.55	10	20
Ht 6	Shields, Tresarrieu, Woodifield, Ondrasik, 55.32	11	25
Ht 7	Bird, Tresarrieu, Gordon, Simmonds, 55.00	12	30
Ht 8	Watt, Ondrasik (GD), G.Phillips, Woodifield, 55.94	16	34
Ht 9	Tresarrieu, Shields, Wolff, Courtney, 55.29	17	39
Ht 10	Bird, Woodifield, Ondrasik, G.Phillips, 55.06	20	42
Ht 11	Watt, Gordon, Simmonds, Morton (ret), 56.24	23	45
Ht 12	Bird, Tresarrieu, Wolff, S.Phillips, 55.44	24	50
Ht 13	Woodifield, Ondrasik, Shields, Morton (ret), 56.30	29	51
Ht 14	Gordon, Bird, Courtney, G.Phillips, 55.47	33	53
Ht 15	(Nominated) Shields, Morton, Ondrasik, Gordon, 56.43	34	58

Tuesday 25 September, 2001 – Premier League
TRELAWNY 'TIGERS' 50 SWINDON 'ROBINS' 40

TRELAWNY			
Pavel Ondrasik	3 1'3 1 1'- -	9	2
Brett Woodifield	0 2 3 2'- - -	7	1
Richard Wolff	1 1'1'1'2 - - -	5	2
Mark Courtney	3 2 2 1 - - -	8	
Seemond Stephens	2 2'3 X T - -	7	1
Graeme Gordon	3 3 1 3 2 - -	12	
Simon Phillips	0 1 1'1 0 - -	2	1

SWINDON			
Paul Fry	1'0 0 3 0 - -	4	1
Alun Rossiter	2 3 0 2 2 3 -	12	
Oliver Allen	2 1 1 - - - -	4	
Claus Kristensen	0 0 0 - - - -	0	
Alan Mogridge	3 0 3 3 2'X -	11	1
Ritchie Hawkins	2 3 0 1 0 - -	6	
Martin Dixon	1'F 2 - - - -	3	1

PROGRAMME CHANGES:-
Ht 12: T/S Mogridge for Allen; Ht 14: T/S Rossiter for Kristensen; T/S Fry for Dixon; Ht 15: Gordon replaced Stephens in the re-run; Hawkins replaced Mogridge in the re-run

Note: In Heat-13, Seemond Stephens suffered engine failure, whilst leading on the back straight. The closely following Paul Fry was unable to react in time and piled into the stricken rider. Thankfully, there were no serious injuries, but it was Stephens who was excluded as a result of the incident.

Note: Heat-15 was initially re-run after a bunching incident on the first turn. At the second attempt, both Seemond Stephens and Alan Mogridge were excluded at the same time, for nudging the tapes and delaying the start respectively. Both teams elected to use reserves, rather than reinstate the excluded riders from a 15-metre handicap.

		Tigers	Swin
Ht 1	Ondrasik, Rossiter, Fry, Woodifield, 55.36	3	3
Ht 2	Gordon, Hawkins, Dixon, Phillips, 55.65	6	6
Ht 3	Courtney, Allen, Wolff, Kristensen, 56.24	10	8
Ht 4	Mogridge, Stephens, Phillips, Dixon (fell), 55.59	13	11
Ht 5	Rossiter, Courtney, Wolff, Fry, 55.07	16	14
Ht 6	Hawkins, Woodifield, Ondrasik, Mogridge, 56.10	19	17
Ht 7	Gordon, Stephens, Allen, Kristensen, 55.29	24	18
Ht 8	Woodifield, Dixon, Phillips, Rossiter, 56.14	28	20
Ht 9	Mogridge, Courtney, Wolff, Hawkins, 56.01	31	23
Ht 10	Ondrasik, Woodifield, Allen, Kristensen, 55.84	36	24
Ht 11	Stephens, Gordon, Fry, 55.15	40	26
Ht 12	Mogridge, Wolff, Hawkins, Phillips, 56.36	42	30
Ht 13	(Re-Run) Fry, Mogridge, Ondrasik, Stephens (ex), 56.74	43	35
Ht 14	Gordon, Rossiter, Courtney, Fry, 55.84	47	37
Ht 15	(Nominated – Re-Run Twice) Rossiter, Gordon, Ondrasik, Hawkins, Stephens (ex, tapes), Mogridge (ex, delaying start), 55.28	50	40

Tuesday 2 October, 2001 – 4 Team Tournament
TRELAWNY 16, THE CHECKS 23, GT MOTORCYCLES 28, THE KANGAROOS 29

TRELAWNY
Mark Courtney	0 0 0 0 - - -	0
Frank Smart	2 1 0 1 - - -	4
Graeme Gordon	2 2 1 2 - - -	7
Chris Neath	3 0 1 1 - - -	5

THE CHECKS
Josef Franc	2 3 1 1 - - -	7
Richard Wolff	1 1 2 3 - - -	7
Adrian Rymel	1 0 0 R - - -	1
Michal Makovsky	0 3 2 3 - - -	8

GT MOTORCYCLES
Brent Werner	3 3 2 3 - - -	11
Billy Janniro	2 0 0 X - - -	2
David Howe	3 2 3 2 - - -	10
Glenn Cunningham	1 3 1 0 - - -	5

THE KANGAROOS
Shane Parker	0 2 3 2 - - -	7
Brett Woodifield	0 1 3 2 - - -	6
Nigel Sadler	1 1 3 3 - - -	8
Craig Watson	3 2 2 1 - - -	8

Meeting Reserves:-
Simon Phillips	- - - - - - -	-
Gerry Sims	- - - - - - -	-

PROGRAMME CHANGES:-
None!

The Check team were interestingly titled so, on account of their ingenious check-style race-jacket!

		Tr	Ch	GT	Ka
Ht 1	(Re-Run) Neath, Franc, Cunningham, Woodfield, 57.66	3	2	1	0
Ht 2	Howe, Gordon, Wolff, Parker, 56.27	5	3	4	0
Ht 3	Werner, Smart, Sadler, Makovsky, 56.78	7	3	7	1
Ht 4	Watson, Janniro, Rymel, Courtney, 56.56	7	4	9	4
Ht 5	Werner, Watson, Wolff, Neath, 56.35	7	5	12	6
Ht 6	Franc, Gordon, Sadler, Janniro, 55.57	9	8	12	7
Ht 7	(Re-Run) Cunningham, Parker, Smart, Rymel, 55.99	10	8	15	9
Ht 8	Makovsky, Howe, Woodifield, Courtney, 56.44	10	11	17	10
Ht 9	Parker, Makovsky, Neath, Janniro, 56.28	11	13	17	13
Ht 10	Woodifield, Werner, Gordon, Rymel, 56.20	12	13	19	16
Ht 11	Howe, Watson, Franc, Smart, 55.59	12	14	22	18
Ht 12	Sadler, Wolff, Cunningham, Courtney, 56.37	12	16	23	21
Ht 13	Makovsky, Gordon, Watson, Cunningham, 55.54	14	19	23	22
Ht 14	Sadler, Howe, Neath, Rymel (ret), 56.04	15	19	25	25
Ht 15	(Awarded) Wolff, Woodifield, Smart, Janniro (f,ex), No Time	16	22	25	27
Ht 16	Werner, Parker, Franc, Courtney, 55.84	16	23	28	29

Tuesday 9 October, 2001
CORNISH BEST PAIRS

Pavel Ondrasik	1'2 3 2'2 3 -	13	2
Graeme Gordon	2 1'2'3 1'2'-	11	4
Brett Woodifield	3 3 3 2 2 2 -	15	
Wayne Barrett	0 1 1 0 1 1'1'-	4	2
Richard Wolff	3 2 1 2 2 2 -	12	
Jimmy Jansson	0 0 0 1'0 0 -	1	1
Mark Courtney	1'1 2 2 0 2 -	8	1
Krister Marsh	2 R 0 1'1 F -	4	1
Craig Watson	2 3 2 3 3 3 -	16	
Gary Phelps	1'2'1'1 X 1 -	6	3
Shaun Tacey	3 3 1 3 3 3 -	16	
Tristan Brewer	0 0 0 0 - - -	0	
Seemond Stephens	3 2 3 3 3 3 -	17	
Lee Herne	R 1'0 0 0 1 0 -	2	1
Gerry Sims (Res)	0 F - - - - -	0	

PROGRAMME CHANGES:-
Ht 16: Sims replaced Brewer;
Ht 21: Sims replaced Brewer

1st PAVEL ONDRASIK & GRAEME GORDON 24-pts
2nd CRAIG WATSON & GARY PHELPS 22-pts;
3rd SEEMOND STEPHENS & LEE HERNE 19-pts

Ht 1	Woodifield, Gordon, Ondrasik, Barrett, 55.05
Ht 2	(Re-Run) Wolff, Marsh, Courtney, Jansson, 55.44
Ht 3	Tacey, Watson, Phelps, Brewer, 55.56
Ht 4	Stephens, Ondrasik, Gordon, Herne (ret), 55.48
Ht 5	Woodifield, Wolff, Barrett, Jansson, 56.04
Ht 6	Watson, Phelps, Courtney, Marsh (ret), 56.28
Ht 7	Tacey, Stephens, Herne, Brewer, 55.94
Ht 8	Ondrasik, Gordon, Wolff, Jansson, 56.14
Ht 9	Woodifield, Courtney, Barrett, Marsh, 55.09
Ht 10	Stephens, Watson, Phelps, Herne, 55.17
Ht 11	Gordon, Ondrasik, Tacey, Brewer, 55.74
Ht 12	(Re-Run) Watson, Woodifield, Phelps, Barrett, 55.74
Ht 13	Tacey, Wolff, Jansson, Brewer, 55.30
Ht 14	Stephens, Courtney, Marsh, Herne, 55.34
Ht 15	(Re-Run Twice) Watson, Ondrasik, Gordon, Phelps (f,ex), 56.06
Ht 16	Tacey, Woodifield, Barrett, Sims, 56.36
Ht 17	Stephens, Wolff, Herne, Jansson, 56.78
Ht 18	Ondrasik, Gordon, Marsh, Courtney, 57.20
Ht 19	Stephens, Woodifield, Barrett, Herne, 56.37
Ht 20	Watson, Wolff, Phelps, Jansson, 56.77
Ht 21	Tacey, Courtney, Marsh (fell), Sims (fell), 56.73
Ht 22	(3rd Place Run-Off) Stephens, Woodifield, 56.45